OF GREAT AMERICAN FOOD & DRINK

THE

OF GREAT AMERICAN FOOD & DRINK

FROM THE RECIPE FILES OF
THE STOUFFER CORPORATION

COMPILED, EDITED, AND TESTED BY
JOY GRAWEMEYER, R.D.
DIRECTOR OF QUALITY CONTROL
STOUFFER'S RESTAURANTS & INNS

Random House / Garret Press / New York

Published in the United States by Random House, Inc., New York, and simultaneously in Canada by Random House of Canada Limited, Toronto

Library of Congress Cataloging in Publication Data
Stouffer Corporation
The Stouffer cookbook of great American food and drink.

2. Cookery. 2. Beverages. I. Title.
TX715.S884 1973 641.5 73-3998
ISBN 0-394-48810-5

Designed by Antonina Krass
Illustrations by Cal Sacks
Calligraphy by Carole Lowenstein

Manufactured in the United States of America
2468B97531

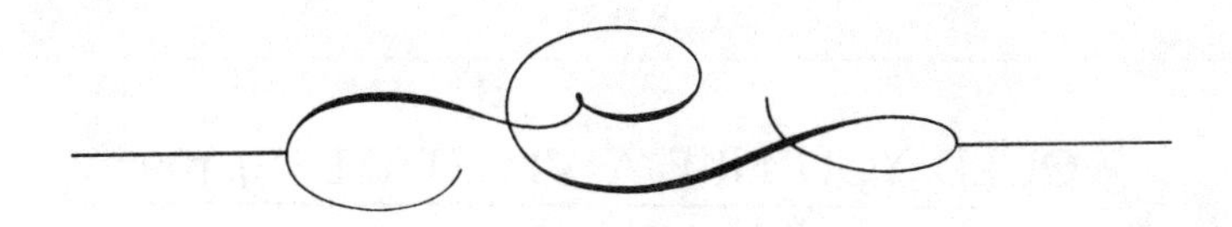

CONTENTS

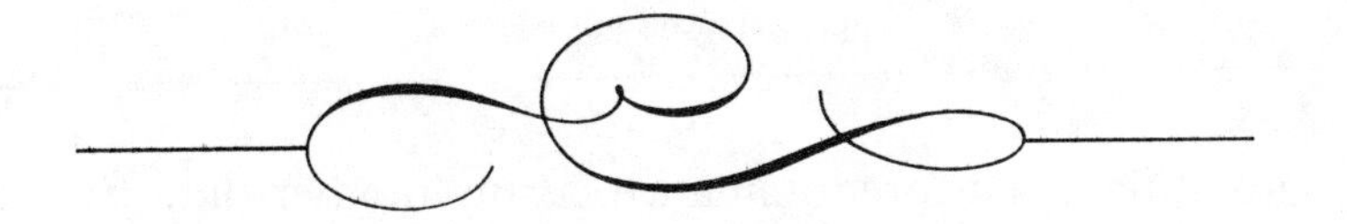

BEFORE YOU BEGIN...

I want to tell you why we at Stouffer's finally decided to share some of our secret recipes. This is our fiftieth year, and as we talked about the ways we could thank our customers, it occurred to us that the best birthday gift we could give would be the recipes that you have enjoyed.

So we reached back into our files . . . and along with interesting recipes we came up with some tender memories . . .

Our business began when my father, A. E. Stouffer, opened a Stouffer stand-up dairy counter in the Arcade in downtown Cleveland. He sold buttermilk fresh from the churn, premium crackers, and—later—an open-grilled cheese sandwich on one-inch-thick toasted home-style bread. When customers began asking for a dessert, my mother sent down her own Dutch Apple Pies. Now, Mother's pies were not just ordinary apple pies; they were something special: open-faced, and made of fresh apples baked with cream and cinnamon sauce. We still use the recipe in our restaurants, and we have indicated it here on page 153.

By May 1924, my brother Gordon and I had joined Dad in business. That year we opened our first restaurant, Stouffer Lunch, on East Ninth Street in downtown Cleveland. Later in the year we started a Stouffer's in Detroit on Shelby Street, and in May 1925 another new restaurant was opened in Cleveland's Citizens' Building.

To build our dinner business in the new restaurant, we expanded the menu to include tenderloin steaks, which we broiled over charcoal embers right in the dining room. Later we added broiled lamb chops and then Virginia baked ham with candied sweet potatoes. In 1925 we were serving our guests a choice of entrée, baked potato, iced head-lettuce salad with our own Thousand Island Dressing, along with hot biscuits and honey . . . all for 65 cents.

Well, the prices have changed, but the basic philosophy has not. We still try to have good, fresh, clean flavors in our foods. We still strive to keep natural flavors in predominance, as my mother did. (She always cautioned against overseasoning.) From our early years until now, we at Stouffer's have operated under one set of quality standards that were established in our test kitchens by home economists and put into practice by our women cooks.

The desire for Stouffer's kind of food at home led us to early development of a quality line of frozen foods. Today we have more than forty different restaurant recipes cooked and frozen for home use, including some of our best-known menu items: Lobster Newburg, Macaroni and Cheese, Spinach Soufflé, hearty soups, and thirty bakery items, such as cupcakes and French Crumb Cakes. We sell Stouffer Frozen Foods in supermarkets throughout the United States and Canada.

In 1960 we opened the first Stouffer Inn, in Fort Lauderdale. Today we are located in major cities throughout the United States, and you will soon find new Stouffer Inns in Houston and Washington, D.C.

Our Management Food Service Division provides Stouffer-type food service to colleges, universities, hospitals, factories and offices.

So that is Stouffer's today. Restaurants, frozen foods, inns, management food service.

And in this book are the recipes that have built this business.

A few random thoughts before you start cooking . . .

Recipes must be followed accurately so you make the right product each time. For example, if cake flour is indicated, be sure you use cake flour and no substitutions.

In baking, Stouffer's has always used a double-action baking powder; it makes a real difference in the lightness of the baked product. And oven temperatures are often in need of checking for accuracy; a faulty temperature can ruin your cake.

Most homemakers taste the finished dish before serving it to their family. We know you're one who also likes to follow this practice. It gives the pride and confidence which is so important in serving nicely prepared food.

Since Stouffer Frozen Foods provide a real kitchen help, we have included some interesting recipes using various frozen foods as the base. Every recipe that uses a Stouffer Frozen Food is marked with an asterisk (*).

You will see that we have also included a section in the book on Stouffer cocktails as well as nonalcoholic drinks. In mixing drinks, as in cooking, it is important to use exact amounts of quality ingredients.

Among the pleasures of life is the time spent with good friends. And we would hope that good food and drink can add to that enjoyment. We offer you this cookbook with our warm wishes and our thanks to all of you for helping us reach this golden anniversary.

Cleveland, Ohio
January/1974

Vernon Stouffer

Hors d'oeuvres,
Canapés,
and
Dips

We have started our recipes where good dinners begin: with a drink and something to eat with it. If you follow the recipes exactly (and observe oven temperatures carefully), you should have success every time.

All through the book you'll find special little Stouffer ways of doing things that work at home, too. For instance, one of our special procedures involves the way we cook shrimp. We have definite ideas about the importance of serving plump, moist shrimp. What we do is cook the cleaned raw shrimp in boiling, salted water. Then we plunge the freshly cooked shrimp in salted ice water (one-quarter cup of salt to two quarts of water).

Another word before we start. At Stouffer's we are sticklers for garnishes, and in each section we'll tell you how we add to the appearance of the restaurant food. The idea of garnishes, of course, is to increase appetite appeal. Somehow things that look good taste better.

To garnish canapé trays we suggest any of the following: drained capers, thin-sliced unpeeled cucumbers scored with a fork, sliced hard-cooked eggs, grated hard-cooked egg yolks, wedges of ripe olives sliced lengthwise, slices of stuffed olives, paprika lightly sprinkled, parsley chopped fine or sprigs of parsley, pieces of canned pimiento, sliced radishes . . . and even cooked, chilled shrimp.

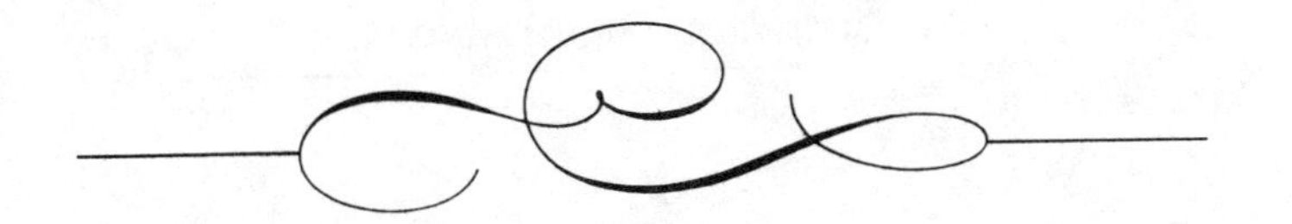

SEAFOOD

❦

You'll notice that the recipe makes approximately 40; that means we suggest it for pre-dinner cocktails for sixteen people. If it's part of a cocktail party . . . well, you'll have to make judgment based on the time of day and the appetites of your friends.

LOBSTER-STUFFED SHRIMP

(Makes approximately 40)

1—6-1/2-ounce package Frozen Lobster Newburg, defrosted*
1-1/2 pounds raw shrimp, in shell
Salt
1/3 to 1/2 cup bread crumbs (day-old bread trimmed of crusts, cut in 1/8″ pieces)
3/4 cup butter, melted

1. Preheat oven to 375°F.
2. Wash shrimp quickly in cold water. Remove shell and black vein from shrimp but leave tail intact.
3. Split shrimp at center for 2/3 of its length beginning at the head end. Cut completely through only as far as necessary so shrimp will lie flat. Sprinkle shrimp lightly with salt.
4. Combine defrosted Lobster Newburg with the bread crumbs. Mixture should hold its shape—add more crumbs if needed.
5. Place a rounded teaspoon of stuffing on opening of each shrimp, covering center area only. Place in an aluminum-foil-lined pan and drizzle with melted butter.
6. Bake as needed for 8 to 10 minutes just until shrimp is cooked through. Run under broiler to brown lightly. Serve immediately.

KING CRABMEAT BALLS

(Makes approximately 32)

1 tablespoon minced onion
2 tablespoons butter
2 tablespoons all-purpose flour
1/4 cup hot milk
2 tablespoons cold milk
2-1/4 slices stale bread, crusts trimmed and cut in 1/8" pieces
1 egg, beaten
1 tablespoon finely chopped parsley
1/2 teaspoon Worcestershire sauce
Few grains cayenne
1-1/2 teaspoons salt
1/4 teaspoon granulated sugar
1-1/2 teaspoons freshly squeezed lemon juice
1—12-ounce package king crabmeat, cut in 1/4" cubes
1/2 cup dry bread crumbs
Melted shortening or oil for deep frying

Egg Batter:
1 egg, beaten
2 tablespoons water
1/4 teaspoon salt

1. Sauté onions in butter until tender but not browned.
2. Add flour and stir to form a smooth paste.
3. Gradually add hot milk and cook 3 to 5 minutes; remove from heat and reserve.
4. Combine cold milk and bread pieces; let stand until milk has been absorbed.
5. Add beaten egg, parsley, Worcestershire sauce, cayenne, salt, sugar and lemon juice to bread mixture; mix thoroughly. Add reserved thick cream sauce and mix well; stir diced crab meat into mixture to evenly distribute. Chill thoroughly.
6. Shape into 1-inch balls.
7. Combine beaten egg, water and salt; blend thoroughly to make egg batter.
8. Dip balls in egg batter, then in bread crumbs.
9. Fry in 360° F. deep fat until golden brown; drain on absorbent paper and serve piping hot.

CRABMEAT QUICHE

(Serves 6 to 8)

1—9″ unbaked pie shell
3 eggs
2 tablespoons all-purpose flour
1/8 teaspoon salt
4—6-1/2-ounce packages Frozen Alaska King Crab Newburg, defrosted*
1/4 cup grated Cheddar cheese
2 teaspoons chopped parsley
1/4 cup chopped green onion

1. Preheat oven to 400° F.
2. Prebake pie shell for 10 minutes. Remove from oven and lower oven temperature to 350° F.
3. In a medium bowl, beat eggs, flour and salt until well combined. Add Crab Newburg, cheese, parsley and onion; stir.
4. Spoon crab mixture into pie shell. Bake for 60 to 70 minutes or until set and lightly browned.

CRAB-STUFFED MUSHROOMS

(Makes 12)

12 large mushrooms
1—6-1/2-ounce package Frozen Alaska King Crab Newburg, defrosted*
3/4 cup seasoned stuffing mix
1 teaspoon chopped parsley
1-1/4 teaspoons chopped onion
Salt
3 tablespoons grated Cheddar cheese

1. Preheat oven to 400° F.
2. Wash mushrooms and remove stems. Drain well and pat dry.
3. In a small bowl, combine Crab Newburg, stuffing mix, parsley, and the onion.
4. Sprinkle each mushroom lightly with salt.
5. Stuff mushrooms with crab mixture; sprinkle with cheese. Bake for 20 to 25 minutes or until cheese is lightly browned.

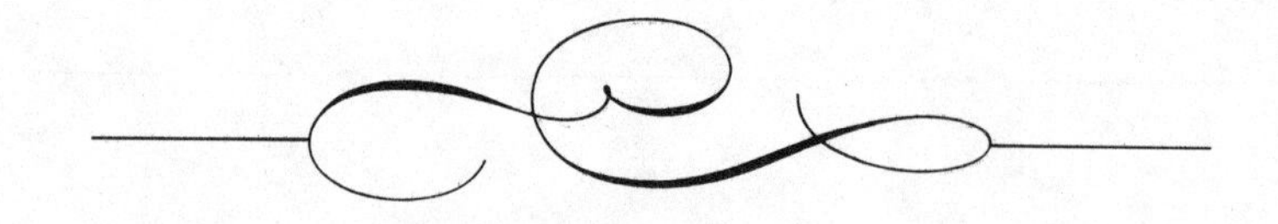

MEATS

This is one of the recipes we used when we opened our Polynesian-style restaurant, Top of the Flame, *in Detroit. Well, as things turned out, we changed the restaurant . . . but kept the riblets and now serve them in most Stouffer cities.*

SWEET AND SOUR RIBLETS

(Makes approximately 50)

2-1/2 pounds pork riblets, cut in 2" long pieces
2 teaspoons salt
1/8 teaspoon pepper

Sweet and Sour Sauce:
1-3/4 cups very hot water
1 tablespoon margarine
1 small onion, sliced 1/8" thick
1-1/2 tablespoons brown sugar
2 tablespoons cornstarch
1/4 teaspoon salt
1/4 cup pineapple juice
3 tablespoons cider vinegar
1-3/4 teaspoons soy sauce

1. Place pork riblet pieces on a rack in a roasting pan. Sprinkle with salt and pepper; brown in a 400° F. oven for 30 minutes. Set riblets aside and save drippings. Reduce oven temperature to 350° F.
2. Add hot water to drippings in pan and stir while heating. Cook down until you have 1 cup of pork broth. Set aside.
3. Melt margarine in heavy skillet. Add sliced onion and sauté over medium heat until golden and almost tender, but not brown, stirring occasionally. Set aside.
4. Mix brown sugar, cornstarch and salt together. Add pineapple juice to make a smooth paste.
5. Place pork broth, cider vinegar and soy sauce in a heavy saucepan and bring to a boil. Remove from heat and add cornstarch paste mixture gradually, beating until smooth. Cook over medium heat until

sauce thickens and becomes clear. Turn heat to low. Add undrained sautéed onions and stir to combine. Simmer 5 to 10 minutes.
6. Place browned riblet pieces, one layer deep, in a large baking pan. Cover riblets with Sweet and Sour Sauce and bake in a 350°F. oven for 30 minutes or until tender. Serve hot with the sauce.

NOTE: These riblets may be refrigerated and then placed on 9-inch bamboo skewers for reheating over a hibachi.

This started in Detroit, too.

TERIYAKI STEAK ON A SKEWER
(Makes approximately 45)

1-1/2 pounds top sirloin steak, 1/4″ thick

Teriyaki Sauce:
1/2 cup soy sauce
1 clove garlic, crushed
1 teaspoon powdered ginger
2 tablespoons granulated sugar

1. Cut steak into strips 3/4-inch wide and 3 inches long.
2. Mix all ingredients for sauce together. Let stand for 30 minutes to allow flavors to blend.
3. Marinate raw sirloin strips in the sauce for 30 minutes; drain thoroughly. Do not leave in marinade any longer or meat will be too salty.
4. Thread each marinated strip onto a 9-inch bamboo skewer. Cover and refrigerate until needed.
5. Cook raw Teriyaki Steaks over a hibachi.

NOTE: Make sauce fresh each time. Unused sauce becomes too strong upon standing.

More people order sauerkraut balls than any other hors d'oeuvres in our restaurants, and they are just as successful at home. If you're preparing for a big cocktail party, these are terrific because you can make and freeze them weeks in advance.

SAUERKRAUT BALLS

(Makes approximately 75)

1/4 pound ground pork sausage
1/4 pound ground cooked ham
1/4 pound ground cooked corned beef
1/4 cup finely chopped onion
1/2 teaspoon finely chopped parsley
1 cup all-purpose flour
1/2 teaspoon salt
1/2 teaspoon dry mustard
1 cup milk
3 cups firmly packed sauerkraut, drained and chopped fine
3 cups fresh bread crumbs
Melted shortening or oil for deep frying

Egg Batter:
2 eggs, beaten
2/3 cup water
1 teaspoon salt

1. Break up pork sausage into small bits and fry in a heavy skillet until lightly browned.
2. Add ground ham and corned beef, chopped onion and parsley; continue to cook, stirring frequently with a fork until hot.
3. Sift flour, salt and dry mustard together once; add to meat mixture, stirring constantly to combine.
4. Add milk and continue to cook over low heat until mixture is thickened. Remove from heat.
5. Stir in chopped sauerkraut and mix well. Chill mixture thoroughly. For rapid chilling, spread in a shallow pan and place in freezer for 30 minutes.
6. Shape mixture into 3/4-inch balls. Roll lightly in flour.
7. Combine beaten eggs, water and salt and blend to make egg batter. Dip floured balls into egg batter, then in fresh bread crumbs.
8. Deep fry in 360° F. fat for 1-1/2 to 2 minutes or until golden brown. Drain on absorbent paper and serve hot with Mustard Sauce (page 203).

NOTE: Balls may be frozen after shaping. Defrost for 30 to 45 minutes before breading.

MEAT BALLS STROGANOFF

(Makes approximately 25)

Meat Balls:
14 single or 7 double soda crackers
1/4 cup milk
1 egg, beaten
2 tablespoons finely chopped onion
1 teaspoon salt
1/16 teaspoon pepper
1/16 teaspoon dried, crushed thyme
1/16 teaspoon dried, crushed oregano
3/4 pound ground beef
1/4 pound ground pork
(have beef and pork ground together, if possible)

Sauce:
3 tablespoons butter
1/3 cup thinly sliced mushrooms
3 tablespoons all-purpose flour
2-1/2 cups beef broth
1 teaspoon tomato ketchup
Dash Worcestershire sauce
1/2 cup dairy sour cream
1 teaspoon all-purpose flour
Dash pepper
Salt to taste

1. Crush crackers very fine and combine with the milk, egg, onions, salt, pepper, thyme and oregano. Allow to stand until crackers become soft.
2. Add ground beef and pork and mix to combine ingredients thoroughly.
3. Shape mixture into balls the size of walnuts and place one layer deep and close together in a shallow baking pan.
4. Bake uncovered in a 425° F. oven for 20 to 25 minutes until browned, turning once.
5. Meanwhile make sauce. Melt butter, add mushrooms and sauté a few minutes over low heat until lightly browned.
6. Add the 3 tablespoons of flour and stir to combine. Heat beef broth and add gradually, stirring constantly, to make a smooth sauce.
7. Add ketchup and Worcestershire sauce and simmer for 5 to 8 minutes until flour taste disappears.
8. Combine the sour cream with the 1 teaspoon of flour and add to the hot sauce, stirring constantly. Add pepper and salt to taste.
9. Add browned meat balls to sauce and simmer 10 to 15 minutes until meat is cooked through and hot. Serve hot in a chafing dish.

NOTE: *Do not boil* sauce after adding sour cream or it may curdle.

BURGUNDY BEEF BALLS

(Makes approximately 40)

Meat Balls:
1 egg
6 tablespoons coffee cream
1/4 cup dry bread crumbs
2 tablespoons finely chopped onion
3/4 teaspoon salt
1/2 teaspoon cornstarch
1/8 teaspoon allspice
3/4 pound lean ground beef

Sauce:
2 tablespoons beef fat or shortening
1/4 cup cornstarch
2-2/3 cups hot beef broth
1 teaspoon granulated sugar
1 cup Burgundy wine

1. Combine egg and cream, blend well and pour over dry bread crumbs, onion, salt, cornstarch and allspice. Mix to combine.
2. Add ground meat and mix so that mixture holds its shape.
3. Form meat balls the size of walnuts. Place in a single layer in a well greased baking pan.
4. Bake in a 425° F. oven for 15 to 20 minutes to brown meat balls. Remove from oven and lower oven temperature to 375° F. Drain off excess fat.
5. Meanwhile make sauce. Melt beef fat or shortening in a heavy saucepan. Blend in cornstarch and heat.
6. Gradually add hot beef broth, beating constantly. Add sugar and bring to a boil. Reduce heat and simmer until sauce is clear.
7. Remove from heat. Add Burgundy and blend well.
8. Pour sauce over meat balls and bake, uncovered, in a 375° F. oven for 20 to 25 minutes. Serve in a chafing dish.

NOTE: The meat balls can be prepared hours in advance and the heated sauce added just before serving.

TOASTED HAM AND CHEESE ROLLS

(Makes 12)

12 slices white bread
1—4-ounce jar sharp Cheddar cheese spread
12 thin slices baked ham

1. Trim crusts from bread slices to make 4-inch squares.
2. Spread each slice of bread with 2 teaspoons of cheese spread.
3. Cover cheese with a slice of ham; trim ham to fit bread.
4. Roll bread very tightly and secure with toothpicks at each end.
5. Toast rolls 2 to 3 inches from medium broiling heat for 2 minutes, turning once. Or, toast in a 450°F. oven for 10 minutes, turning rolls after 5 minutes. Remove toothpicks and serve immediately.

CHILI MEAT BALLS

(Makes approximately 25)

Meat Balls:

12 single or 6 double soda crackers
1 teaspoon salt
1-1/4 teaspoons chili powder
2 tablespoons milk
1 small egg, beaten
3 tablespoons finely chopped onion
1 tablespoon butter
1 pound ground beef

Sauce:

1 tablespoon butter
1/4 cup finely chopped onion
1-1/2 tablespoons all-purpose flour
2-1/2 cups beef broth
3/4 cup canned tomato sauce
1/4 teaspoon salt
1/16 teaspoon pepper
1 teaspoon chili powder

1. Crush crackers very fine and combine with salt, chili powder, milk and egg. Let stand until crackers are soft.
2. Sauté onions in butter until soft.
3. Add the onions and beef to cracker mixture and mix to combine ingredients thoroughly.
4. Shape mixture into balls the size of walnuts and place one layer deep and close together in a shallow baking pan.
5. Bake uncovered in a 400°F. oven for 20 to 25 minutes or until browned, turning once.
6. Remove from oven and drain off excess fat.
7. To prepare sauce, sauté onion in the butter until soft; add flour and stir to combine thoroughly.
8. Heat the beef broth and add gradually, stirring constantly.
9. Add tomato sauce and seasonings. Simmer 15 to 20 minutes to thicken and blend.
10. Add browned meat balls and continue simmering 10 to 15 minutes until meat is cooked through and hot. Serve hot in a chafing dish.

When we instituted Sunday Brunch at our Tack Room *in Shaker Heights, Ohio, we designed this version of chicken livers. It's been so popular that it has stayed on our menus for thirty years.*

SHERRIED CHICKEN LIVERS

(Serves 8–10)

2 pounds chicken livers
1/2 cup all-purpose flour
1-1/2 tablespoons salt
1/3 cup Clarified Butter (page 200)
1 cup hot chicken broth
2/3 cup sherry

1. Wash chicken livers in salted water (one teaspoon of salt to a quart of water). Remove loose connective tissue. Drain well.
2. Mix flour and salt together. Roll chicken livers lightly in flour.
3. Heat Clarified Butter in a heavy skillet. Add chicken livers and sauté until they are barely cooked through and are browned on all sides.
4. Use a slotted spoon to lift chicken livers out of skillet, draining off as much butter as possible.
5. Place cooked livers in a chafing dish. Pour chicken broth and sherry over livers and heat thoroughly. Serve at once.

CHICKEN LIVER PÂTÉ

(Serves 8–12)

1-1/2 pounds chicken livers
4 teaspoons diced raw onion
1/4 pound butter, room temperature
1/4 cup fresh chicken fat
1-1/2 teaspoons salt
1/2 teaspoon dry mustard
Few grains cayenne
Lettuce, chopped onion and hard-cooked eggs for garnish

1. Rinse chicken livers in salted water. Simmer in lightly salted water for 5 minutes or until livers are cooked through and tender. Drain well.
2. Grind cooked chicken livers and raw onion together.
3. Combine soft butter, chicken fat, salt, dry mustard and cayenne. Add ground liver mixture and blend thoroughly.
4. Pack pâté into a lightly oiled 1-quart mold and chill overnight.
5. Unmold onto a chilled lettuce-lined platter. Garnish with chopped onion and grated hard-cooked egg. Serve with assorted crackers.

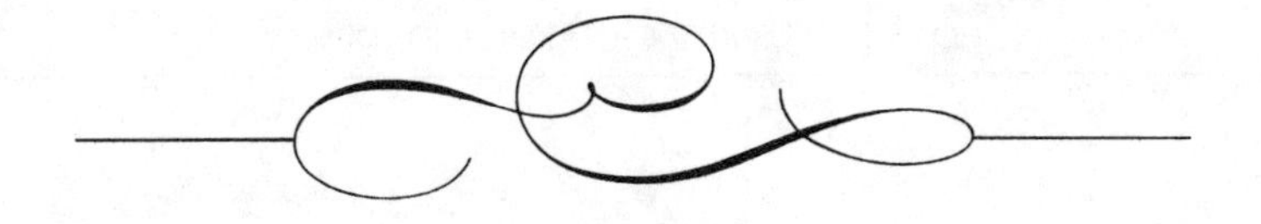

CHEESE, ETC.

We created this recipe for serving at our Top of the Rockies *in Denver because we figured the Rockies were the closest thing in America to the Swiss Alps.*

SWISS FONDUE

(Serves 10–12)

2 pounds natural (not processed) Swiss cheese
1 tablespoon all-purpose flour
3 cups imported Rhine wine
Salt to taste
1 ounce kirsch (optional)

1. Dice the cheese in 1/2-inch pieces and toss with the flour.
2. Heat the wine in a fondue pot over an alcohol burner. Keep the heat low.
3. When wine is bubbly, add the cheese in four batches, stirring with a wooden spoon in one direction at all times. Allow cheese to melt completely each time before adding more. Heat until fondue begins to bubble.
4. Add salt to taste. Add kirsch, if desired. Serve immediately.

NOTE: When serving, provide chunks of French bread or hard rolls, each having a crust on one side. Guests spear the bread through the crust side with long-handled forks and dunk it in fondue in a stirring motion. If fondue becomes too thick, stir in a little more wine. The brown crust that forms on the bottom and sides of the dish should be eaten with a fork, traditionally the prize part of this Swiss meal.

If you use Stouffer's Frozen Welsh Rarebit and a prebaked pie shell, you'll have a gourmet dish everybody will think took days to prepare.

QUICHE LORRAINE

(Serves 8)

4 eggs
1—10-ounce package Frozen Welsh Rarebit, defrosted*
1/2 teaspoon salt
1/4 teaspoon pepper
5 slices bacon, fried and cut in 1" pieces
1—8" baked pie shell

1. Preheat oven to 350° F.
2. Beat eggs in a medium bowl; add defrosted Welsh Rarebit, salt and pepper; beat until well blended.
3. Stir bacon pieces into mixture and pour into pie shell.
4. Bake for 40 minutes or until a silver knife inserted in the center comes out clean.
5. Cut into wedges and serve at once.

NOTE: To serve as hors d'oeuvres, bake the mixture in 16 prebaked tart shells 30 to 35 minutes.

SPINACH QUICHE

(Serves 8)

1—8" unbaked pie shell
3 eggs
2—12-ounce packages Frozen Spinach Soufflé, defrosted*
1/4 teaspoon salt
1/4 teaspoon nutmeg
2 tablespoons grated Parmesan cheese
3 tablespoons finely chopped green onion

1. Preheat oven to 400° F.
2. Prebake pie shell for 10 minutes. Remove from oven and lower oven temperature to 350° F.

3. In a medium bowl, beat eggs slightly. Add defrosted Spinach Soufflé, salt, nutmeg, cheese and onion; mix to combine.
4. Pour mixture into pie shell. Bake in 350° F. oven for 35 to 40 minutes or until a silver knife inserted in the center comes out clean.
5. Cut into wedges and serve at once.

NOTE: To serve as hors d'oeuvres, bake in 16 prebaked tart shells 30 to 35 minutes.

Here's another easy one if you use Stouffer's Frozen Welsh Rarebit.

CHEESE PASTRIES

(Makes approximately 3 dozen)

1—11-1/4-ounce package pastry mix
1/2 teaspoon dehydrated, minced onion
1—10-ounce package Frozen Welsh Rarebit, defrosted*

1. Place pastry mix into a medium bowl.
2. Stir onion into pastry mix.
3. Add defrosted Welsh Rarebit and mix until well blended.
4. Roll out 1/8-inch thick on a lightly floured board. Cut into strips 1/2-inch wide by 1-1/2 inches long. Place on an ungreased baking sheet.
5. Bake in a 425° F. oven for 10 to 15 minutes. Serve warm.

NOTE: For added flavor, sprinkle with poppy seeds or sesame seeds before baking, if desired.

COCKTAIL CHEESE SNACKS

(Makes approximately 24)

1—10-ounce package Frozen Welsh Rarebit, defrosted*
1/2 cup all-purpose flour
1/4 teaspoon baking soda
1/8 teaspoon salt
2 cups dry flaked cereal

1. Place defrosted Welsh Rarebit in a bowl and sift flour, baking soda and salt into bowl; mix well.
2. Add cereal and stir to combine ingredients thoroughly.
3. Shape tablespoons of the mixture into rolls, approximately 2 inches long and 1/2-inch in diameter.
4. Place on an ungreased cookie sheet. Press each roll with the tines of a fork to flatten.
5. Bake in a 375° F. oven for 12 minutes. Serve hot.

SWISS-CHEESE BALLS

(Makes approximately 40)

3 tablespoons butter
1/2 cup all-purpose flour
1/8 teaspoon salt
Few grains cayenne
1 egg, room temperature
1/2 cup hot milk
12 ounces finely grated Swiss cheese
2 cups dry bread crumbs
Melted shortening or oil for deep frying

Egg Batter:
1 egg
2/3 cup milk
3/4 teaspoon salt

1. Melt butter in a heavy saucepan. Add flour, salt and cayenne and blend until smooth. Simmer 2 to 3 minutes, stirring constantly.
2. Remove from heat and add slightly beaten egg. Beat with an egg beater or mixer for 2 to 3 minutes until well blended.
3. Add hot milk gradually, beating for 3 to 4 minutes until smooth. Add cheese and beat to combine thoroughly. Chill overnight or until firm.
4. Shape cold mixture into balls the size of walnuts. Roll lightly in flour.
5. Combine egg, milk and salt to make egg batter.
6. Dip cheese balls in egg batter and drain. Roll in bread crumbs; refrigerate.
7. Fry in deep fat at 350° F. for 2 minutes. Serve hot.

HOT MUSHROOM CANAPÉS

(Makes approximately 24)

1/2 pound fresh mushrooms
3 tablespoons butter
1-1/3 tablespoons all-purpose flour
1/3 cup milk
1/4 teaspoon salt
Dash pepper
12 thin slices white bread

1. Wash mushrooms in cold water; drain and pat dry. Chop fine.
2. Sauté mushrooms in butter until lightly browned. Add flour and mix well. Stir in milk, salt and pepper; simmer, stirring constantly, until mixture thickens and holds its shape. Remove from heat.
3. Trim crusts from bread. Divide mushroom filling onto six slices of bread. Spread filling evenly to edge of bread and top with remaining six slices of bread.
4. Cut each sandwich into four pieces (squares, triangles, diamonds or fingers).
5. Toast on both sides under a hot broiler. Serve hot.

FRENCH-FRIED MUSHROOMS

(Makes approximately 75)

2-1/2 pounds fresh medium mushrooms
3 tablespoons salt
2-1/2 cups all-purpose flour
3 cups dry bread crumbs
Melted shortening or oil for deep frying
Salt

Egg Batter:
4 eggs
1/2 cup water
1/2 teaspoon salt
Few grains pepper

Red Dipping Sauce (page 201)

1. Wash mushrooms and pat dry. Trim stems to within 1/2 inch of caps.
2. Combine salt and flour.
3. Beat eggs, water, salt and pepper together to make egg batter.
4. Roll mushrooms lightly in flour mixture.
5. Dip in egg batter and drain on a wire rack.
6. Roll in dry bread crumbs.
7. Deep fry in 350° F. fat for 3 minutes, or until golden brown. Drain and sprinkle lightly with salt. Serve hot with Red Dipping Sauce.

STUFFED CUCUMBER SLICES

(Makes approximately 16)

1 small cucumber
1—3-ounce package cream cheese, room temperature
2 tablespoons mayonnaise or salad dressing
1 tablespoon finely chopped chives
1 teaspoon finely chopped fresh parsley
Dash Tabasco
Dash Worcestershire sauce
Salt to taste
Butter
Cocktail rye bread

1. Wash cucumber well and dry. Draw the tines of a fork lengthwise up and down cucumber to give a decorative effect. Cut off one end of the cucumber. Using an apple corer, remove the seed part from the center.
2. Cream the remaining ingredients together well.
3. Stuff the hollowed-out cucumber with the cheese mixture. Chill thoroughly.
4. To serve, cut the cucumber in 3/8-inch to 1/2-inch thick slices and place on 1/8-inch thick slices of buttered cocktail rye bread.

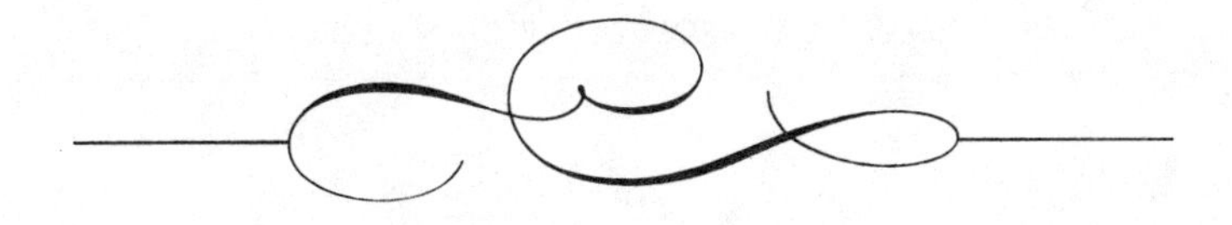

COLD DIPS

This is especially good with raw cauliflower and celery, although it works harmoniously with carrots, radishes, and cherry tomatoes, too. And instead of the usual potato chips, why not try serving Rye Chips (page 201)?

GREEN GODDESS DIP
(Makes 1 cup)

1/2 cup salad dressing or mayonnaise
1/4 cup dairy sour cream
1 tablespoon tarragon vinegar
1 teaspoon lemon juice
1 tablespoon finely chopped green onion
2 tablespoons finely chopped fresh parsley or 1-1/2 teaspoons finely chopped dried parsley flakes
1/2 ounce anchovy paste
Few grains garlic salt

1. Combine all ingredients and chill thoroughly. Refrigerate.
2. Remove dip from refrigerator about 15 minutes before serving time.

HORSERADISH CREAM CHEESE DIP
(Makes approximately 2 cups)

12 ounces cream cheese, room temperature
3/4 teaspoon Worcestershire sauce
3/4 teaspoon finely chopped onion
3 tablespoons prepared horseradish
1/2 cup coffee cream

1. Beat cream cheese until soft and creamy.
2. Add all other ingredients except the cream and beat to combine thoroughly.
3. Add cream gradually while beating. Dip should have a soft, dipping consistency. Refrigerate.
4. Remove dip from refrigerator about 15 minutes before serving time.

AVOCADO CREAM CHEESE DIP

(Makes approximately 2 cups)

1— 8-ounce package cream cheese, room temperature
1 cup peeled, mashed avocado
1-1/2 teaspoons lemon juice
1-1/2 teaspoons onion juice
3/4 teaspoon salt

1. Beat cream cheese until soft and creamy.
2. Add all other ingredients and beat to combine thoroughly. Refrigerate.
3. Remove dip from refrigerator about 15 minutes before serving time.

ROQUEFORT OR BLEU CHEESE DIP

(Makes approximately 2 cups)

1—8-ounce package cream cheese, room temperature
6 ounces crumbled Roquefort or bleu cheese
2 teaspoons lemon juice
2 tablespoons finely chopped onion
3/4 teaspoon salt
1/2 cup coffee cream

1. Beat cream cheese until soft and creamy.
2. Add all other ingredients except the cream; beat to combine thoroughly.
3. Add cream gradually while beating. Dip should have a soft, dipping consistency. Refrigerate.
4. Remove dip from refrigerator about 15 minutes before serving time.

SMITHFIELD HAM, CHIVE AND CREAM CHEESE DIP

(Makes approximately 2 cups)

12 ounces cream cheese, room temperature
1 teaspoon finely snipped fresh chives
2 tablespoons deviled Smithfield Ham Spread
1/2 cup coffee cream

1. Beat cream cheese until soft and creamy.
2. Add all other ingredients except the cream; beat to combine thoroughly.
3. Add cream gradually while beating. Dip should have a soft, dipping consistency. Refrigerate.
4. Remove dip from refrigerator about 15 minutes before serving time.

GUACAMOLE DIP

(Makes 1 cup)

1 large very ripe avocado
1 teaspoon lemon juice
1/4 teaspoon salt
1/4 teaspoon chili powder
2 teaspoons finely chopped onion
3 tablespoons mayonnaise or salad dressing

1. Cut avocado in half. Remove stone and strip off peel. Force avocado through a fine sieve (there should be one cup of pulp). Sprinkle immediately with lemon juice.
2. Add salt, chili powder and onion to pulp and mix well.
3. Place mixture in a bowl and spread the salad dressing over the top of mixture in a thin layer to prevent discoloration.
4. Just before serving, stir dressing into avocado mixture. Serve as a dip with corn chips, tortillas, potato crackers, etc.

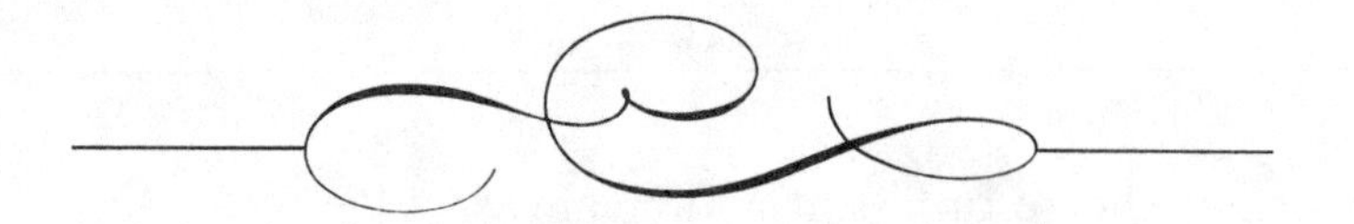

HOT DIPS

Two of our Stouffer's Frozen Foods combined and you have a simple, hot dip.

IMPERIAL CHEESE DIP

(Makes approximately 3 cups)

2—10-ounce packages Frozen Welsh Rarebit, defrosted*
2—6-1/2-ounce packages Frozen Alaska King Crab Newburg, defrosted*

1. Remove Welsh Rarebit and Crab Newburg from containers; place in top of double boiler over rapidly boiling water and heat for 25 to 30 minutes or until hot.
2. Stir lightly to combine, so as not to break up crabmeat. Serve hot as a dip.

BACON TOMATO RAREBIT DIP

(Makes 2-1/2 cups)

1— 10-ounce package Frozen Welsh Rarebit, defrosted*
1— 10-1/2-ounce can tomato soup
6 bacon strips, raw
1/2 teaspoon finely chopped parsley
1/2 teaspoon dried, crushed oregano or 1/2 teaspoon dried, crushed basil

1. Place Welsh Rarebit in top of double boiler over rapidly boiling water and heat for 15 minutes, stirring occasionally.
2. Add tomato soup and mix well. Continue heating until very hot.
3. Fry or broil bacon slices. Drain on absorbent paper to crisp; cut in 1/2-inch pieces.
4. Add bacon, parsley and herbs to hot mixture and stir to combine.
5. Serve hot as a dip with Rye Chips (page 201) or Melba toast sticks.

SPICY WELSH RAREBIT

(Makes approximately 2-1/2 cups)

2—10-ounce packages Frozen Welsh Rarebit, defrosted*
1/4 cup tomato sauce

1. Remove Welsh Rarebit from containers; place in top of double boiler over rapidly boiling water and heat for 20 to 25 minutes.
2. Stir in tomato sauce and heat for another 5 minutes.
3. Serve hot over Melba toast or serve as a dip with crackers or chips.

MEXICALI RAREBIT DIP

(Makes 1-1/2 cups)

1—10-ounce package Frozen Welsh Rarebit, defrosted*
1—4-ounce can green chilies

1. Place Welsh Rarebit in top of double boiler over rapidly boiling water and heat for 15 minutes, stirring occasionally.
2. Drain chilies. Remove seeds and any burned spots. Chop in 1/4-inch pieces and add to Rarebit. Heat thoroughly.
3. Serve hot with corn chips, Rye Chips (page 201) or tortillas.

CREAMY WELSH DIP

(Makes approximately 1-1/2 cups)

1—10-ounce package Frozen Welsh Rarebit, defrosted*
1—3-ounce package cream cheese
1/4 cup dairy sour cream

1. Place Welsh Rarebit in top of double boiler over rapidly boiling water and heat for 20 minutes.
2. Add cream cheese and sour cream (do not allow mixture to boil after sour cream has been added). Blend well with a mixer for a light and fluffy dip.

Here's our old friend, onion dip, done a new way: HOT.

ONION CHEESE DIP

(Makes approximately 1-1/2 cups)

1—10-ounce package Frozen Welsh Rarebit, defrosted*

2 tablespoons dry onion soup mix

1/2 cup dairy sour cream

1. Place Welsh Rarebit in top of double boiler over rapidly boiling water and heat for 20 minutes.
2. Add onion soup mix and sour cream (do not allow mixture to boil after sour cream has been added); stir well to combine. Heat another 5 minutes and serve piping hot with bread sticks for dipping.

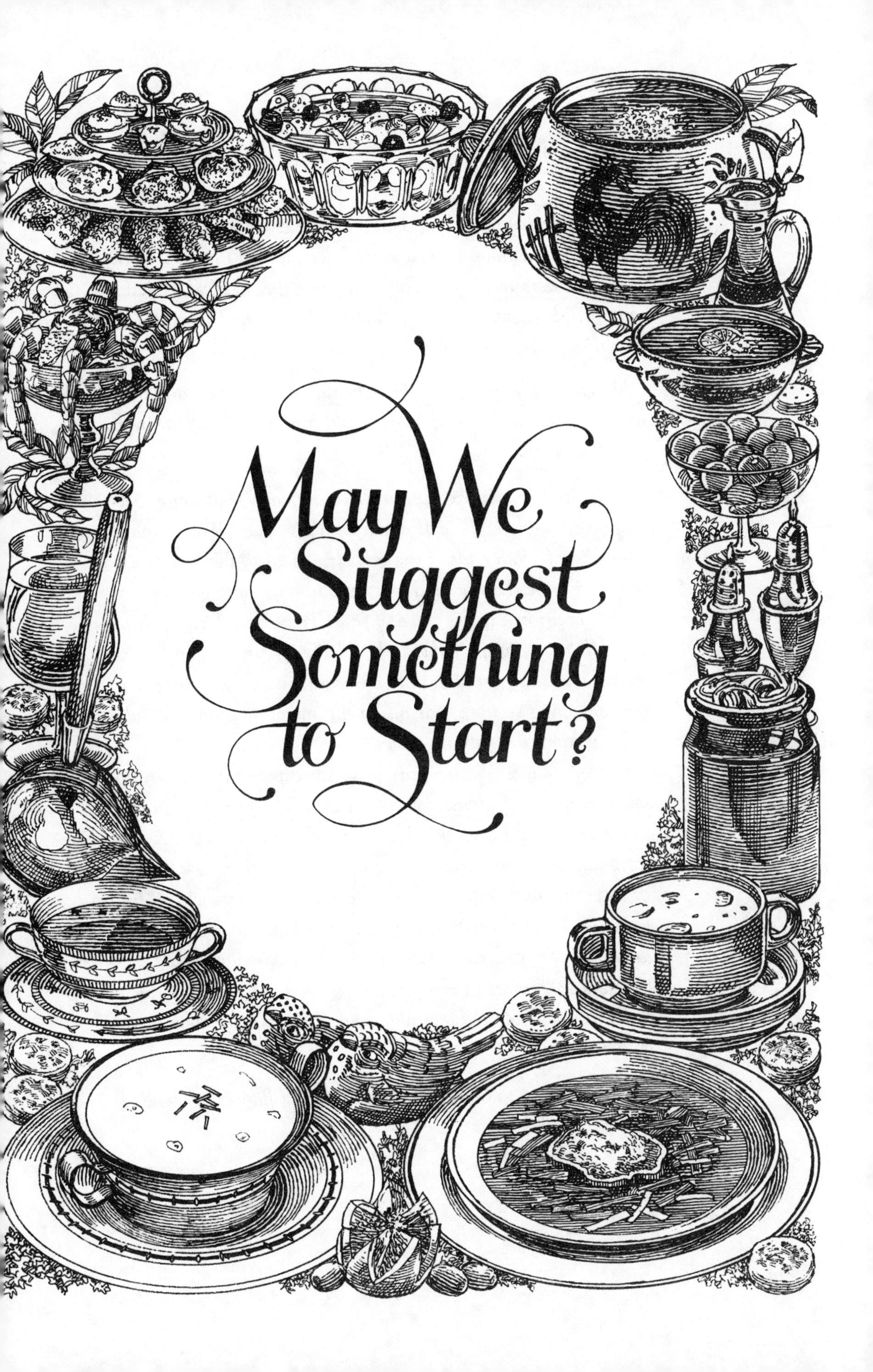
May We
Suggest
Something
to Start?

That's the phrase every Stouffer girl uses when she comes to your restaurant table, and we have divided this section in two: appetizers and soups. There are some special tricks we have to improve the taste and appearance of both, and we'd like to pass them on to you.

Many of our appetizers call for the use of fresh fruit, and over the years we have developed tried and true procedures for fresh fruit preparation.

Grapefruit or Orange: *Use a well-sharpened fruit knife, cutting board, table knife, and a pan with a strainer. With a sharp knife, cut off both ends of the grapefruit skin so the fruit is exposed; remove the rind and white membrane cutting in sawing motion and rotating the piece of fruit. To section: Pick up fruit with left hand, insert table knife (blade up), and remove first section by cutting on both sides of section inside membrane. For the remaining sections, cut inside the membrane on one side only. Sections will flip out easily.*

Frosted Grapes: *Wash grapes by gently dipping the bunch up and down in a container of cold water. Portion grapes in size bunches desired for service. Use scissors to cut grape stems. Redip grape bunches in cold water and drain on a wire rack for two or three minutes. Frost grapes by gently rolling bunch in dry, granulated sugar as near to service time as possible. Place frosted grapes on wire rack to prevent sugar from becoming soaked.*

Bananas, Peaches, Pears, Apples or Avocados: *To prevent them from discoloring, sprinkle with fresh orange, lemon or grapefruit juice.*

Another hint: to bring out individual fruit flavors in blended fruit juices, add salt.

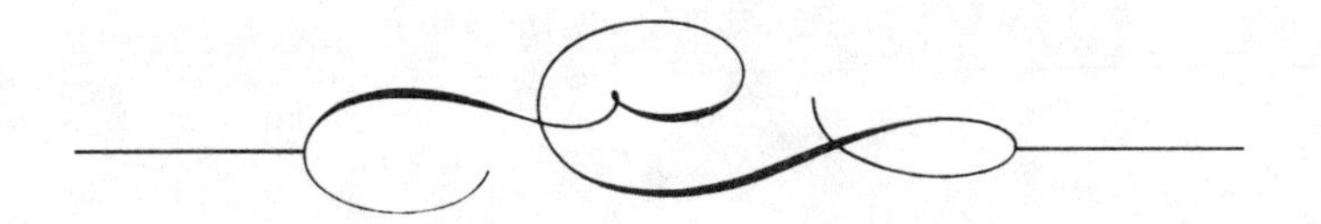

APPETIZERS

ORANGE COCKTAIL AU RHUM

(Serves 6)

1/2 cup orange juice
1/4 cup Simple Syrup (page 223)
1/4 cup light rum
4 cups fresh orange sections

1. Combine orange juice, Simple Syrup and light rum.
2. Add oranges and mix gently to combine. Chill for several hours.
3. Serve in frosted glass dishes garnished with sprigs of fresh mint.

NOTE: To frost glass dishes, dip edges of dishes into lemon juice, then in granulated sugar. Chill thoroughly.

We put this on our menu early in our history, and it's practically a fixture now. Nice simple idea that leads into meat dishes well.

FROSTED CRANBERRY SHRUB

(Serves 6)

2-1/2 cups cranberry juice
1 tablespoon freshly squeezed lemon juice
1/2 cup orange juice
1/2 pint lemon sherbet
6 fresh mint sprigs

1. Combine fruit juices and chill.
2. Chill stemmed juice glasses.
3. Place a small scoop of sherbet in each glass and fill glasses with fruit juice. Garnish with fresh mint sprigs. Serve at once.

There's more to our fresh fruit appetizers than fresh fruit. A particular favorite is the champagne variation.

FRESH FRUIT SUPREME

(Serves 6)

Select five (5) of the following fruits depending on the season of the year and your color scheme. Prepare one cup of each fruit selected. Combine all fruit with compote juice and chill thoroughly. Garnish each serving with a sprig of fresh mint.

Grapefruit sections: cut in half
Grapes: whole green, or halves of black or red
Melon: balls, sticks or small wedges
Orange sections: cut in half
Peaches: peeled and sliced
Pineapples: wedges or sticks
Plums: in 1/4-inch slices
Strawberries: cut in half

COMPOTE JUICE

1/2 cup Simple Syrup (page 223)
2 tablespoons freshly squeezed lemon juice
1 tablespoon freshly squeezed lime juice
Few grains salt
1/3 cup water

1. Combine all ingredients and chill. Pour over fresh fruits.

Variations:

Sherried Fruit: Reduce water to 2-1/2 tablespoons and add 3 tablespoons cream sherry.

Minted Fruit: Add 2 tablespoons crème de menthe and one drop green food coloring.

Grenadine: Reduce Simple Syrup to 3 tablespoons; add 1/3 cup maraschino cherry juice, 1-1/2 teaspoons grenadine and 1 tablespoon of lemon juice.

Champagne: Add 1/2 cup of cold champagne just before serving.

Lime: Add 3 tablespoons freshly squeezed lime juice; garnish each serving with a thin slice of fresh lime.

MINTED GRAPEFRUIT COCKTAIL

(Serves 6)

1/4 cup fresh grapefruit juice
1/2 cup Simple Syrup (page 224)
1/4 cup cold water
3 to 4 drops peppermint extract
3 drops green food coloring
3 cups grapefruit sections, approximately 4 grapefruits

1. Combine grapefruit juice, Simple Syrup, cold water, peppermint extract and green food coloring.
2. Add grapefruit sections which have been cut in half. Stir gently to combine. Chill thoroughly.
3. Serve garnished with sprigs of fresh mint.

The first time we ever served this was at the Top of the Six's, *our New York restaurant at 666 Fifth Avenue.*

HOT OYSTERS EN RAMEKIN

(Serves 4)

6 tablespoons butter, melted
1/4 teaspoon onion salt
3/4 cup crushed oyster crackers
1/4 cup butter
2 dozen raw oysters, drained well
4 ovenproof ramekins

1. Combine melted butter and onion salt. Pour butter over the crushed crackers and toss lightly.
2. Melt 1/4 cup butter in a skillet. Add drained oysters and sauté over low heat for approximately 2 minutes, just until edges of the oysters begin to curl. Remove oysters from skillet and save broth.
3. Arrange six oysters in each ramekin. Pour one tablespoon cooking broth over oysters. Sprinkle 3 tablespoons crumb mixture over each ramekin and pack firmly.
4. Place ramekins under broiler until crumbs are golden brown.

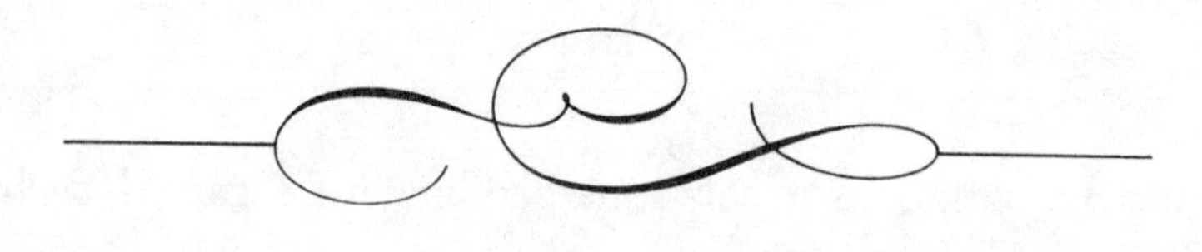

SOUPS

Soup is still one of life's better one-dish meals. Make a nice, big tureen, then fill the soup bowls. Along with the soup, try crusty French bread and a crisp green salad. Fresh fruit and cheese make a satisfying dessert.

Garnishes always add the professional finishing touch. Try paprika sprinkled lightly, chopped parsley or unsweetened whipped cream.

Sometimes even a careful cook finds that things don't go quite right, so we have a couple of ideas for correcting some common problems.

Vichyssoise or Cream of Mushroom: *If this soup starts to curdle, vigorously whip a small amount of white sauce into the soup. Use medium-thick sauce for vichyssoise; thin sauce for cream of mushroom.*

Oversalting: *If your soup broth (or gravy) seem slightly oversalted, put in a piece of raw potato; it will absorb some of this excess salt.*

FRESH MUSHROOM BISQUE

(Serves 4)

2 tablespoons butter
3 tablespoons all-purpose flour
3/4 teaspoon salt
Few grains white pepper
1-1/3 cups hot coffee cream
1/3 cup hot chicken broth
1-1/4 cups hot milk
2 teaspoons butter
1/3 cup sliced fresh mushrooms
1/2 cup chopped fresh mushrooms
1/8 teaspoon grated onion
1/4 cup milk

1. Melt first amount of butter in a heavy saucepan. Blend in flour, salt, and pepper. Beat to a smooth paste and simmer for 2 minutes to partially cook flour.
2. Combine hot cream, hot chicken broth and first amount of hot milk. Gradually add to flour mixture, beating constantly until smooth.

Cook over medium heat until thickened and the flour taste disappears. Remove from heat.

3. Melt second amount of butter in a large skillet. Add chopped and sliced mushrooms and grated onion; cook uncovered 6 to 8 minutes, stirring occasionally.
4. Add second amount of milk to mushrooms and heat to simmering. Add to soup and heat thoroughly. Taste for salt. Serve at once.

When the weather gets cold we make extra batches of this soup because it sounds good on the menu, tastes even better than it sounds.

OLD-FASHIONED NAVY BEAN SOUP

(Serves 4)

3/4 cup navy beans
1-1/4 cups water
3/4 pound smoked (picnic) ham or shoulder
1 ham bone
3 quarts water
1 whole, small onion
3/4 teaspoon granulated sugar
Dash pepper
Salt to taste

1. Wash navy beans under cold running water and drain well. Combine beans with 1-1/4 cups water and soak overnight in the refrigerator.
2. Cut ham into 1-inch pieces and place in a heavy kettle; add ham bone and 3 quarts of water. Simmer 2 hours. Skim off fat. Lift ham bone and pieces from broth; reserve.
3. Drain beans and place in heavy kettle. Add 1 quart of ham broth.
4. Tie ham bone, ham pieces and onion in a cheesecloth bag. Add to broth. Heat to boiling; reduce heat, cover and simmer for 2 to 3 hours or until beans begin to break.
5. Remove cheesecloth bag; discard bone and onion. Chop 1/4 cup ham and set aside.
6. Strain 1/2 cup of beans from soup and force them through a fine sieve; return bean purée to soup.
7. Add sugar, pepper and chopped cooked ham; taste for salt. Heat thoroughly.

Since our French Onion Soup is served in the hearty French style, individual salads will be all you need to complete your meal. A word about the onions you use, however. After careful testing we have found that large, white onions have a better browning quality than yellow onions and suggest you use white onions for a better-tasting soup.

FRENCH ONION SOUP AU GRATIN

(Serves 4)

2 teaspoons butter or margarine
1-1/2 teaspoons beef fat
1-1/3 cups thinly sliced white onions
1/2 teaspoon salt
Few grains pepper
4-1/4 cups beef broth
1/2 cup Madeira wine (optional)
4 oven proof individual tureens
4 Parmesan croutons (below)
1/2 cup coarsely shredded Swiss cheese

1. Melt butter or margarine and beef fat in a heavy skillet. Heat until bubbling hot.
2. Add sliced onions. Cover and cook until onions are heated through (approximately 5 minutes). Uncover and cook until onions are tender and dark brown. Onions should be well browned before broth is added so that soup will have a full-bodied flavor and rich appearance.
3. Combine cooked onions, salt, pepper and beef broth and heat thoroughly. (If canned bouillon is used in place of homemade beef broth, omit the salt and add 1/2 cup water.) Let stand on very low heat for 30 minutes to allow flavors to blend. Taste for seasoning and add more salt if necessary.
4. Measure 2 tablespoons of Madeira wine into each individual preheated tureen. Ladle soup into tureens and top each serving with one crouton. Mound 2 tablespoons shredded Swiss cheese on each crouton. Bake in a 400°F. oven for 15 minutes or until cheese is melted and golden brown. Serve at once.

PARMESAN CROUTONS

4—3/4" thick white bread slices (French bread makes good croutons, too)
1/4 cup butter, melted
2 teaspoons grated Parmesan cheese

1. Cut bread into 3-inch rounds using a large biscuit cutter.
2. Generously butter a baking tray. Arrange bread rounds on tray leaving some space between pieces. Brush top surfaces of bread rounds with butter to saturate bread lightly.
3. Sprinkle each crouton evenly with grated Parmesan cheese.
4. Bake in 350°F. oven for 10 to 15 minutes or until dry and lightly browned.

Some people can't spell it. Some people can't say it. But anybody can make it with this recipe. The apple and curry flavor really gets to you.

MULLIGATAWNY SOUP

(Serves 4–6)

2 tablespoons chicken fat
2 tablespoons chopped onion
1/4 cup carrots, cut in 1/2" cubes
1/4 cup celery, cut in 1/2" cubes
1 teaspoon diced green pepper
1 large apple, pared and cored, cut in 1/2" cubes
1/2 cup chicken broth
1/4 cup all-purpose flour
3/4 cup canned tomatoes, broken
1/4 teaspoon salt
Few grains pepper
1/4 teaspoon curry powder
3-1/2 cups chicken broth
1 cup cooked chicken, cut in 1/2" cubes

1. Melt chicken fat in a heavy kettle; add onion, carrots, celery, green pepper and apples. Simmer 10 to 15 minutes or until vegetables are tender but not brown.
2. Combine 1/2 cup chicken broth with flour and mix well. Add to vegetables, stirring constantly to blend.
3. Add tomatoes, salt, pepper, curry powder and 3-1/2 cups chicken broth. Blend; heat to boiling; reduce heat and simmer one hour.
4. Add cubed, cooked chicken and simmer 5 to 10 minutes longer. Serve at once.

CREAM OF TOMATO SOUP

(Serves 4)

2 cups canned tomatoes, sieved
1/4 cup tomato purée
1 tablespoon granulated sugar
1/8 teaspoon baking soda
1 tablespoon margarine
1-1/2 tablespoons all-purpose flour
1 teaspoon salt
Dash pepper
1/4 cup hot milk
1-3/4 cups hot coffee cream

1. Combine sieved tomatoes and tomato purée. Add granulated sugar. Heat tomato mixture, but do not boil. Add soda and mix well. Keep hot for combining with cream mixture.
2. Melt margarine in a saucepan. Blend in flour, salt and pepper until smooth. Reduce heat and simmer for 1 to 2 minutes. Gradually add hot milk and cream, stirring constantly until smooth. Cook over medium heat until sauce thickens slightly.
3. Add the hot tomato mixture gradually to the hot cream mixture, beating constantly. *Be sure that both mixtures are hot before combining or soup will curdle.* Serve at once.

NOTE: If soup does begin to curdle, vigorously whip 2 tablespoons crushed ice into the mixture; the ice and beating will smooth the texture.

CHICKEN GUMBO SOUP

(Serves 4)

1/4 cup salt pork, cut in 1/4" pieces
2 tablespoons fat (drained from pork)
1/2 cup cooked chicken, cut in 1/4" pieces
1-1/2 teaspoons chopped onion
1/4 cup canned okra
2-1/3 cups chicken broth
1 cup canned tomatoes, broken into 1" pieces
1/2 teaspoon salt
3 tablespoons cooked rice

1. Sauté salt pork in a heavy saucepan until crisp and brown. Drain and save required amount of fat; reserve salt pork.
2. Return fat to saucepan. Add chicken and onion; simmer 5 minutes.
3. Add okra, sauteed salt pork, chicken broth and tomatoes; heat to boiling. Taste for salt. Lower heat and simmer 20 minutes.
4. Add cooked rice and heat thoroughly.

VIENNESE CHICKEN SOUP

(Serves 4)

2 tablespoons chicken fat
3-1/2 tablespoons all-purpose flour
1/2 teaspoons salt
2-1/3 cups hot chicken broth
1-1/4 cups hot coffee cream
1/4 cup finely chopped cooked chicken

1. Melt chicken fat in a heavy saucepan. Add flour and salt; beat smooth and simmer 2 minutes to partially cook flour.
2. Gradually add hot chicken broth, beating constantly until smooth. Cook over medium heat until flour taste disappears, stirring occasionally.
3. Add hot cream gradually, stirring constantly. Add cooked chicken and heat thoroughly.
4. Taste for seasoning. Serve at once.

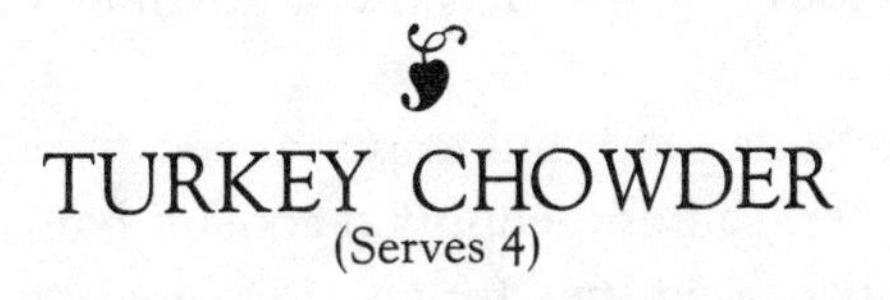

TURKEY CHOWDER

(Serves 4)

2 tablespoons butter or margarine
1 teaspoon chopped onion
1 medium potato, peeled and cut in 1/2" cubes
1/2 cup diced celery
1/2 cup cream-style corn
1 cup hot turkey broth
3/4 cup cooked turkey, cut in 1/4" pieces
1/4 teaspoon salt
Dash pepper
1/8 teaspoon paprika
1/8 teaspoon ginger
1/2 cup hot milk
1 cup hot coffee cream
2 teaspoons finely chopped parsley

1. Melt butter or margarine; add chopped onion and sauté for 5 minutes or until onion is tender but not brown.
2. Add potato, celery, corn, turkey broth and cooked turkey; cover and simmer 20 minutes or until potatoes and celery are tender.
3. Add salt, pepper, paprika, ginger, hot milk and cream; blend and heat thoroughly.
4. Garnish each serving with 1/2 teaspoon finely chopped parsley.

OLD-FASHIONED SPLIT PEA SOUP

(Serves 4)

3/4 cup dry split peas
1-2/3 cups water
2 pounds smoked (picnic) ham or shoulder
4 quarts water
1 ham bone
1 whole, small onion
1/2 teaspoon granulated sugar
Dash pepper
1/4 teaspoon salt

1. Wash peas under cold running water and drain well. Combine peas and 1-2/3 cups of water and soak overnight in the refrigerator.
2. Cut ham into 1-inch pieces and place in a heavy kettle; add ham bone and 4 quarts of water. Simmer for 2 hours. Skim off fat. Lift ham bone and pieces from broth; reserve.
3. Drain peas; place in a heavy kettle and add 3-1/2 cups of ham broth.
4. Tie ham bone, ham pieces and onion in a cheesecloth bag. Heat to boiling; reduce heat, cover, and simmer one hour or until peas are soft.
5. Remove cheesecloth bag; discard bone and onion. Chop 1/4 cup ham and set aside.
6. Strain soup through a food mill to purée peas.
7. Add sugar, pepper, salt and chopped cooked ham; heat thoroughly. Garnish with thinly sliced frankfurters, if desired.

This is an old Stouffer family favorite, and sometimes is called Pennsylvania Dutch Chicken Corn Soup.

LANCASTER CHICKEN CORN SOUP

(Serves 4)

3-1/2 cups chicken broth
2-1/2 tablespoons chopped onion
1/2 cup chopped celery
1/4 teaspoon salt
Dash pepper
1/4 cup cooked chicken, cut in 1/4" pieces
1/3 cup uncooked, wide noodles
1/4 cup whole-kernel corn
2 tablespoons diced hard-cooked egg
2 teaspoons finely chopped parsley

1. Combine chicken broth, onion, celery, salt and pepper; simmer one hour.
2. Add chicken, uncooked noodles and corn; cook until noodles are just tender.
3. When ready to serve, stir in hard-cooked egg. Garnish each serving with 1/2 teaspoon finely chopped parsley.

Cold soups are not simply for hot weather; they can be served all year round and are on our menus . . . so why not on yours?

CRÈME VICHYSSOISE

(Serves 6)

1-1/4 cups boiling water
2 teaspoons salt
Few grains white pepper
3/4 cup hot chicken broth
1-1/2 cups instant potato buds
1-1/2 tablespoons butter
1 cup finely chopped onion
3/4 cup chicken broth
2 cups hot coffee cream
2 tablespoons finely snipped fresh chives

1. Measure boiling water into mixing bowl.
2. Add salt, pepper, first amount of hot chicken broth, and potato buds. Mix on medium speed of an electric mixer to blend.
3. Melt butter in a heavy saucepan. Add finely chopped onion and cook until onion is tender but not brown.
4. Add second amount of chicken broth and bring to a boil. Add potato mixture; blend and bring to a boil.
5. Add hot cream and heat but do not boil.
6. Strain through a fine sieve and discard onions.
7. Chill soup thoroughly. It should be icy cold when served.
8. Garnish each serving of soup with 1 teaspoon finely snipped fresh chives.

This is one of Mother Stouffer's original recipes and has been served in the restaurants as long as any of us can remember.

CHILLED FRESH TOMATO BISQUE

(Serves 4)

1-1/3 cups chicken broth
2/3 cup canned tomatoes
1/2 cup chopped celery
1 teaspoon chopped onion
1/2 cup carrots, cut in 1/2" pieces
1/4 teaspoon salt
1-1/2 tablespoons butter
2 tablespoons all-purpose flour
1-1/3 cups hot coffee cream
1 large fresh tomato
1-1/2 tablespoons butter
1 tablespoon granulated sugar
1/4 teaspoon salt
Pinch baking soda

1. Combine chicken broth, canned tomatoes, celery, onion, carrots, and first amount of salt. Heat to boiling and simmer 20 minutes.
2. Strain and discard vegetables. Reserve broth.
3. Melt first amount of butter and blend in flour. Simmer over low heat for 2 minutes to partially cook flour.
4. Gradually add hot cream, beating constantly until thickened. Remove from heat; blend in reserved hot broth. Keep hot.
5. Peel fresh tomato and cut into 1/2-inch pieces.
6. Melt second amount of butter in skillet. Add fresh, diced tomatoes and sauté 2 to 4 minutes.
7. Add sugar, second amount of salt, and soda; mix well.
8. Pour hot fresh tomato mixture into hot cream mixture, stirring constantly to blend.
9. Chill thoroughly.

From
the
Dinner
Menu

Of course, in the restaurants we offer a great deal of variety to satisfy everyone from vegetarian to steak-and-potato lover. That's why you find so many different kinds of entrées on our menus. We offer an interesting balance, and what we present on a daily menu often makes up a week of interesting eating for a family.

Most of the recipes are fairly simple to prepare and take on a festive look when garnished with crisp, fresh sprigs of watercress, parsley, chicory or endive.

In putting together some of our favorites, we've given you some shortcuts by using our frozen foods as the base. So in each section you'll find the last few recipes especially designed for easy preparation. We don't think anyone should spend all their time in the kitchen, and we do think that people who cook infrequently should be confident of good results. So when you're short of time and/or experience, try some of these short-cuts. We call them Stouffer Shorties.

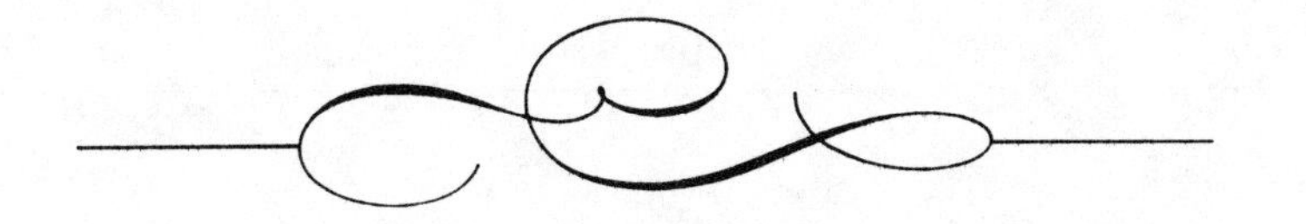

MEATS

POLYNESIAN PEPPER STEAK

(Serves 4–6)

1-1/4 pounds sirloin of beef, sliced 3/8″ thick
1-1/2 tablespoons beef fat or margarine
1/2 teaspoon salt
1-1/2 teaspoons beef fat or margarine
1/4 cup chopped green pepper
1/3 cup chopped onion
1/2 clove garlic, crushed
3/4 cup pan drippings
3/4 cup beef broth
1 cup canned tomatoes, broken
1/2 teaspoon salt
Dash pepper
1 tablespoon cornstarch
1/4 cup cold water
2 teaspoons soy sauce
1-1/2 large green peppers, cut in strips 1/4″ wide by 2-1/2″ long

1. Cut beef slices into strips 1 inch wide and 1-1/2 inches long.
2. Melt first amount of beef fat or margarine in heavy skillet; add 1/2 teaspoon of salt, and beef; brown quickly. Remove from heat. Drain meat; reserve. Save drippings.
3. Melt 1-1/2 teaspoons of fat in a heavy kettle; add chopped green pepper, onion and garlic; sauté 8 to 10 minutes or until onion is tender but not brown.
4. Add meat, pan drippings, beef broth, tomatoes, 1/2 teaspoon salt and pepper; heat to boiling, reduce to simmering and cook 1-1/2 hours or until meat is tender.
5. Blend cornstarch with cold water and add to meat mixture, stirring constantly. Simmer 3 to 5 minutes.
6. Add soy sauce and blend. Keep warm.
7. Cover green pepper strips with boiling water and simmer 1 minute. Drain immediately. Add to meat mixture just before serving.
8. Serve over fluffy rice.

This is on the menu at almost all our Tops restaurants, and we think one of the reasons for its success is the Mustard Sauce marinade. Little tricks make big hits, we find.

STEAK AU POIVRE

(Serves 4)

1/4 cup Mustard Sauce (page 203)
4 sirloin strip steaks (12 to 14 ounces each)
3 tablespoons cracked black peppercorns
1/2 cup Clarified Butter (page 200)
Cognac Mustard Sauce (below)

1. Spread 1 teaspoon Mustard Sauce on one side of each steak; then sprinkle 1 teaspoon cracked peppercorns evenly over entire surface. Press peppercorns into steaks using the palm of your hand. Turn steaks over on waxed paper and repeat this procedure on the other side of the steaks.
2. Cover steaks and refrigerate overnight or for at least 8 hours.
3. Heat Clarified Butter in a heavy skillet. Pan fry steaks, turning only once with tongs, to the desired degree of doneness:

Rare	4–5 minutes/each side
Medium rare	5–6 minutes/each side
Medium	6–7 minutes/each side

4. Serve with Cognac Mustard Sauce.

COGNAC MUSTARD SAUCE

2 tablespoons butter
1 tablespoon freeze-dried chives
1/4 cup cognac
1/2 cup Mustard Sauce (page 203)
1/4 cup coffee cream

1. Place butter and freeze-dried chives in a stainless steel saucepan. Cook for 2 to 3 minutes, stirring frequently, until hot.
2. Add the cognac and boil rapidly for 1 to 2 minutes to evaporate the alcohol. Remove from heat.
3. Add the Mustard Sauce and stir to combine; then add cream and stir again.
4. Place over low heat until mixture starts to bubble. Remove from heat and serve immediately.

LONDON BROIL

(Serves 4)

1 flank steak, about 2 pounds
1 cup White French Dressing
Mushroom Sauce (below)

1. Trim transparent membrane from steak and score both sides 1/8-inch deep and 1 inch apart.
2. Place scored steak in a shallow, oblong container. Cover with White French Dressing.
3. Cover and refrigerate 24 hours.
4. Drain marinade from steak and reserve for basting.
5. Broil to desired doneness, basting occasionally with remaining marinade.
6. Slice steak across the grain into 1/8-inch thick slices. Hold knife at a 45° angle so that slices will be approximately 2 inches wide. Serve with Mushroom Sauce.

MUSHROOM SAUCE

2 tablespoons beef fat or margarine
2 tablespoons all-purpose flour
1/4 teaspoon salt
Few grains pepper
1 cup hot beef broth
2 teaspoons butter
3 mushrooms, washed and thinly sliced

1. Melt fat or margarine in a heavy saucepan. Blend in flour, salt and pepper and simmer 2 minutes to partially cook flour.
2. Gradually add hot beef broth, stirring constantly. Cook until thickened and flour taste has disappeared. Reduce heat.
3. Heat butter in a skillet until bubbling. Add sliced mushrooms and saute uncovered over medium heat until mushrooms are tender and brown.
4. Add mushrooms to hot gravy and blend. Serve hot.

TENDERLOIN OF BEEF MADEIRA

(Serves 4)

1/2 cup all-purpose flour
1/2 teaspoon salt
1/8 teaspoon pepper
Few grains paprika
1/4 teaspoon dry mustard
1-1/4 pounds tenderloin of beef, sliced 1/2″ thick
1/4 cup butter
1/4 cup finely chopped onion
1/4 clove garlic, minced
3 cups beef broth
1 tablespoon tomato purée
1/3 cup Madeira wine (pale dry)
1/4 pound small mushroom caps

1. Combine flour, salt, pepper, paprika and dry mustard. Roll tenderloin slices in mixture to coat all sides. Reserve excess flour mixture.
2. Melt butter in heavy skillet. Add meat slices a few at a time and brown over high heat. Remove meat slices and reserve.
3. Add flour to skillet along with onion and garlic; simmer 5 minutes until onion softens.
4. Gradually add beef broth and tomato purée, stirring constantly, until slightly thickened.
5. Add meat slices and simmer 10 minutes.
6. Stir in Madeira and mushroom caps. Simmer over low heat until mushrooms are tender.
7. Cover and bake in a 350° F. oven for 40 minutes. Sauce should have rich color and consistency of thin gravy.
8. Serve over parsley buttered noodles or rice.

BEEF TENDERLOIN EN BROCHETTE

(Serves 8)

3-1/2 pounds beef tenderloin, cut into 72 1" cubes
2-1/2 cups White French Dressing
32 pieces green pepper, cut in 1" squares (approximately 2 peppers)
32 fresh mushroom caps or 32 cherry tomatoes
3/4 pound bacon, partially cooked, cut in 1" pieces
32 small, whole white onions, drained (approximately 2—1-pound cans)
8 metal skewers
Melted butter for basting
Salt

1. Place beef tenderloin cubes in a shallow pan; pour White French Dressing evenly over meat and refrigerate for 1-1/2 to 2 hours, basting occasionally. Drain thoroughly.
2. Blanch green pepper squares in boiling water for 1 minute; drain immediately.
3. Cover mushroom caps with hot water and simmer 4 to 5 minutes; drain well.
4. Assemble each brochette as follows:

   1 beef cube
   1 pepper square
   1 mushroom cap or cherry tomato
   1 beef cube
   1 piece bacon
   1 whole onion

   and continue threading ingredients in this order, ending with the ninth cube of meat.
5. Broil 3 inches from heat for 5 to 6 minutes; turn brochettes several times brushing each time with melted butter.
6. Remove from broiler and sprinkle with salt; brush with butter or garlic butter.
7. Serve over a bed of Rice Pilaf (page 118). Place rice on heated plates. Hold skewers over rice and gently push ingredients from skewers so that the row of ingredients stays in line.

TENDERLOIN OF BEEF BURGUNDY

(Serves 4)

1-1/4 pounds beef tenderloin, sliced 1/4" thick
2 tablespoons shortening
1 medium onion, thinly sliced
1/2 clove garlic, minced
1/4 cup all-purpose flour
3/4 teaspoon salt
1/8 teaspoon pepper
Dash paprika
3 cups hot beef broth
1 tablespoon tomato paste
1 drop red food coloring
1/3 pound sliced fresh mushrooms
1/2 cup Burgundy wine

1. Cut beef slices in pieces 1-1/2 inches wide and 2 inches long.
2. Melt shortening in heavy skillet over high heat; brown meat slices quickly and remove from skillet with a slotted spoon.
3. Reduce heat; add onion and garlic to shortening and sauté until tender but not brown.
4. Blend in flour; add salt, pepper, paprika, hot beef broth and tomato paste, stirring constantly.
5. Heat to boiling point; reduce heat and cook, stirring occasionally, for 20 minutes.
6. Add a drop of red food coloring to give reddish brown color.
7. Add mushrooms, wine and sautéed meat slices. Simmer 10 to 15 minutes.
8. Serve over fluffy rice or buttered noodles.

TENDERLOIN OF BEEF CONTINENTAL

(Serves 6)

2 teaspoons beef fat
2 teaspoons butter
4 teaspoons all-purpose flour
3-3/4 teaspoons cornstarch
Few grains pepper
1/8 teaspoon garlic salt
2 beef bouillon cubes
1 cup boiling water
2/3 cup warm coffee cream
3 to 4 drops gravy seasoning
2-1/4 pounds beef tenderloin, cut into 12 steaks
6 ovenproof ramekins
3/4 pound fresh mushroom caps, sautéed

1. Melt beef fat and butter in a saucepan. Blend in flour, cornstarch,

pepper and garlic salt. Simmer 2 minutes.
2. Dissolve bouillon cubes in boiling water; gradually add to flour mixture, beating constantly until smooth; bring to a boil. Reduce heat and blend in warm cream.
3. Simmer 5 minutes. Add gravy seasoning to give a medium brown color.
4. Broil tenderloin steaks to desired doneness.
5. Arrange two steaks in each heated ramekin; top with 1/4 cup of hot sauce and garnish with sautéed mushrooms.

You don't have to be Hungarian to love this dish. It's an all-family all-American favorite.

HUNGARIAN GOULASH

(Serves 4–6)

1-1/2 tablespoons margarine
1-1/4 pounds boneless beef chuck, cut in pieces 1/4″ thick by 3/4″ wide by 1″ long
3 tablespoons butter
2 cups sliced onion
1 clove garlic, minced
2-1/2 cups canned tomatoes, broken
2-1/4 teaspoons granulated sugar
1-1/2 teaspoons paprika
1-1/2 teaspoons salt
1/8 teaspoon pepper
1/2 teaspoon barbecue seasoning
1/8 teaspoon leaf tarragon
3 tablespoons dairy sour cream, room temperature
1/2 teaspoon all-purpose flour

1. Melt margarine in a heavy kettle. Add meat and brown quickly, stirring frequently. Lift meat from kettle and reserve.
2. Add butter and melt; add onion and garlic, and sauté until onion is golden brown.
3. Add browned meat, tomatoes, sugar, paprika, salt, pepper, barbecue seasoning and tarragon; heat to boiling; reduce heat and simmer until meat is tender but not shredding. Remove from heat.
4. Combine room-temperature sour cream with flour and beat smooth; gradually add to goulash. Do not allow mixture to boil after sour cream has been added.
5. Serve over parsley buttered noodles.

Simple-sounding foods sometimes surprise us by becoming standout favorites, such as this Stouffer super speciality.

HAM LOAF WITH FRESH RHUBARB SAUCE

(Serves 4)

1 egg
1/2 cup milk
2-1/2 slices stale bread, trimmed and cut in 1/8″ flakes
3/4 pound lean ground pork
3/4 pound ground cooked smoked ham
1/2 cup finely diced celery
Fresh Rhubarb Sauce (below)

1. Beat egg slightly; add milk and blend. Pour egg mixture over flaked bread and mix well. Allow to stand until bread absorbs all the liquid.
2. Combine pork, ham, bread mixture and celery. Mix thoroughly.
3. Shape into loaf or pat into lightly oiled loaf pan.
4. Bake in 350° F. oven for 1 hour. When done, juice on top of the loaf will be clear.
5. Remove from oven and let stand 15 minutes to set. Unmold onto a heated platter and serve with Fresh Rhubarb Sauce.

FRESH RHUBARB SAUCE

1 cup water
1/3 cup granulated sugar
1 tablespoon cornstarch
Dash salt
3/4 cup fresh rhubarb, cut in 1/2″ cubes
2 drops red food coloring

1. Heat water to boiling.
2. Combine sugar, cornstarch and salt. Gradually add to boiling water, stirring constantly until mixture becomes clear. Add red food coloring. Remove from heat.
3. Stir in rhubarb. Cover and let stand away from heat until rhubarb is tender.

TENDERLOIN OF PORK PROVINCIAL

(Serves 6)

1/2 cup all-purpose flour
1-1/2 teaspoons salt
2-1/4 pounds pork tenderloin, cut into 18 steaks
3 tablespoons butter
2 tablespoons vegetable shortening
1/4 cup chicken fat
3 tablespoons all-purpose flour
2-1/2 cups hot chicken broth
1/2 teaspoon salt
1 drop yellow food coloring
1-1/4 cups hot coffee cream
Oranges for garnish

1. Combine first amount of flour and salt. Coat steaks lightly with flour mixture.
2. Melt butter and shortening in a heavy skillet. Sauté steaks until well browned.
3. Place steaks in a single layer in a shallow 2-quart baking dish.
4. Melt chicken fat in a saucepan. Blend in second amount of flour. Simmer 2 minutes.
5. Gradually add hot broth, beating constantly until smooth. Bring to a boil; reduce heat and cook until gravy thickens slightly.
6. Add salt and a drop of yellow food coloring.
7. Add hot cream and combine thoroughly.
8. Pour hot cream gravy over steaks. Cover and bake in a 350° F. oven for 1 hour or until tender. Uncover and bake 10 minutes longer to brown top of meat.
9. Garnish with very thin slices of unpeeled oranges.

VEAL PARMESAN

(Serves 4)

Tomato Sauce:
2/3 cup tomato juice
1/3 cup tomato purée
1 teaspoon granulated sugar
Few grains salt
1/8 teaspoon sweet basil
1/8 teaspoon Worcestershire sauce
Few grains garlic salt
1-1/2 teaspoons butter

1 egg, beaten
2 tablespoons water
4—5-ounce veal cutlets, 1/4" thick
1/2 cup dry bread crumbs
3/4 teaspoon salt
Vegetable shortening as needed
2 tablespoons grated Parmesan cheese
4 slices Mozzarella cheese, 1/8" thick

1. To make tomato sauce, combine first eight ingredients in a saucepan. Simmer 10 minutes to blend flavors. Keep sauce hot.
2. Combine beaten egg and water to make egg batter.
3. Dip veal cutlets into egg batter. Drain on a rack.
4. Combine dry bread crumbs and salt. Dip cutlets into crumbs to coat lightly on both sides.
5. Melt vegetable shortening to a depth of 1/4 inch in a heavy skillet. Sauté cutlets until golden brown on both sides. Drain on absorbent paper.
6. In a shallow 9-inch square baking dish, place the four cutlets; do not overlap.
7. Pour the hot tomato sauce over the cutlets.
8. Sprinkle grated Parmesan cheese over the sauce. Cover and bake in a 325°F. oven for 1 to 1-1/4 hours until veal is tender.
9. Remove from oven and uncover. Place one slice of Mozzarella cheese over each cutlet and return to oven just long enough for the cheese to melt.

VEAL SCALOPPINE AL MARSALA

(Serves 6)

3 tablespoons butter
3/4 pound mushrooms, sliced 1/4" thick
1/2 teaspoon salt
1/2 cup all-purpose flour
2 tablespoons salt
3/4 teaspoon pepper
Few grains cayenne
2-3/4 pounds veal, sliced 1/4" thick by 2" wide by 3" long
1 cup butter, melted
1-1/2 cups chicken broth
1 cup dry Marsala wine

1. Melt butter in a skillet. Add sliced mushrooms. Cover and sauté over low heat until mushrooms are tender. Uncover mushrooms, increase heat to medium and brown mushrooms slightly. Add salt and mix gently; set aside. Do not drain off broth.
2. Combine flour, salt, pepper and cayenne. Flatten veal slices to 1/8-inch thickness. Dip slices into flour mixture to coat all sides evenly.
3. Pour melted butter to a depth of 1/4-inch in a large heavy skillet. Heat until butter bubbles. Add some of the veal slices and sauté until veal is golden brown on both sides. Remove and drain on absorbent paper. Add additional melted butter when necessary and continue until all veal has been browned. Return veal slices to the skillet; cover and simmer over low heat until veal is tender, approximately 7 to 10 minutes. Remove veal from pan to heated serving dish, leaving the butter in the pan.
4. Add chicken broth and wine; heat to bubbling, stirring well. Simmer 1 to 2 minutes to blend flavors. Remove from heat.
5. Add sautéed mushrooms and broth.
6. Pour pan sauce and mushrooms over veal slices in serving dish.
7. Garnish with parsley and serve at once.

VEAL CORDON BLEU

(Serves 4)

8 veal cutlets, 2-1/2 ounces each
Salt
4 slices processed Swiss cheese (approximately 1/4 pound)
4 slices boiled ham (approximately 1/4 pound)
1/2 cup all-purpose flour
3 eggs, slightly beaten
3 tablespoons salad oil
1 cup fresh bread crumbs
1/2 cup Clarified Butter (page 200)

1. Flatten cutlets, using a meat mallet or flat side of cleaver so that each slice of meat will measure 3 inches wide by 8 inches long by 1/8-inch thick.
2. Sprinkle both sides of veal slices lightly with salt.
3. Place 4 slices of veal on a tray; arrange 1 slice of Swiss cheese and 1 slice of ham on top of each veal slice, leaving a 1/2-inch rim of veal uncovered.
4. Place remaining veal slices on top of ham and cheese; hit edges of cutlets lightly with mallet or flat side of cleaver to seal.
5. Dip cutlets in flour to coat lightly.
6. Combine beaten eggs and oil; dip cutlets in egg mixture and drain slightly; coat cutlets lightly with bread crumbs. Chill thoroughly.
7. Heat Clarified Butter in an electric fry pan or large skillet. Fry cutlets for 3 minutes on first side or until a deep golden brown; using two spatulas, carefully turn cutlets and fry on second side for 3 minutes or until browned.
8. Drain cutlets on absorbent paper and serve at once.

VEAL À LA BONNE FEMME

(Serves 4)

12 canned whole onions
3 tablespoons butter, melted
1 cup fresh mushroom caps, stems cut off
3 tablespoons butter, melted
1/2 cup all-purpose flour
1 tablespoon salt
1/4 teaspoon pepper
1-1/2 pounds veal, sliced 1/4" thick by 4-1/2" wide by 3" long
1/2 cup butter
1-2/3 cups hot water
3/4 cup dry sauterne (domestic)
1/4 cup Haut Sauternes (imported)

1. Sauté canned whole onions, uncovered, in 3 tablespoons of melted butter until onions are a very light golden brown. Set aside.
2. Sauté mushroom caps, covered, in second 3 tablespoons of melted butter until mushrooms are lightly browned and almost cooked through. Set aside.
3. Combine flour, salt and pepper thoroughly. Dip veal slices into flour mixture to coat lightly.
4. Melt 1/2 cup of butter in a heavy skillet over medium heat. When butter bubbles, add veal slices and sauté until veal is golden brown on both sides. Add sautéed onions and mushrooms, including mushroom broth, hot water and first amount of sauterne. Cover and reduce heat. Cook until veal is tender, approximately 6 to 7 minutes.
5. Arrange veal slices in a shallow serving dish. Pour pan sauce with mushrooms and onions over veal. Pour Haut Sauternes over all. Garnish with parsley sprigs. Serve immediately.

Now for those Stouffer Shorties:

SALISBURY BURGUNDY

(Serves 4)

2—12-ounce packages Frozen Salisbury Steaks, defrosted*

2—3-1/4-ounce cans mushrooms, drained

1/4 cup Burgundy wine

1. Preheat oven to 400°F.
2. Remove Salisbury Steaks from onion gravy and place in a shallow 2-quart baking dish.
3. Combine onion gravy from the steaks, mushrooms and Burgundy wine.
4. Pour mixture over steaks. Bake for 30 to 35 minutes.

SALISBURY STEAK WITH MUSHROOM GRAVY

(Serves 4)

2—12-ounce packages Frozen Salisbury Steaks, defrosted*

1—10-1/2-ounce can mushroom soup, undiluted

1. Preheat oven to 400° F.
2. Remove Salisbury Steaks from onion gravy. Place steaks in an 8-inch square baking dish.
3. Combine onion gravy and mushroom soup; pour over steaks.
4. Bake for 30 minutes. Serve with whipped potatoes or buttered noodles.

SALISBURY ROMANOFF

(Serves 4)

2—12-ounce packages Frozen Noodles Romanoff, defrosted*

2—12-ounce packages Frozen Salisbury Steaks, defrosted*

4 slices cooked bacon

1. Preheat oven to 400° F.
2. Place Noodles Romanoff in a lightly buttered 2-quart casserole.
3. Top with Salisbury Steaks and onion gravy. Bake for 25 to 30 minutes.
4. Garnish each steak with one strip of bacon before serving.

SALISBURY STROGANOFF

(Serves 4)

2—12-ounce packages Frozen Salisbury Steaks, defrosted*

1/3 cup dairy sour cream

2 teaspoons Worcestershire sauce

2—3-1/4-ounce cans mushrooms, undrained

1. Preheat oven to 400° F.
2. Remove Salisbury Steaks from onion gravy and place in a 1-quart casserole.

3. Combine onion gravy, sour cream, Worcestershire sauce, mushrooms and liquid.
4. Pour over steaks. Bake covered for 20 to 25 minutes.

SWEET AND SOUR STEAKS

(Serves 4)

2—11-ounce packages Frozen Swiss Steaks, defrosted*
4 teaspoons cornstarch
1/4 cup cold water
1 tablespoon cider vinegar
2 tablespoons soy sauce
2 tablespoons granulated sugar
1—13-ounce can pineapple tidbits and liquid
1 green pepper, cut into strips 1/4" wide

1. Preheat oven to 400° F.
2. Arrange Swiss Steaks in an 8-inch square baking dish.
3. Combine cornstarch, water, vinegar, soy sauce and sugar in a saucepan.
4. Cook over medium heat, stirring constantly until thickened and smooth.
5. Add pineapple tidbits with juice and blend.
6. Pour sauce over steaks.
7. Arrange green pepper strips on top of steaks and sauce.
8. Cover loosely and bake for 30 minutes. Serve with fluffy steamed rice.

BEEF STEAK PAPRIKASH

(Serves 4)

2—11-ounce packages Frozen Swiss Steaks, defrosted*
1/2 cup dairy sour cream
1/4 teaspoon paprika

1. Preheat oven to 400° F.
2. Remove Swiss Steaks from gravy and place in an 8-inch square baking dish.
3. Place gravy in a small mixing boil; blend in sour cream and paprika. Pour gravy over steaks; cover and bake for 20 to 25 minutes.

BEEF HASH ROUNDS

(Serves 6)

2—10-ounce packages Frozen Welsh Rarebit*
2—11-1/2-ounce packages Frozen Roast Beef Hash, defrosted*
1 egg, slightly beaten
1/4 cup chopped green pepper
1/4 cup chopped onion
2 tablespoons all-purpose flour
2 cups cornflake crumbs
1/4 cup melted shortening

1. Heat Welsh Rarebit following package directions.
2. In a medium bowl, combine Roast Beef Hash, beaten egg, chopped green pepper, chopped onion, flour and cornflake crumbs. Mix well.
3. Form hash mixture into patties; fry in melted shortening until golden brown on both sides. Drain on absorbent paper.
4. Transfer browned hash rounds to heated plates. Ladle hot Welsh Rarebit over patties.

CREAMED CHIPPED BEEF OMELET

(Serves 2)

1—11-ounce package Frozen Creamed Chipped Beef*
6 eggs, whole
1/2 teaspoon salt
2 tablespoons cold water
3 tablespoons butter
2 tablespoons chopped green onion

1. Heat Creamed Chipped Beef following package directions.
2. Beat eggs, salt and water until foamy.
3. Heat butter in omelet pan or skillet over low heat. Add egg mixture. As omelet sets, loosen edges to let uncooked egg mixture flow underneath. Cook until dry on top. Fold and slide out of skillet onto heated platter.
4. Ladle Creamed Chipped Beef over omelet. Sprinkle with chopped green onion.

CREAMED CHIPPED BEEF AND CABBAGE

(Serves 4–6)

1—2-pound head cabbage

2—11-ounce packages Frozen Creamed Chipped Beef*

1. Cut cabbage into six wedges; partially core each wedge. Wash and drain. Cook uncovered in boiling, salted water just until tender. Drain well.
2. Heat Creamed Chipped Beef following package directions.
3. Transfer cabbage wedges to heated serving dish.
4. Ladle hot Creamed Chipped Beef over cabbage.

HARVEST MACARONI AND BEEF

(Serves 4)

2 acorn squash
1 teaspoon salt
2 cups hot water
1/4 cup butter, melted

2—11-1/2-ounce packages Frozen Macaroni and Beef, defrosted*
1/4 cup buttered bread crumbs (optional)

1. Preheat oven to 350° F.
2. Scrub squash. Cut in half crosswise; scoop out seeds and stringy portion. Sprinkle squash with salt. Place squash cut side down in a shallow baking pan. Add hot water.
3. Bake uncovered 1 hour, or until squash is tender. Remove from oven and drain well.
4. Brush cut sides of squash with butter. Fill each half of squash with 1/2 package Macaroni and Beef. Return to oven and bake for 30 minutes.
5. Sprinkle with buttered bread crumbs and broil 4 to 5 minutes, if desired.

SAUERBRATEN STEW

(Serves 4)

4—10-ounce packages Frozen Beef Stew, defrosted*
1/4 cup cider vinegar
4 teaspoons dehydrated minced onion
1/4 cup brown sugar
Pinch ground cloves
1/2 teaspoon ground ginger
1/2 cup beef bouillon
1/2 cup dairy sour cream, room temperature

1. Place Beef Stew in the top of a double boiler over rapidly boiling water.
2. Add remaining ingredients, except sour cream. Stir to combine and heat for 20 to 25 minutes, or until piping hot. Stir in sour cream and heat, but do not boil.

BEEF RAGOUT

(Serves 4)

4—10-ounce packages Frozen Beef Stew, defrosted*
1/2 cup Burgundy wine

1. Place Beef Stew in the top of a double boiler over rapidly boiling water and simmer for 15 minutes.
2. Stir in wine and continue to simmer for 5 minutes or until hot. Serve over parsley buttered or caraway noodles.

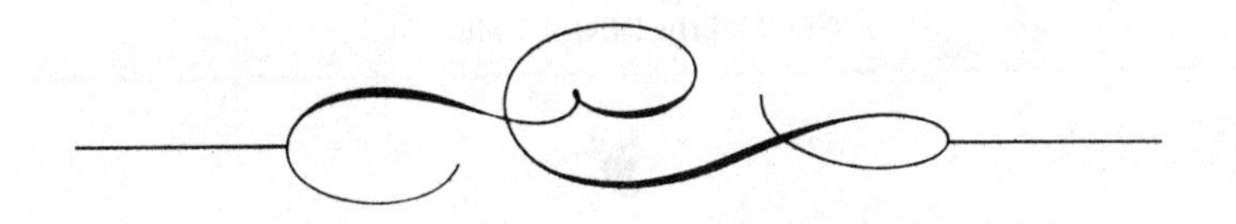

POULTRY

CHINESE CHICKEN

(Serves 8)

24 pieces chicken (breasts, legs and thighs)
1 cup all-purpose flour
3 tablespoons salt
1-1/2 cups (or 1—17-ounce jar) apricot preserves
1 teaspoon paprika
1 tablespoon soy sauce
4 cups apricot nectar
4 teaspoons soy sauce
1/4 cup cider vinegar
1/2 cup brown sugar
1/3 cup slivered, toasted almonds

1. Wash chicken parts under cold running water. Drain and pat dry.
2. Blend flour and salt. Coat each piece of chicken thoroughly with flour mixture. Place chicken pieces, not touching, in a greased baking pan. Bake in a 400° F. oven for 25 minutes. Remove from oven; reduce oven temperature to 350° F.
3. Combine apricot preserves, paprika and first amount of soy sauce. Spread evenly over each piece of chicken.
4. Combine apricot nectar, second amount of soy sauce, vinegar and brown sugar. Pour around chicken pieces.
5. Bake uncovered in a 350° F. oven for 35 to 40 minutes, basting once after 15 minutes.
6. Transfer chicken to a heated platter and sprinkle with slivered, toasted almonds. Pour sauce into serving bowl. Serve with fluffy rice.

This recipe has been on our menu almost as long as apple pie, and it's loved almost as much.

SESAME FRIED CHICKEN

(Serves 6)

18 pieces chicken (breasts, legs and thighs)
2 eggs, beaten
1/4 cup water
1/2 teaspoon salt
Few grains pepper
1/2 cup sesame seeds
3/4 cup all-purpose flour
1 tablespoon salt
Vegetable shortening and Clarified Butter (page 200), for frying
Salt

1. Wash chicken under running water and drain well.
2. Combine beaten eggs, water, first amount of salt and pepper to make egg batter.
3. Combine sesame seeds, flour and second amount of salt and mix well.
4. Dip chicken pieces in egg batter and roll each piece lightly in sesame seed/flour mixture.
5. Place pieces of chicken on a wire rack in a roasting pan. Pour 1/2 cup of water in the bottom of the pan. Cover and bake at 350° F. for 20 to 30 minutes. Remove from oven.
6. Melt equal parts of shortening and Clarified Butter in a heavy skillet or electric fry pan to a depth of 1/2 inch. Fry chicken until golden brown. Drain on absorbent paper and sprinkle lightly with salt.

BREAST OF CHICKEN JUBILEE

(Serves 8)

2—#303 cans whole, pitted Bing cherries, drained
1/4 cup brandy
8 chicken breasts
2 teaspoons salt
1/4 cup all-purpose flour
1-1/2 teaspoons salt
Melted shortening or oil for deep frying
2 cups chicken broth
3/4 cup currant jelly
1/8 teaspoon dry mustard
1-1/2 tablespoons cornstarch
1-1/2 tablespoons cold water
2/3 cup brandy

1. Combine drained cherries with first amount of brandy and allow to stand one hour, stirring occasionally.
2. Wash chicken breasts and dry thoroughly. Sprinkle each piece with 1/4 teaspoon salt.
3. Combine flour and second amount of salt. Coat entire outside surfaces of chicken with flour mixture.
4. Deep fry chicken, 2 or 3 pieces at a time, in 375°F. fat, just until golden brown—about 4 minutes. Drain on absorbent paper. Place chicken in a single layer in a casserole dish. Pour chicken broth in the bottom of the pan. Cover and bake in a 350°F. oven for one hour or until fork tender. Drain off broth.
5. Melt currant jelly in a heavy saucepan, beating constantly with a wire whip, until smooth. Beat in dry mustard.
6. Combine cornstarch and cold water; mix to a smooth paste. Gradually add to jelly, whipping constantly, and cook until clear. Remove from heat and blend in brandy.
7. Brush the surface of each piece of chicken with 2 teaspoons sauce. Place pan under broiler for 2 to 3 minutes to glaze. Repeat this step once more.
8. Transfer glazed chicken breasts to a heated serving casserole or platter. Scatter brandied cherries around chicken and pour remaining sauce over all.

TURKEY DIVAN

(Serves 4)

1—10-ounce package frozen asparagus spears or 1— 10-ounce package frozen broccoli spears
2 tablespoons butter
2-1/2 tablespoons minced onion
2 tablespoons all-purpose flour
1/2 teaspoon salt
Few grains thyme
1/4 teaspoon paprika
2 cups hot coffee cream
1 egg yolk, beaten
2 tablespoons grated Parmesan cheese
8 slices cooked turkey breast
1/4 cup grated Parmesan cheese

1. Cook asparagus spears or broccoli spears according to package directions; drain.
2. Melt butter in a heavy saucepan. Add onion and sautê 5 minutes. Add flour, salt, thyme and paprika; simmer 2 minutes to partially cook flour.
3. Gradually add hot cream, beating constantly until smooth; simmer 8 to 10 minutes until thickened.
4. Whip a small amount of the hot sauce into the beaten egg yolk. Return to pan, stirring constantly. Remove from heat and blend in first amount of Parmesan cheese.
5. Arrange cooked vegetable in a shallow serving casserole. Place turkey slices over stem ends of vegetable. Ladle sauce over turkey and stem part of vegetable, leaving tips exposed.
6. Sprinkle remaining Parmesan cheese over sauce and broil until cheese is golden brown and the sauce is bubbly.

TURKEY STUFFED HAM ROLLS

(Serves 6)

3 tablespoons chicken fat
1/4 cup all-purpose flour
3/4 cup hot chicken or turkey broth
1/4 cup hot coffee cream
1/8 teaspoon salt
1 drop yellow food coloring (optional)
3 tablespoons chopped, unblanched almonds
1-1/4 cups cooked turkey, cut in 1/4″ pieces
1/2 cup celery, cut in 1/4″ pieces
6 slices canned ham, 1/8″ thick
Parsley for garnish

1. Melt chicken fat in a heavy saucepan. Blend in flour and simmer 2 minutes to partially cook flour.
2. Gradually add hot broth, beating constantly until smooth. Cook until thickened and the flour taste disappears. Remove from heat.
3. Blend in hot cream and salt; add yellow food coloring, if desired.
4. Sprinkle almonds on a well buttered baking pan and toast in a 350° F. oven for 6 to 8 minutes.
5. Combine almonds, turkey and celery and toss lightly. Add 1/3 cup hot sauce and mix well.
6. Place 1/3 cup turkey mixture across one end of each ham slice and roll tightly. Secure with toothpicks if necessary.
7. Arrange rolls in a shallow, oblong casserole dish. Pour remaining sauce over rolls and bake at 350° F. for 15 to 20 minutes or until hot. Remove toothpicks. Garnish with chopped parsley.

The Stouffer Shorties with chicken are almost never-ending. We included the ones that have been most popular, but you can probably devise some things we haven't even thought about:

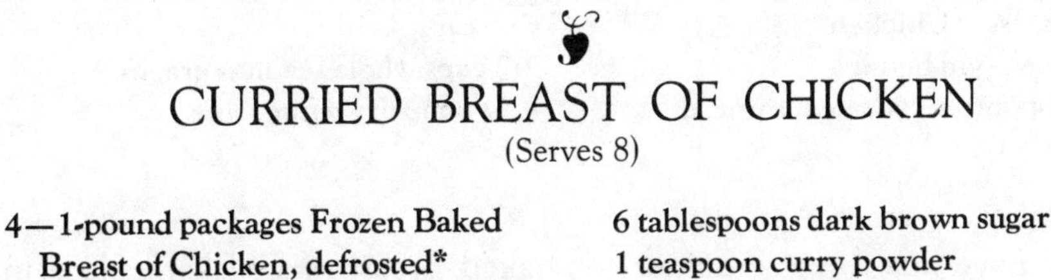

CURRIED BREAST OF CHICKEN

(Serves 8)

4—1-pound packages Frozen Baked Breast of Chicken, defrosted*
2—6-ounce cans frozen orange juice concentrate, defrosted
6 tablespoons dark brown sugar
1 teaspoon curry powder
1/2 cup shredded coconut
3/4 cup cornflake crumbs

1. Remove Baked Breast of Chicken from gravy and set gravy aside. Place chicken breasts in a shallow baking dish.
2. Combine gravy, undiluted orange juice concentrate, brown sugar, and 1/2 teaspoon curry powder. Pour mixture over chicken.
3. Combine coconut, cornflake crumbs and remaining curry powder. Toss lightly and sprinkle over chicken breasts. Bake at 400° F. for 35 to 40 minutes. Serve over steamed rice.

CREAMED CHICKEN VIRGINIA STYLE

(Serves 4)

4—6-1/2-ounce packages Frozen Creamed Chicken*
4 cornbread squares or corn muffins
1/2 cup deviled Smithfield Ham Spread
Pimiento or parsley for garnish

1. Heat Creamed Chicken following package directions.
2. Split cornbread squares or muffins.
3. Spread cornbread squares or muffins with deviled ham mixture; top with hot Creamed Chicken. Garnish with drained pimiento chips or finely minced fresh parsley.

BAKED BREASTS OF CHICKEN AND GRAPE CASSEROLE

(Serves 4)

2— 1-pound packages Frozen Baked Breast of Chicken*
1 tablespoon butter
1 teaspoon dehydrated, minced onion
3—4-ounce cans tiny mushroom caps
2 cups whole seedless grapes
3/4 cup dry white wine

1. Preheat oven to 400° F.
2. Remove lids from containers of Baked Breast of Chicken; place in oven for 25 to 30 minutes. Remove from oven.
3. In a medium skillet, melt butter and sauté onion and mushrooms.
4. Remove chicken from gravy; place in a single layer in a shallow baking dish.
5. In a medium mixing bowl, combine gravy from the chicken, sautéed mushrooms and onion, grapes, and wine. Mix lightly and pour over chicken.
6. Place casserole in oven and bake 8 to 10 minutes. Garnish with toasted almonds and grape clusters, if desired.

CHICKEN 'N ALMONDS IN PATTY SHELLS

(Serves 6)

6—6-1/2-ounce packages Frozen Creamed Chicken*
3/4 cup slivered almonds
3 tablespoons melted butter
6 patty shells

1. Heat Creamed Chicken according to package directions.
2. Lightly brown almonds in butter, stirring often.
3. Place patty shells on heated serving platter; ladle Creamed Chicken over all. Garnish with toasted slivered almonds.

CHICKEN TAHITIAN

(Serves 6)

3—1-pound packages Frozen Baked Breast of Chicken*
1—6-ounce can frozen pineapple juice concentrate
2 tablespoons lemon juice
1/4 cup butter
1 teaspoon ground ginger
1/2 cup macadamia, almond or cashew nuts
4 cups cooked rice
1 peeled, sliced avocado
1 unpeeled orange, thinly sliced

1. Heat Baked Breast of Chicken according to package directions.
2. Combine undiluted pineapple juice concentrate, lemon juice, butter and ginger in a saucepan and heat until well blended.
3. When chicken is golden brown and gravy is bubbly, remove from gravy and place in an attractive baking dish. Set cream gravy aside for later use.
4. Spoon 1/2 of the citrus sauce over chicken and return to 375° F. oven for 15 to 20 minutes or until glazed, basting occasionally.
5. Add nuts to remaining citrus sauce; set aside.
6. Place rice in electric skillet or on a large warm serving platter; arrange chicken over rice, "pyramid" or "spoke" fashion and garnish with slices of avocado and orange between them.
7. Pour remaining citrus sauce and nuts over all.
8. Reheat cream gravy from step #3 and pour into sauce boat to be served at the table, if desired.

CHICKEN À LA KING

(Serves 4)

1 tablespoon butter or margarine
2 tablespoons diced pimiento
2 tablespoons diced green pepper
1—3-1/4-ounce can sliced mushrooms, drained
1 tablespoon diced onion
2—6-1/2-ounce packages Frozen Creamed Chicken, defrosted*

1. Melt butter in a medium skillet; add pimiento, green pepper, mushrooms and onion; sauté on low heat for 5 to 6 minutes.
2. Place sauteed vegetables and Creamed Chicken in top of a double boiler over rapidly boiling water; heat for 15 to 20 minutes or until piping hot. Serve in flaky patty shells or over steamed rice.

CHICKEN-FILLED CRÊPES

(Serves 4)

Crêpes:
3 eggs, separated
1 tablespoon granulated sugar
1-1/2 teaspoons salad oil
1/3 cup all-purpose flour
1/2 teaspoon salt
3/4 cup milk

Chicken Filling:
4—6-1/2-ounce packages Frozen Creamed Chicken, defrosted*
1/2 teaspoon dehydrated, minced onion
2 tablespoons sherry
2 tablespoons grated Parmesan cheese

1. Beat egg whites until soft peaks form; set aside.
2. Place egg yolks in mixing bowl; add sugar, oil, flour, salt and milk; beat until smooth. Fold into beaten egg whites.
3. Heat a 6- to 7-inch crêpe pan or frying pan over medium heat; brush lightly with oil coating the pan evenly. For each crêpe, use a large utility spoon to dip batter and quickly smooth over pan bottom. Brown quickly on both sides.
4. Carefully remove crêpe from pan and set aside to cool. Repeat for remaining crêpes.
5. To make filling, combine Creamed Chicken, onion and sherry. Place a rounded 1/4 cup Creamed Chicken mixture across center of each

crêpe and roll. Place crêpes seam-side down in a 7-inch by 11-inch baking dish.

6. Sprinkle with Parmesan cheese. Bake at 400°F. for 20 to 25 minutes until piping hot. Serve at once.

CHICKEN IN LOBSTER SAUCE

(Serves 4)

2—1-pound packages Frozen Baked Breast of Chicken, defrosted*
2—6-1/2-ounce packages Frozen Lobster Newburg, defrosted*
1 teaspoon paprika

1. Preheat oven to 400°F.
2. Remove Baked Breast of Chicken from gravy and place chicken in a baking dish. Save gravy.
3. Combine Lobster Newburg and chicken gravy; pour over chicken breasts.
4. Sprinkle with paprika.
5. Bake for 30 minutes.

BREAST OF CHICKEN KIEV

(Serves 4)

2—1-pound packages Frozen Baked Breast of Chicken, defrosted*
1/8 teaspoon granulated garlic
1 teaspoon minced chives
1 tablespoon chopped parsley
1/8 teaspoon rosemary
2 tablespoons dry sherry
1/4 cup grated Parmesan cheese
Dash pepper

1. Remove Baked Breast of Chicken from gravy and arrange in a 1-1/2-quart baking dish; save gravy.
2. Combine gravy, garlic, chives, parsley, rosemary, sherry, 1/2 of the cheese, and pepper; pour gravy mixture over chicken; sprinkle with remaining cheese.
3. Bake at 400°F. for 25 to 30 minutes. Serve chicken over wild rice; top with gravy.

CHICKEN AVOCADO OMELET

(Serves 4)

4—6-1/2-ounce packages Frozen Creamed Chicken*
8 eggs, separated
2 tablespoons all-purpose flour
3 tablespoons milk
2 teaspoons minced chives
1/2 teaspoon salt
Dash pepper
1 avocado, thinly sliced or cubed

1. Heat Creamed Chicken following package directions.
2. Beat egg yolks until creamy; add flour, milk, chives, salt and pepper; mix until combined.
3. Beat egg whites until stiff but not dry.
4. Fold beaten egg whites and avocado into yolk mixture.
5. Pour mixture into a greased 1-1/2-quart baking dish and bake at 400°F. for 15 to 20 minutes.
6. Spoon hot Creamed Chicken over omelet before serving.

CHICKEN CHEESE STACK-UPS

(Serves 4)

2—6-1/2-ounce packages Frozen Creamed Chicken, defrosted*
1—2-1/2-ounce can sliced mushrooms, drained
1/4 cup dairy sour cream
1 tablespoon grated Cheddar cheese
2 teaspoons chopped green pepper
1 tablespoon chopped onion
8 pancakes
1—1-pound can whole cranberry sauce

1. Place Creamed Chicken in a medium bowl; add mushrooms, sour cream, cheese, green pepper and onion; stir to combine.
2. Arrange four cooked pancakes on a large baking tray. Spoon 1/3 cup chicken mixture onto each pancake. Top with four more pancakes; cover tray with aluminum foil.
3. Bake covered in a 350°F. oven for 15 to 20 minutes.
4. Heat cranberry sauce in a double boiler.
5. Transfer stack-ups to heated platter.
6. Spoon hot cranberry sauce over all just before serving.

CHICKEN CURRY
(Serves 4)

4—6-1/2-ounce packages Frozen Creamed Chicken, defrosted*
2 teaspoons curry powder
1/2 teaspoon seasoned salt
2 cups cooked rice
3 tablespoons finely chopped green onion

1. Combine Creamed Chicken with curry powder and seasoned salt.
2. Place in top of double boiler over rapidly boiling water and heat for 25 to 30 minutes.
3. Serve over rice and top with finely chopped green onion.

PLANTATION CHICKEN
(Serves 4)

2— 17-ounce packages Frozen Chicken and Dumplings*
4 slices baked ham or 8 slices Canadian bacon
2 tablespoons butter
1 teaspoon minced parsley

1. Heat Chicken and Dumplings according to package directions.
2. Sauté ham slices or Canadian bacon in melted butter until lightly browned.
3. Place meat slices on heated serving plate. Top with baked Chicken and Dumplings. Garnish each serving with 1/4 teaspoon minced parsley.

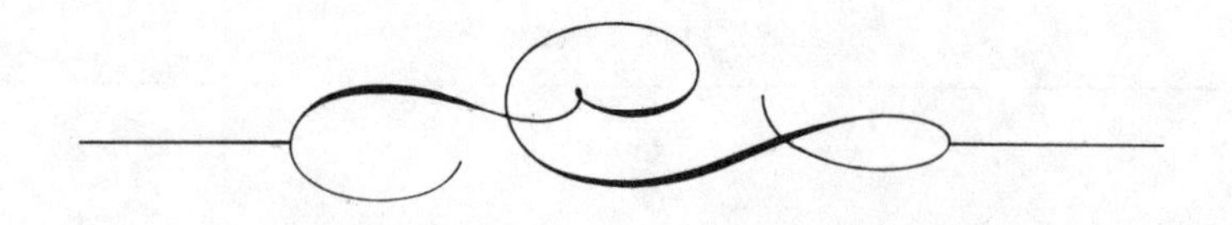

FROM THE SEAS AND LAKES

Every once in a while, a cook must take the diners upstream. Fish is not only a good way to vary a menu; it's also a healthful and satisfying way. We have avoided including the typical amandine and plain broiled recipes (either you know them or will find them somewhere else). What we have done is give you some unusual dishes to appeal to people who think fish is uninteresting.

BAKED STUFFED FLOUNDER

(Serves 4)

4 whole dressed flounder (9 to 11 ounces each)
1 teaspoon salt
1 tablespoon butter
1 tablespoon all-purpose flour
3/4 teaspoon salt
Few grains cayenne
1-1/8 cups hot coffee cream
3 cups (approximately 1 pound) king crabmeat, cut in 3/8" pieces
1-1/2 tablespoons sauterne
2 slices stale bread, crusts trimmed and cut in 1/8" cubes
2-1/2 teaspoons capers
1/4 cup Clarified Butter (page 200)
Salt
Paprika
Parsley
Lemon crowns

1. Remove skin from top of fish; split the fish by making a 4-1/2-inch to 5-inch slit along the natural crease—cutting through flesh to the bone. To make a pocket, use a small knife to separate flesh from both sides of the bone.
2. Wash fish under cold running water and drain well; sprinkle top and inside of each fish with 1/4 teaspoon salt.
3. Heat butter to bubbling in a heavy saucepan; add flour, salt and cayenne; beat smooth and simmer 1 minute.

4. Gradually add hot cream, beating constantly; simmer over low heat until thickened and flour taste disappears. Remove from heat.
5. Stir in crabmeat and sauterne. Cool to room temperature.
6. Fold in bread cubes and capers.
7. Stuff each fish with 2/3 cup of crab mixture.
8. Arrange stuffed fish, skin side down, in a lightly buttered baking pan. Do not overlap fish. Brush tops of fish with Clarified Butter; sprinkle with 1/4 teaspoon salt and paprika.
9. Pour hot water into pan—just enough to cover the bottom. Cover loosely and bake at 350° F. for 15 minutes. Uncover, sprinkle again with paprika and bake 5 to 10 minutes longer or until fish is firm to the touch.
10. Brush fish again with Clarified Butter and sprinkle with paprika.
11. Broil 2 to 3 inches below a medium broiler until golden brown.
12. Transfer to heated plates; garnish with bouquets of parsley and lemon crowns; serve at once.

BUTTER BROILED SHRIMP

(Serves 4)

1-1/2 pounds raw shrimp, peeled and deveined
1/2 cup Clarified Butter (page 200)
2 teaspoons salt
1/2 teaspoon garlic salt
Few grains pepper
Paprika
Lemon wedges
Parsley

1. Clean shrimp and butterfly them by cutting each shrimp down the back without cutting through. Press flat.
2. Place flattened shrimp in a single layer in a shallow pan (not a broiler rack) which will fit under the broiler.
3. Combine Clarified Butter, salt, garlic and pepper.
4. Brush shrimp with butter mixture using full amount.
5. Broil close to heat for 2 minutes; baste with pan butter. Sprinkle lightly with paprika and continue broiling 2 to 3 minutes until just cooked through. Baste again with pan butter.
6. Serve at once with lemon wedges and parsley to garnish.

Try this once, and it will become a regular on your menus. At least that's what happened to us in the restaurants.

SALMON LOAF WITH FRESH CUCUMBER SAUCE

(Serves 6)

2—1-pound cans red salmon
1 cup salmon liquid and milk
3-1/2 slices dry bread, crusts trimmed, cut in 1/8" cubes
2 eggs, beaten
1 teaspoon finely chopped onion
3/4 teaspoon salt
Fresh Cucumber Sauce (below)

1. Drain salmon and reserve liquid.
2. Measure salmon liquid and add milk to make 1 cup; pour over bread cubes and let stand until liquid is completely absorbed.
3. Add eggs, onion, salt and flaked salmon to bread mixture; mix to combine.
4. Pour mixture into a buttered 9-inch loaf pan and spread even on top. Set loaf pan in another pan containing 1/2-inch hot water.
5. Place loaf pan and hot water bath in a 325°F. oven and bake for 1 to 1-1/4 hours or until firm in the center. Remove from oven. Let stand 10 minutes; remove loaf pan from hot water bath.
6. Invert loaf pan onto heated serving platter to unmold.
7. Ladle Fresh Cucumber Sauce across loaf. Garnish with sliced unpeeled cucumbers, if desired.

FRESH CUCUMBER SAUCE

1/2 cup peeled cucumber, cut in 1/2" by 1/8" cubes
1 teaspoon salt
1 tablespoon butter
2 tablespoons all-purpose flour
3/4 teaspoon salt
1/2 cup hot milk
2/3 cup hot coffee cream
1-1/2 tablespoons cider vinegar
1/4 cup dairy sour cream, room temperature

1. Sprinkle salt over cucumbers and mix gently. Allow to stand for 10 minutes; drain thoroughly.
2. Melt butter in a heavy saucepan; blend in flour and salt; simmer 2 minutes to partially cook flour.

3. Gradually whip in hot milk and cream; cook, stirring constantly until thickened and flour taste has disappeared.
4. Slowly beat vinegar into sauce and heat thoroughly.
5. Stir sour cream into hot sauce; do not boil after addition of sour cream.
6. Stir in drained cucumbers and serve hot.

When we opened Top of the Flame *in Detroit we had a Japanese cook who made Shrimp Tempura at the bar, and it was served only as an appetizer. But our guests liked it so much we increased the quantities and began serving it as an entrée.*

SHRIMP TEMPURA

(Serves 6)

2-1/2 pounds raw shrimp (approximately 26–30 count)
1-3/4 teaspoons salt
1 cup all-purpose flour
3/4 teaspoon salt
3/4 teaspoon granulated sugar
1 whole egg
3/4 cup water
Melted shortening or oil for deep frying
Red Dipping Sauce (page 201)

1. Remove shell from shrimp down to tail. Leave tail shell on. Wash and remove vein.
2. Butterfly shrimp by cutting down the back without cutting through. Press shrimp flat, Sprinkle with salt.
3. Sift flour, 3/4 teaspoon salt and sugar together.
4. Whip egg and water until frothy.
5. Add liquid to dry ingredients and blend. Mixture will be slightly lumpy and thin.
6. Heat deep fat to 400°F.
7. Dip shrimp into batter, holding it by the tail; do not drain. Immediately drop shrimp into hot fat and fry 2 to 3 minutes.
8. Drain on absorbent paper and sprinkle lightly with salt. Serve with Red Dipping Sauce.

BAKED STUFFED TROUT

(Serves 6)

6 rainbow trout, dressed and boned
1-1/2 teaspoons salt
2 tablespoons butter
2 tablespoons all-purpose flour
3/4 teaspoon salt
Few grains cayenne
1 cup hot coffee cream
1 pound cooked lobster meat, cut in 3/8″ pieces
2 tablespoons sauterne
2 slices stale bread, crusts trimmed and cut into 1/4″ cubes
1 tablespoon capers
Melted butter for basting
Salt
Paprika

1. Wash trout inside and outside under cold running water; drain well and pat dry. Sprinkle inside of each fish evenly with 1/4 teaspoon salt.
2. Melt butter in a heavy saucepan; stir in flour, salt and cayenne; simmer 2 minutes to partially cook flour.
3. Gradually whip in hot cream; cook, stirring constantly, until thickened and flour taste disappears. Remove from heat.
4. Stir in lobster meat and sauterne. Cool to room temperature.
5. Gently fold bread cubes and capers into cooled sauce.
6. Stuff each fish with 1/2 cup filling; secure opening with wooden toothpicks.
7. Place fish in a well-buttered baking dish; do not overlap. Brush skin with melted butter; sprinkle each fish with 1/4 teaspoon salt, then with paprika.
8. Pour hot water into pan—just enough to cover the bottom.
9. Cover loosely and bake in a 350° F. oven for 15 to 20 minutes; uncover and continue baking 10 minutes longer or until fish is firm to the touch.
10. Just before serving, brush again with melted butter and sprinkle with paprika; broil 2 to 3 inches away from heat just until skin is glazed.

CRABMEAT STUFFED SHRIMP

(Serves 4)

1-1/2 pounds raw shrimp (approximately 15–20 count)
1-1/4 teaspoons salt
2 tablespoons butter or margarine
2-1/2 tablespoons all-purpose flour
3/4 teaspoon salt
Few grains cayenne
1-1/4 cups hot coffee cream
1 drop yellow food coloring
1/2 pound king crabmeat, cut in 1/4″ pieces
2 tablespoons sauterne
4 slices stale bread, crusts trimmed, cut in 1/8″ pieces
2 tablespoons butter, melted
1/2 teaspoon barbecue seasoning (optional)

1. Wash shrimp in cold water. Remove shell leaving tail on. Remove vein. Partially split shrimp down the back without cutting through. Open shrimp out flat. Sprinkle with first amount of salt.
2. Melt butter or margarine in a heavy saucepan.
3. Blend in flour, salt and cayenne; simmer 2 minutes to partially cook flour.
4. Gradually add hot cream, beating constantly until smooth. Cook 8 to 10 minutes over low heat until thick and the flour taste disappears. Remove from heat.
5. Add yellow food coloring and blend.
6. Add crabmeat and sauterne; blend.
7. Add bread crumbs and mix gently; chill mixture thoroughly.
8. In the center of each flattened shrimp, mound 2 tablespoons of crab mixture. Place stuffed shrimp in a lightly buttered shallow baking dish. Drizzle with melted butter.
9. Sprinkle barbecue seasoning over each stuffed shrimp, if desired.
10. Bake in a 375° F. oven for 15 to 18 minutes or until shrimp are cooked and filling is hot.
11. Place under medium broiler to brown lightly. Serve at once.

CRABMEAT CRÊPES SUPREME WITH ARTICHOKES

(Serves 4)

Crêpes:
1/2 cup all-purpose flour
1-1/2 teaspoons granulated sugar
1/2 teaspoon salt
1 egg
1/2 cup cold water
1/4 cup coffee cream
1 tablespoon salad oil

Filling:
3-1/2 tablespoons butter
5 tablespoons all-purpose flour
1/8 teaspoon salt
Few grains white pepper
3 cups hot coffee cream
1-3/4 cups king crabmeat, cut into 1/4″ cubes
3 tablespoons sauterne

12 artichoke hearts
2 tablespoons toasted, slivered almonds

1. Sift dry ingredients together twice.
2. Beat egg slightly. Add cold water and cream; blend.
3. Add liquid to sifted dry ingredients and beat until smooth.
4. Heat a 6- to 7-inch crêpe pan or frying pan. For each crepe, brush pan lightly with oil to barely coat bottom. Measure two tablespoons batter into pan; tilt pan to coat bottom evenly. Cook over medium heat approximately 1/2 minute on each side or until golden brown. Carefully remove crêpe from pan, and repeat for remaining crêpes. There should be eight in all.
5. Cool crêpes and save.
6. Melt butter in a heavy saucepan. Blend in flour, salt and white pepper. Cook over medium heat for 2 minutes to partially cook flour. Reduce heat.
7. Gradually whip in hot cream and cook over low heat, stirring constantly, until thickened and the flour taste has disappeared. Remove from heat. Divide into two equal amounts and cool to room temperature.
8. Combine diced crabmeat, 1-1/2 tablespoons sauterne and half of the room-temperature cream sauce; mix well.
9. Butter individual ramekins or an oblong casserole dish.
10. Lay one crêpe on waxed paper. Place 3 tablespoons of crab mixture on crêpe. Overlap opposite sides of crêpe toward center. The mixture will ooze out of the ends slightly. Repeat this step until all crêpes are filled.

11. Place two crêpes in each ramekin or place eight crêpes in oblong casserole with seam sides on top. Arrange 3 artichoke hearts in each ramekin or all artichoke hearts in the casserole.
12. Bake in 350° F. oven for 25 to 30 minutes or until heated through.
13. Heat remaining cream sauce. Add 1-1/2 tablespoons sauterne and blend.
14. When ready to serve, ladle 3 tablespoons hot sauce over each ramekin or ladle all hot sauce over casserole leaving ends of crêpes showing.
15. Garnish with toasted, slivered almonds.

Even with seafood specialities we have the Stouffer Shorties:

LOBSTER AND SHRIMP MILANO

(Serves 4–6)

2—6-1/2-ounce packages Frozen Lobster Newburg, defrosted*
2—6-1/2-ounce packages Frozen Shrimp Newburg, defrosted*
5 tablespoons grated Parmesan cheese
1—8-ounce package spaghetti
3 tablespoons butter
2 tablespoons chopped onion
1-1/2 teaspoons chopped parsley

1. Place Lobster Newburg and Shrimp Newburg into top of double boiler over rapidly boiling water and heat for 25 to 30 minutes. Add 2 tablespoons grated Parmesan cheese. Stir to combine.
2. Cook spaghetti following package directions. Drain. In a saucepan, melt butter; add onion; sauté 3 to 4 minutes. Add cooked spaghetti and remaining Parmesan cheese. Toss quickly with a fork over low heat until well coated with butter and cheese.
3. Stir chopped parsley into hot sauce.
4. Lift spaghetti onto a heated serving platter and top with lobster/shrimp sauce. Serve at once.

QUICK LOBSTER THERMIDOR

(Serves 4)

4—6-1/2-ounce packages Frozen Lobster Newburg*

1/2 cup grated Cheddar cheese

2 teaspoons dehydrated, chopped onion

1-1/2 tablespoons dry, toasted bread crumbs

1. Preheat oven to 350° F.
2. Heat Lobster Newburg following package directions.
3. Place hot Lobster Newburg into a small bowl; add cheese and onion. Stir to combine.
4. Spoon mixture into a 1-quart baking dish; sprinkle with crumbs.
5. Bake 10 to 15 minutes.

KEMMA CURRY OF LOBSTER

(Serves 4)

2 tablespoons butter

1/2 cup finely chopped onion

1/2 clove garlic, crushed

2 chili pequines, crushed

1/4 teaspoon ginger

1/4 teaspoon turmeric

1/4 teaspoon coriander

1/8 teaspoon pepper

1/8 teaspoon ground cumin

1/8 teaspoon ground cloves

2 fresh peeled tomatoes, cut in 1/2" cubes

4—6-1/2-ounce packages Frozen Lobster Newburg, defrosted*

2 cups hot cooked rice

2 peeled, sliced avocados

1. Melt butter in a heavy saucepan; add chopped onions and seasonings; sauté over medium heat until onion is tender but not brown.
2. Add tomatoes and cook 5 minutes longer.
3. Stir in defrosted Lobster Newburg and heat to boiling.
4. Place hot rice on serving platter; arrange avocado slices over rice. Ladle sauce over all.
5. Serve with chutney, chopped raisins, toasted coconut, salted peanuts, and minced green onions passed in individual bowls as accompaniments.

LOBSTER SOUFFLÉ

(Serves 6)

4—6-1/2-ounce packages Frozen Lobster Newburg, defrosted*

2—12-ounce packages Frozen Cheese Soufflé, defrosted*

1. Preheat oven to 325° F.
2. Place defrosted Lobster Newburg into a small bowl.
3. Spoon one package defrosted Cheese Soufflé into an ungreased 2-quart casserole or soufflé dish.
4. Spoon pieces of lobster meat from Newburg over Cheese Soufflé in casserole. Reserve remaining lobster and sauce.
5. Spoon remaining package of defrosted Cheese Soufflé over lobster meat.
6. Bake for 50 to 55 minutes or until a silver knife inserted in the center comes out clean.
7. Heat remaining sauce in top of a double boiler over rapidly boiling water for 20 minutes.
8. Serve soufflé at once; pass hot sauce.

CLAM CHEESE SOUFFLÉ

(Serves 4)

2—12-ounce packages Frozen Cheese Soufflé, defrosted*

1-1/2 cups canned minced clams, drained

1/4 cup chopped green onion

1. In a small bowl, combine Cheese Soufflé, clams and onion.
2. Pour into a lightly buttered 1-1/2-quart casserole or soufflé dish. Bake at 350° F. for 1-1/4 hours or until a silver knife inserted in the center comes out clean. Serve at once.

OYSTER AND SPINACH CASSEROLE

(Serves 4)

1—8-ounce can frozen oysters, defrosted

2—12-ounce packages Frozen Spinach Soufflé, defrosted*

1-1/2 teaspoons minced onion

1. Preheat oven to 350° F.
2. Place defrosted oysters and juice in a small skillet; simmer over medium heat *just* until edges begin to curl. Do not overcook. Drain and cut into 1/2-inch pieces.
3. Place Spinach Soufflé in a medium mixing bowl; add cooked oysters and onions; stir well to combine.
4. Pour mixture into a lightly buttered 1-quart casserole; bake for 35 to 40 minutes, or until a silver knife inserted in the center comes out clean.

OYSTER CHEESE SOUFFLÉ

(Serves 4)

2—8-ounce cans frozen oysters, defrosted

2—12-ounce packages Frozen Cheese Soufflé, defrosted*

4 teaspoons white wine

1. Preheat oven to 325° F.
2. Place defrosted oysters and juice in a small skillet; simmer over medium heat *just* until edges begin to curl. Do not overcook.
3. Drain oysters and cut in half.
4. Place Cheese Soufflé in a mixing bowl; fold in cooked oysters and white wine.
5. Spoon mixture into a buttered 1-1/2-quart soufflé dish.
6. Bake for 1-1/2 hours or until a silver knife inserted in the center comes out clean. Serve immediately.

SHRIMP AND WILTED GREENS SALAD

(Serves 4–6)

4—6-1/2-ounce packages Frozen Shrimp Newburg, defrosted*
1/4 cup minced onion
2 teaspoons Worcestershire sauce
6 tablespoons cider vinegar
4 teaspoons granulated sugar
1/4 cup bacon bits
4 to 6 cups cut salad greens

1. Combine Shrimp Newburg with onion, Worcestershire sauce, vinegar, sugar and bacon bits in top of double boiler over rapidly boiling water and heat for 20 to 25 minutes or until hot.
2. Place cut salad greens in serving dish.
3. Pour hot mixture over greens; garnish with sieved hard-cooked egg yolk, if desired.
4. Serve at once.

SHRIMP 'N ARTICHOKE

(Serves 4)

4—6-1/2-ounce packages Frozen Shrimp Newburg*
4 cooked artichokes, choke removed

1. Heat Shrimp Newburg following package directions.
2. Stand hot artichokes upright on heated plates; spread leaves slightly and pour hot Shrimp Newburg over all.
3. Serve at once.

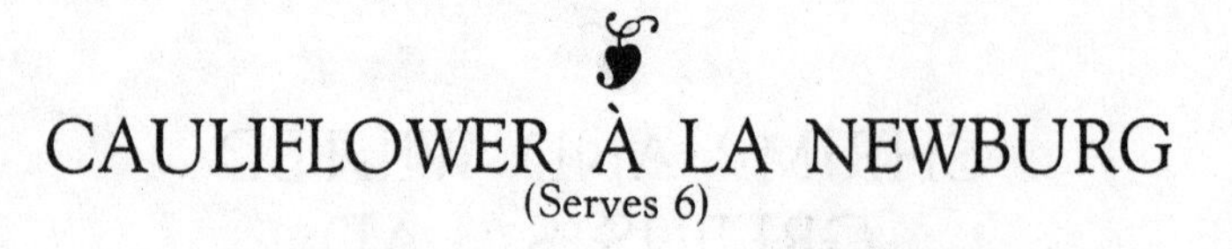

CAULIFLOWER À LA NEWBURG

(Serves 6)

2—10-ounce packages Frozen Cauliflower au Gratin, defrosted*

2—6-1/2-ounce packages Frozen Alaska King Crab Newburg, defrosted*

1/4 cup grated Cheddar cheese

1. Preheat oven to 350° F.
2. In a small bowl, combine Cauliflower au Gratin and King Crab Newburg.
3. Spoon mixture into a 1-quart casserole and sprinkle with cheese. Bake for 20 to 30 minutes.

TWO-PEAR NEWBURG

(Serves 4)

4—6-1/2-ounce packages Frozen Alaska King Crab Newburg*

4 halves canned Bartlett pears

1 peeled avocado pear

2 tablespoons lemon juice

4 toast rounds

1. Heat Alaska King Crab Newburg following package directions.
2. Slice pear halves and avocado lengthwise into 1/2-inch slices. Sprinkle lemon juice over avocado slices.
3. Place toast rounds in individual ramekins.
4. Arrange pear and avocado slices alternately around toast in a circular pattern.
5. Top with hot Alaska King Crab Newburg.
6. Serve at once.

CRAB-ASPARAGUS NEWBURG

(Serves 4)

2—6-1/2-ounce packages Frozen Alaska King Crab Newburg*
1—10-ounce package frozen asparagus spears
4 English muffins, split and toasted

1. Heat Alaska King Crab Newburg following package directions.
2. Cook asparagus following package directions; drain well.
3. Place split and toasted English muffins on dinner plates. Top with asparagus spears; spoon hot King Crab Newburg over all.
4. Serve at once.

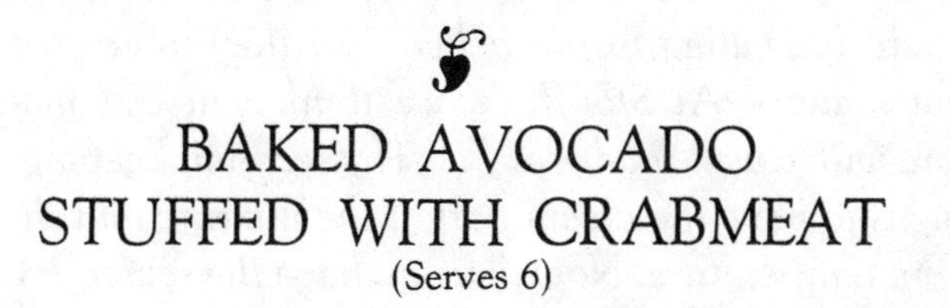

BAKED AVOCADO STUFFED WITH CRABMEAT

(Serves 6)

3 firm avocados
Salt to taste
Juice of one lemon
2—6-1/2-ounce packages Frozen Alaska King Crab Newburg, defrosted*
6 tablespoons grated Cheddar cheese

1. Preheat oven to 350° F.
2. Peel avocados; cut in half lengthwise and remove pits. Sprinkle with salt and lemon juice.
3. Pour one package of King Crab Newburg into bottom of a shallow baking dish; arrange avocado halves on top, cut side up. Spoon remaining package King Crab Newburg into avocados. Sprinkle one tablespoon cheese on each avocado half. Bake for 30 to 35 minutes.
4. Serve hot.

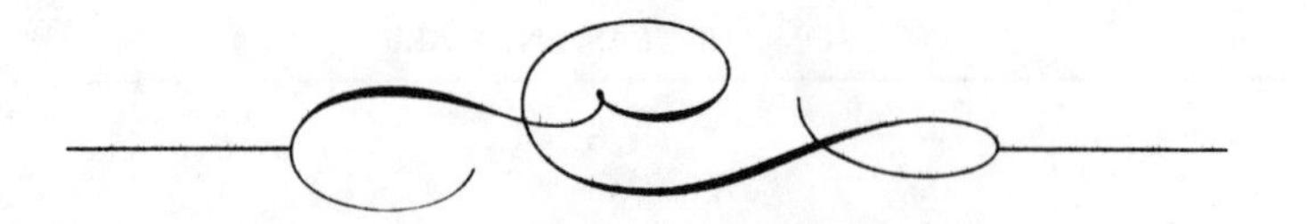

SOUFFLÉS, CASSEROLES AND GOOD DISH ONE-DISH FAVORITES

Nothing makes a cook more uptight than the thought of a soufflé. Soufflés are made for falling, some believe, so they never try them for a dinner that matters. At Stouffer's, we think you can make a dinner matter more with a well-made soufflé. The secret in keeping your soufflé from falling is to have the cream part of the mixture and the egg whites both at room temperature. Now that you have the secret, try the recipes.

Incidentally, in this section we start with the Stouffer Shorties, mainly because these are the most requested kinds of recipes, particularly by women who work.

VEGETABLE SOUFFLÉ

(Serves 4)

1—12-ounce package Frozen Cheese Soufflé, defrosted*

1—12-ounce package Frozen Spinach Soufflé, defrosted*

1. Preheat oven to 350°F.
2. Spoon Cheese Soufflé and Spinach Soufflé into a medium bowl; stir well to combine.
3. Pour mixture into a 1-quart soufflé dish.
4. Bake 45 minutes or until a silver knife inserted in the center comes out clean and soufflé is golden brown.
5. Serve at once with tomato sauce, if desired.

MACARONI SOUFFLÉ

(Serves 6)

3 eggs
3/4 cup milk
1 chopped pimiento
1 teaspoon chopped parsley
1-1/2 teaspoons chopped onion
1/2 teaspoon salt
1/8 teaspoon pepper
2—12-ounce packages Frozen Macaroni and Cheese, defrosted*
2—11-ounce packages Frozen Creamed Chipped Beef*

1. Preheat oven to 350° F.
2. Beat eggs lightly; add milk, pimiento, parsley, onion, salt and pepper. Stir well.
3. Add Macaroni and Cheese; stir until combined.
4. Pour into a 1-1/2-quart casserole or soufflé dish. Bake 45 to 50 minutes or until set and golden brown.
5. Top with Creamed Chipped Beef which has been heated according to package directions.
6. Serve at once.

CHEESE SOUFFLÉ WITH MUSHROOMS

(Serves 4)

2—8-ounce cans mushrooms, drained
2 teaspoons butter
2—12-ounce packages Frozen Cheese Soufflé, defrosted*
4 teaspoons pale dry sherry

1. Preheat oven to 325° F.
2. Chop drained mushrooms into 1/4-inch pieces.
3. Sauté mushrooms in butter for 5 minutes.
4. Spoon defrosted Cheese Soufflé into a mixing bowl; fold in mushrooms and sherry.
5. Pour mixture into a buttered 1-1/2-quart soufflé dish.
6. Bake for 1-1/2 hours or until a silver knife inserted in the center comes out clean.
7. Serve immediately.

PIMIENTO CORN SOUFFLÉ

(Serves 8)

4—12-ounce packages Frozen Corn Soufflé, defrosted*

1/2 cup chopped pimiento

1. Blend Corn Soufflé and pimiento in a mixing bowl.
2. Pour mixture into a 1-1/2-quart baking dish.
3. Bake at 325° F. for 35 to 40 minutes or until a silver knife inserted in the center comes out clean.
4. Serve at once.

CHEESE PIMIENTO SOUFFLÉ

(Serves 4)

2—12-ounce packages Frozen Cheese Soufflé, defrosted*

1/4 cup chopped pimiento

1. In a small bowl, combine Cheese Soufflé and pimiento.
2. Spoon into a lightly buttered 1-quart casserole or soufflé dish.
3. Bake at 325° F. for 50 to 55 minutes or until a silver knife inserted in the center comes out clean.
4. Serve at once.

SPINACH TOMATO CASSEROLE

(Serves 6)

2—12-ounce packages Frozen Spinach Soufflé, defrosted*
6 tomato slices, 1/2" thick
Few grains salt

2 tablespoons grated Parmesan cheese
2 slices bacon, cut into 2" pieces

1. Preheat oven to 350° F.
2. Spoon Spinach Soufflé into an oblong 1-1/2-quart casserole and arrange tomato slices attractively on top.
3. Sprinkle tomato slices with salt and Parmesan cheese; top each slice with one piece of bacon.

4. Bake for 50 to 60 minutes or until a silver knife inserted in the center comes out clean.
5. Serve at once.

CHEESE QUICHE

(Serves 6–8)

1—8″ or 9″ unbaked pie shell
2—12-ounce packages Frozen Cheese Soufflé, defrosted*
3 tablespoons chopped green onion
1/2 cup chopped mushrooms

1. Prebake pie shell at 400° F. for 10 minutes; remove from oven and lower oven temperature to 350° F.
2. In a medium bowl, combine Cheese Soufflé, onion and mushrooms; pour into prebaked pie shell. Bake 45 to 50 minutes.
3. Cut into wedges and serve warm.

POPEYE PUFFS

(Makes approximately 30)

1-1/4 cups all-purpose flour
1 teaspoon baking powder
3/4 teaspoon salt
1 egg
3/4 teaspoon minced onion
1—12-ounce package Frozen Spinach Soufflé, defrosted*
1-1/4 cups crushed cornflakes
Melted shortening or oil for deep frying
2—10-ounce packages Frozen Welsh Rarebit*

1. Sift flour with baking powder and salt.
2. Beat egg. Add dry ingredients and minced onion; stir to combine.
3. Add defrosted Spinach Soufflé and blend lightly.
4. Form 1/2-teaspoon size balls of mixture; roll in crushed cornflakes.
5. Fry in deep fat at 325° F. until golden brown, approximately 1 to 2 minutes.
6. Serve hot and top with Frozen Welsh Rarebit which has been heated according to package directions.

SPINACH RING WITH NOODLES ROMANOFF

(Serves 8)

4—12-ounce packages Frozen Spinach Soufflé, defrosted*

2—12-ounce packages Frozen Noodles Romanoff*

1. Preheat oven to 350° F.
2. Spoon Spinach Soufflé into a well greased 1-1/2-quart ring mold.
3. Bake 45 to 50 minutes or until a silver knife inserted in the center comes out clean.
4. Put Noodles Romanoff into the same oven the last 30 to 35 minutes of soufflé baking time.
5. Remove Spinach Soufflé ring and Noodles Romanoff from oven.
6. Run a spatula around edges of the spinach mold to loosen. Let stand 5 to 10 minutes.
7. Place warm serving platter over ring mold and invert. Tap lightly to loosen and unmold. Spoon hot Noodles Romanoff into center of spinach ring.
8. Serve at once.

BROCCOLI QUICHE

(Serves 6)

1—8″ or 9″ unbaked pie shell
4 eggs
1/2 teaspoon salt

3 tablespoons grated Parmesan cheese
2—10-ounce packages Frozen Broccoli au Gratin, defrosted*

1. Prebake pie shell at 400° F. for 10 minutes; remove from oven and lower oven temperature to 350° F.
2. In a medium bowl, beat eggs slightly; add salt and 2 tablespoons Parmesan cheese; stir to combine.
3. Drain sauce from broccoli and reserve; cut broccoli into chunks. Stir broccoli and au gratin sauce into egg mixture. Pour into prebaked

pie shell and sprinkle with remaining Parmesan cheese. Bake 45 to 50 minutes or until set.
4. Cut into wedges and serve hot.

TURKEY FLORENTINE

(Serves 4)

1—10-1/2-ounce can cream of chicken soup or 1—10-1/2-ounce can cream of mushroom soup
3 tablespoons sherry
1 tablespoon grated Parmesan cheese
2—12-ounce packages Frozen Spinach Soufflé, defrosted*
1-1/2 cups cooked diced turkey

1. Combine undiluted soup, sherry, and cheese to make sauce.
2. Spoon 1/2 package Spinach Soufflé into a 9-inch by 5-inch baking dish.
3. Place 1/2 cup turkey over soufflé and pour 1/2 cup sauce over turkey; build up alternate layers of soufflé, turkey and sauce, ending with soufflé on top. Sprinkle with additional Parmesan cheese. Bake at 350°F. for 50 to 60 minutes.
4. Serve at once.

ESCALLOPED CHICKEN AND HAM CASSEROLE

(Serves 4)

1—10-ounce package frozen broccoli spears, defrosted and drained
4 ham slices, 1/4" thick
2—11-1/2-ounce packages Frozen Escalloped Chicken and Noodles, defrosted*
2 tablespoons grated Parmesan cheese

1. Divide broccoli into 4 servings.
2. Roll each ham slice around each serving of broccoli; place rolls seam side down in a shallow casserole.
3. Spoon Escalloped Chicken and Noodles over ham rolls; sprinkle with Parmesan cheese.
4. Bake at 400°F. for 30 to 35 minutes.

MUSHROOM CHEESE RAREBIT

(Serves 4)

1—10-ounce package Frozen Welsh Rarebit, defrosted*
1—8-ounce can mushrooms, drained
2 tablespoons dehydrated, chopped onion
2 tablespoons butter or margarine

1. Remove Welsh Rarebit from container and place in top of double boiler over rapidly boiling water and heat for 25 to 30 minutes or until hot.
2. Sauté mushrooms and onion in butter 5 to 10 minutes.
3. Stir mushroom/onion mixture into the heated Welsh Rarebit.
4. Spoon over toast points or Melba toast.

BROCCOLI WITH POACHED EGGS

(Serves 4)

2—10-ounce packages Frozen Broccoli au Gratin, defrosted*
4 eggs
1/4 cup grated Cheddar cheese

1. Preheat oven to 375° F.
2. Spoon Broccoli au Gratin into a 1-quart shallow baking dish. Bake 20 to 25 minutes. Remove from oven.
3. Poach eggs until just set; *drain well;* arrange over Broccoli au Gratin.
4. Sprinkle with grated cheese and broil 4 to 6 inches from heat, just until cheese melts.

GREEN PEPPER NOODLES ROMANOFF

(Serves 4)

2 green peppers
2—12-ounce packages Frozen Noodles Romanoff, defrosted*

1. Preheat oven to 400° F.
2. Cut peppers in half lengthwise; clean, wash and drain thoroughly.
3. Place pepper halves in a 1-quart baking dish, cut side up.

4. Spoon 1/2 package of Noodles Romanoff into each pepper half.
5. Bake for 30 minutes or until noodles are lightly browned.

Instead of just plain hot dogs for Saturday night supper, try this.

FRANKS AND NOODLES ROMANOFF

(Serves 4)

2—12-ounce packages Frozen Noodles Romanoff, defrosted*
1/2 pound frankfurters, sliced
1/2 cup cornflake crumbs
1 tablespoon butter, melted

1. Preheat oven to 400° F.
2. Place defrosted Noodles Romanoff in a medium bowl.
3. Add sliced frankfurters, stirring to combine.
4. Pour into a lightly greased 1-1/2-quart casserole.
5. Combine cornflake crumbs and melted butter; toss lightly. Sprinkle on top of casserole.
6. Bake 25 to 30 minutes.

NOODLES LORRAINE

(Serves 6–8)

2 eggs
1 teaspoon chopped onion
Scant 1/4 teaspoon ground nutmeg
1/2 cup bacon, cooked and coarsely crumbled
2 teaspoons grated Parmesan cheese
1/2 cup milk
2—12-ounce packages Frozen Noodles Romanoff, defrosted*

1. Preheat oven to 350° F.
2. In a medium bowl, beat eggs lightly; add onion, nutmeg, bacon, cheese, milk and Noodles Romanoff. Stir to combine.
3. Pour mixture into a 1-1/2-quart casserole.
4. Bake for 20 to 25 minutes or until lightly browned and piping hot.

The big difference between the Stouffer version and a recipe you may know is that we bake the biscuit on top.

BAKED CHICKEN AND BISCUIT

(Serves 6)

1-1/2 cups biscuit mix
1/3 cup cold water
6 tablespoons chicken fat
1/2 cup all-purpose flour
3-1/4 cups hot chicken broth
1/2 to 3/4 teaspoon salt
1 drop yellow food coloring
1 pound boned, cooked chicken, sliced diagonally 2-1/2" long
1/2 teaspoon salt

1. Place biscuit mix in a mixing bowl. Add cold water. Mix together using a fork, just until well blended.
2. Smooth dough into a ball on a lightly floured surface.
3. Roll dough 1/2-inch thick and cut into six round biscuits, using a 3-inch cutter. Biscuits must not be thicker than 1/2-inch or they will absorb too much gravy and become soggy, and the chicken will be dry from lack of gravy.
4. Refrigerate biscuits until needed.
5. Melt chicken fat in a heavy saucepan. Blend in flour; simmer 2 minutes.
6. Gradually add hot chicken broth, beating constantly until smooth. Bring to a boil; reduce heat and cook until gravy thickens.
7. Add salt to taste and a drop of yellow food coloring. Keep hot.
8. Divide sliced chicken into six equal portions. Place portions in an 8-inch square baking pan.
9. Sprinkle chicken evenly with salt.
10. Pour hot gravy over chicken.
11. Place a biscuit on top of each portion of chicken.
12. Bake in a 375°F. oven for 30 to 35 minutes until biscuits are golden brown on top.

CHICKEN SOUFFLÉ

(Serves 6)

1-1/2 tablespoons chicken fat
2 teaspoons margarine
3 tablespoons all-purpose flour
1-1/2 teaspoons salt
Few grains pepper
2/3 cup hot chicken broth
1/2 cup hot coffee cream
3 egg yolks, slightly beaten
1-3/4 cups cooked chicken, cut in 1/4" cubes
7 tablespoons cold milk
1-3/4 slices stale bread, crusts trimmed, cut in 1/8" cubes
7 egg whites, room temperature

1. Melt chicken fat and margarine in a heavy saucepan. Blend in flour, salt and pepper; simmer 2 minutes to partially cook flour.
2. Gradually add hot chicken broth and cream, beating constantly until smooth. Cook until thickened and the flour taste disappears.
3. Add a small amount of hot sauce to beaten egg yolks, beating constantly. Return egg yolks to sauce, beating until blended. Remove from heat and allow to stand 5 minutes.
4. Add cubed chicken and blend.
5. Pour cold milk over bread cubes and let stand until all liquid is absorbed. Add to chicken mixture and blend.
6. Let chicken mixture stand until it reaches room temperature.
7. Beat room-temperature egg whites until stiff and slightly dry.
8. Fold room-temperature chicken mixture into stiffly beaten egg whites just until combined.
9. Pour mixture into a lightly buttered 1-1/2-quart soufflé dish or round casserole.
10. Set soufflé dish or casserole in a pan containing 1/2-inch of hot water.
11. Set pan in oven and bake at 325°F. for 60 minutes or until soufflé is golden brown and a silver knife inserted in the center comes out clean. Allow the soufflé to stand 15 minutes to set.
12. Serve with hot, creamy mushroom sauce, if desired.

CRABMEAT SOUFFLÉ WITH NEWBURG SAUCE

(Serves 4)

2-1/2 tablespoons butter or margarine
1-1/2 teaspoons finely minced onion
2 tablespoons all-purpose flour
1-1/2 teaspoons salt
1/2 cup hot milk
6 tablespoons hot coffee cream
2 egg yolks
1 cup (approximately 8 ounces) king crabmeat, cut in 1/4″ pieces
1/4 cup cold milk
4 slices stale bread, trimmed and cut in 1/8″ cubes
5 egg whites, room temperature
Newburg Sauce (opposite)

1. Melt butter or margarine in top of double boiler. Add onion and sauté until onion is tender but not brown—about 5 minutes.
2. Add flour and salt; blend smooth. Simmer for 2 minutes to partially cook flour.
3. Add hot milk and cream, beating constantly. Cook over boiling water 8 to 10 minutes or until the flour taste disappears. Reduce heat.
4. Beat egg yolks slightly. Add a small amount of sauce to egg yolks, beating constantly. Return egg mixture to sauce, beating constantly. Continue to cook mixture over barely simmering water until sauce is thickened.
5. Add diced king crabmeat and blend. Cool mixture to room temperature.
6. Pour cold milk over bread cubes and allow to stand until all milk is absorbed. Add to crab mixture and blend thoroughly.
7. Beat room-temperature egg whites until stiff and dry.
8. Gently fold room-temperature crab mixture into egg whites by hand, using a wire whip.
9. Pour soufflé mixture into a lightly buttered 1-1/2-quart soufflé dish and spread even on the top. Set soufflé dish in a pan containing 1/2-inch of hot water.
10. Place pan in oven and bake at 325° F. for one hour or until soufflé is golden brown on top and feels light to the touch. A silver knife inserted in the center should come out almost clean.
11. Let soufflé stand 20 minutes before serving. Pass Newburg Sauce.

NEWBURG SAUCE

2 tablespoons butter
1-1/2 tablespoons all-purpose flour
1/4 teaspoon salt
Few grains cayenne
1 cup hot heavy cream
1 tablespoon sherry
1 drop yellow food coloring

1. Melt butter in a heavy saucepan. Add flour, salt and cayenne; beat smooth.
2. Gradually add hot cream, stirring constantly; cook over low heat until thickened and the flour taste has disappeared.
3. Remove from heat. Add sherry and a drop of yellow food coloring. Blend smooth. Keep hot for serving.

SHORT RIBS OF BEEF IN YORKSHIRE PUDDING

(Serves 4)

2 eggs
1/2 cup all-purpose flour
1/2 cup milk
1/2 teaspoon salt
2—11-1/2-ounce packages Frozen Short Ribs of Beef, defrosted*

1. Preheat oven to 350° F.
2. Beat eggs well. Add flour, milk, and salt; beat until smooth.
3. Grease a 7-inch by 11-inch baking dish generously. Place Short Ribs of Beef and vegetable gravy in the center of baking dish. Pour batter around Short Ribs. Bake for 55 to 60 minutes or until pudding is set and lightly browned.
4. Serve at once.

HAM AND POTATOES AU GRATIN

(Serves 4)

1 cup cooked ham, cut in 1/2" cubes
1/4 teaspoon paprika
2—11-1/2-ounce packages Frozen Potatoes au Gratin, defrosted*
1 can French-fried onion rings

1. Brown ham cubes in skillet in a small amount of butter.
2. Combine ham cubes with paprika and defrosted Potatoes au Gratin in a small bowl.
3. Spoon mixture into a 1-1/2-quart casserole.
4. Bake in a 350° F. oven for 15 minutes. Top with onion rings. Return to oven and bake 10 minutes longer.

Now for two special favorites.

EGGS À LA GOLDENROD

(Serves 4)

1 tablespoon margarine
2 tablespoons all-purpose flour
1-1/2 teaspoons salt
Dash pepper
1 cup hot milk
1 cup hot coffee cream
1 to 2 drops yellow food coloring
4 hard-cooked eggs

1. Melt margarine in a heavy saucepan. Add flour, salt and pepper; blend until smooth. Simmer 2 minutes.
2. Add hot milk and cream gradually, beating constantly until smooth. Cook over medium heat until sauce thickens.
3. Add yellow food coloring and stir to blend.
4. Sieve two of the hard-cooked egg yolks and set aside.
5. Dice remaining yolks and whites into 1/2-inch pieces and add to hot cream sauce.
6. Ladle creamed eggs over asparagus, broccoli spears or toast points.
7. Garnish with sieved egg yolk.

APPLE BLINTZES

(Serves 8–10)

2— 12-ounce packages Frozen Escalloped Apples*
2 eggs
2 tablespoons salad oil
1 cup milk
3/4 cup all-purpose flour
1/2 teaspoon salt
1/2 cup oil
1/2 cup confectioner's sugar
2 cups dairy sour cream

1. Bake Escalloped Apples according to package directions; cool.
2. In a medium bowl, beat eggs, salad oil and milk until well mixed. Add flour and salt; beat until smooth. Cover and refrigerate batter for 30 minutes.
3. For each blintz: Heat 1/2 teaspoon oil in a 10-inch skillet. Pour in 3 tablespoons batter, rotating pan quickly to spread batter evenly. Cook over medium heat until lightly browned on underside; remove from pan.
4. Stack blintzes brown side up. Repeat until all the batter is used.
5. Place 2-1/2 tablespoons of Escalloped Apples on the browned surface of each blintz. Fold two opposite sides over filling and overlap ends, covering filling completely.
6. Heat 1/4 cup oil in skillet. Place blintzes in skillet, seam side down; turn gently to brown on all sides. Keep warm in a low oven.
7. Sprinkle with confectioner's sugar. Serve with sour cream.

From the Late Supper Menu

Sandwiches, hot and cold, are the late night favorites in all our restaurants. Of course, there is no one time for serving these, and you'll find they all make good luncheon dishes, too.

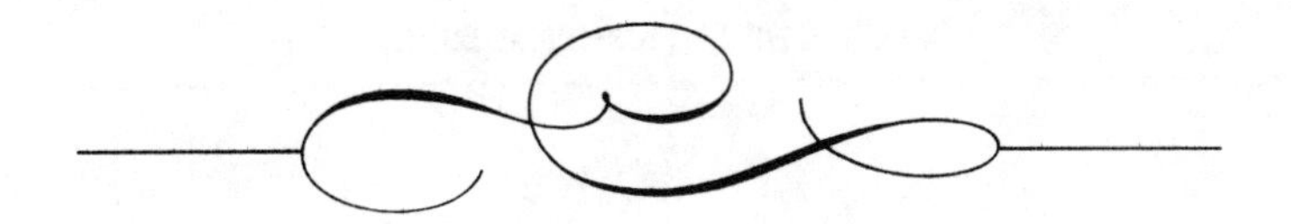

HOT SANDWICHES

You thought no one had a new idea for bacon, lettuce and tomato sandwiches? Well, our idea isn't new because it is Mother Stouffer's original recipe, but since we never before revealed it, it may be new to you. The difference is that both the tomato and the bacon are served hot, and the bacon is grilled right on the bread.

B.L.T. (STOUFFER'S ORIGINAL BACON, LETTUCE, AND TOMATO SANDWICH)

(Makes 4 sandwiches)

8 slices toast
1/4 cup salad dressing
12 slices tomato
12 slices bacon, partially cooked
4 lettuce leaves

1. Spread toast slices with salad dressing.
2. Place 4 slices of toast, dressing side up, on a baking sheet. Arrange 3 slices of tomato on each slice of toast to cover surface; top with 3 slices partially cooked bacon.
3. Place under broiler until bacon is hot and crisp.
4. Cover with lettuce leaves.
5. Top with remaining slices of toast, dressing side down.
6. Cut in half, corner to corner. Serve at once.

We didn't originate the Reuben. It comes from Reuben's Restaurant in New York, but we've adopted it with a Stouffer flavor, and it is our most popular sandwich in every one of our restaurants.

REUBEN GRILL
(Makes 4 sandwiches)

8 slices rye bread
1/2 cup Russian dressing
8 slices Swiss cheese
1 cup sauerkraut, drained
1/2 pound corned beef, sliced very thin
3 tablespoons soft butter

1. Spread each slice of bread with 1 tablespoon Russian dressing.
2. To assemble each sandwich: Place 2 slices Swiss cheese on one slice of bread; add 1/4 cup drained sauerkraut and sliced corned beef. Top with second slice of bread, dressing side down. Spread outside of bread slices with softened butter.
3. Grill on both sides to golden brown. Cut in half and arrange on plates. Garnish with pickle chips and sprigs of parsley.

MONACO GRILL
(Serves 4)

8 slices rye bread
1/2 cup Mustard Sauce (page 203)
8 slices Swiss cheese
1/2 pound sliced turkey breast
1/2 pound sliced baked ham
1/4 cup softened butter

1. To make each sandwich: Spread each slice of bread with Mustard Sauce; cover one slice of bread with one slice Swiss cheese; add turkey and ham; cover ham with one slice Swiss cheese; top with second slice of bread, Mustard Sauce side down. Spread outside of bread with softened butter.
2. Grill on both sides to golden brown. Cut sandwiches in thirds and arrange on plate.
3. Garnish with dill pickle spears.

SALISBURY STEAK TRIPLE DECK SANDWICH

(Serves 4)

2—12-ounce packages Frozen Salisbury Steaks*
2 hamburger buns, cut in half and toasted
8 slices liverwurst, 1/4" thick
4 slices Cheddar cheese

1. Bake Frozen Salisbury Steaks following package directions.
2. On each toasted bun half, place in order:
   2 slices of liverwurst
   1 slice of cheese
   1 Salisbury steak
3. Spoon onion gravy over sandwiches.
4. Serve at once.

SHERRIED RAREBIT OPEN FACE SANDWICH

(Serves 6)

2—10-ounce packages Frozen Welsh Rarebit, defrosted*
6 tablespoons sherry
6 English muffins
4 tomatoes
1 teaspoon salt
1/4 teaspoon pepper
1 cup all-purpose flour
6 tablespoons cooking oil
12 slices crisp bacon

1. Spoon Welsh Rarebit into top of double boiler and heat over rapidly boiling water for 25 minutes. Blend in sherry and heat for 5 minutes.
2. Split and toast English muffins.
3. Cut tomatoes into 1/2-inch thick slices; sprinkle with salt and pepper. Dip in flour and brown on both sides in hot oil.
4. Place two halves of toasted English muffins on each plate; top each half with a fried tomato slice and spoon Welsh Rarebit over tomato.
5. Garnish with crisp bacon strips.

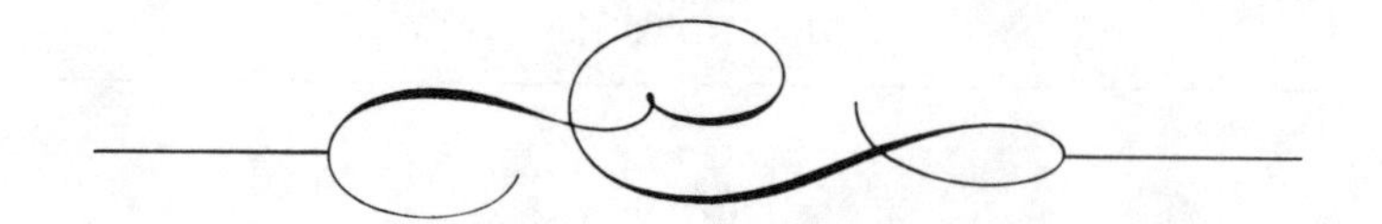

COLD SANDWICHES

This one is a real Stouffer first because it was developed by one of our own people and was a prize-winning entry in a national sandwich contest.

HEIDELBERG OPEN CLUB SANDWICH

(Serves 4)

4 slices rye bread
1/4 cup mayonnaise
4 leaves lettuce
1/2 pound liverwurst, cut into 16 slices
12 thin sweet onion rings
16 thin slices tomato
1/2 cup Russian dressing
2 eggs, hard-cooked and sliced
8 slices crisp bacon

1. Trim crusts from bread. Spread bread with mayonnaise. Place one slice of bread on each plate.
2. Arrange the ingredients on bread slices in the following order so that each layer is visible in the finished sandwich:

   1 leaf lettuce
   4 thin slices of liverwurst
   3 sweet onion rings
   4 tomato slices
   2 tablespoons Russian dressing
   1/2 sliced egg
   2 slices crisp bacon

3. Garnish plate with dill pickle spears, potato chips and a parsley sprig, if desired.

VENETIAN SANDWICH PLATE

(Serves 4)

1 cup cooked chicken, cut in 1/4" cubes
1/4 teaspoon salt
1/2 cup celery, cut in 1/4" cubes
6 tablespoons salad dressing
4 round sandwich buns
3 tablespoons salad dressing
4 lettuce cups
12 slices tomato
8 slices crisp bacon

1. Combine cubed chicken, salt, cubed celery and first amount of salad dressing; mix lightly.
2. Split and toast sandwich buns; place open toasted buns on plates.
3. Spread upper half of each toasted bun with 2 teaspoons salad dressing; top with a lettuce cup and 3 slices of tomato.
4. Spread lower half of each bun with chicken salad mixture; arrange 2 slices of crisp bacon on top. Garnish with potato chips and pickle chips.

VIRGINIAN CLUB SANDWICH

(Serves 4)

12 slices white bread
1/4 cup mayonnaise
1/2 pound sliced turkey breast
1/2 pound sliced baked ham
4 leaves lettuce

1. Spread each slice of bread with mayonnaise.
2. For each sandwich: Place sliced turkey on first slice of bread. Top with second slice of bread, mayonnaise side down. Place sliced ham and lettuce on bread and cover with third slice of bread. Cut sandwich into four quarters. Pierce each quarter with a frilly toothpick to hold it together. Arrange on plate.
3. Serve with potato chips, cole slaw or kidney bean salad.

HUNTER SANDWICH

(Serves 4)

4 Kaiser or round hard rolls
1/3 cup Mustard Sauce (page 203)
4 lettuce leaves
1/2 pound thinly sliced roast beef
Salt
1/2 pound sliced Mozzarella cheese
1-1/3 cups well drained cole slaw
1/4 pound dried chipped beef, pulled apart

1. Slice rolls in half, crosswise; spread each half with 2 teaspoons Mustard Sauce.
2. On bottom half of each roll, arrange ingredients as follows:
   1 leaf lettuce
   Sliced roast beef
   Salt
   Sliced Mozzarella cheese
   1/3 cup cole slaw
   Dried chipped beef
3. Cover with top of roll; cut in half. Garnish plates with dill pickle sticks and watercress. Serve a small lettuce cup filled with additional slaw, if desired.

SEAFOOD OPEN CLUB SANDWICH

(Serves 4)

3/4 cup cooked flaked fish
3/4 cup flaked crabmeat or 3/4 cup king crabmeat cut in 1/4" pieces
1/2 cup cooked shrimp, cut in 1/4" pieces
Salt to taste
3/4 tablespoon lemon juice
1/2 cup finely diced celery
1/2 cup salad dressing
8 slices white bread, crusts trimmed
1/2 cup salad dressing
4 slices lettuce, 1/4" thick
8 slices tomato, 1/2" thick
2 hard-cooked eggs, sliced
2 teaspoons capers

1. Combine cooked fish, crabmeat, diced shrimp, salt, lemon juice, celery and first amount of salad dressing; toss lightly.
2. Spread each slice of bread with 1 tablespoon salad dressing; cut 4 of the slices in half diagonally; arrange on plates so that one full slice

is in the center of each plate with one half slice on each side (points toward edge of the plate).

3. For each sandwich: Center 1 slice of lettuce (slightly pulled apart) across the bread. Top with 1/2 cup seafood salad. Place 2 slices of tomato, side by side, on top of salad mixture. Place one slice of hard-cooked egg on center of each tomato slice; sprinkle 1/4 teaspoon capers over each egg slice.
4. Garnish plates with potato chips, dill pickle spears, lemon wedges, and bouquets of parsley.

EASTERN SHORE CLUB SANDWICH

(Serves 4)

2 cups cooked lobster meat, cut in 1/4″ cubes
1/2 teaspoon lemon juice
1/4 teaspoon salt
2/3 cup celery, cut in 1/4″ cubes
1/2 cup salad dressing
12 slices white bread, crusts trimmed
1/3 cup salad dressing
12 slices tomato
1 large avocado, cut in 1/8″ thick slices
4 leaves lettuce
3 ounces potato chips
8 ripe olives
8 sweet pickle slices

1. Combine lobster, lemon juice, salt, celery and first amount of salad dressing; toss lightly.
2. To make each sandwich: Spread 1 slice of bread with 2/3 cup lobster salad mixture; spread second slice of bread with 2 teaspoons salad dressing and place on top of salad mixture, dressing side down; arrange 3 slices of tomato on second slice of bread; cover with sliced avocado and lettuce; spread third slice of bread with 2 teaspoons salad dressing and place, dressing side down, on lettuce.
3. Cut sandwiches diagonally into quarters. Pierce each quarter with a frilly toothpick and arrange on plates with points up. Place potato chips in the center. Garnish plates with sweet pickles, ripe olives, and a parsley bouquet.

EASTERN SHORE CRAB SANDWICH

Would You Like a Vegetable?

Vegetables used to be boring, but a long time ago we learned that just because something is good for you doesn't mean it has to be unappealing. At Stouffer's we pay as much attention to vegetables as we do to entrees beginning with the lowly potato, which we dress up a hundred different ways. Just a few of the ideas are here, but we also have some new ways for serving everything from corn to tomatoes to zucchini.

Our best advice on vegetables:

1. *Cook any vegetable in the shortest cooking time possible; never, never, never overcook.*
2. *Carefully season vegetables with butter; coat the vegetables . . . don't drown them.*
3. *Sugar added to peas and tomatoes brings out the natural flavors of the vegetables.*
4. *Use a minimum amount of water for all vegetables for nutrient retention.*
5. *Use an open saucepan when preparing green vegetables to retain natural color.*

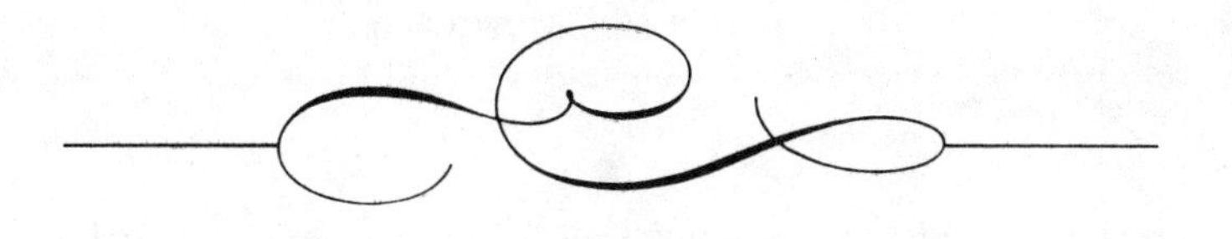

ZESTY CHEESE POTATOES

(Serves 4)

4 baking potatoes
1/2 teaspoon salt
Few grains pepper
1 tablespoon butter
1/4 cup hot milk
1/4 cup grated Cheddar cheese
4 heaping tablespoons (1/3 of a 10-ounce package) Frozen Welsh Rarebit, defrosted*

1. Preheat oven to 400° F.
2. Bake potatoes for one hour (or until soft to touch); remove from oven. Lower oven temperature to 375° F.
3. Immediately cut an oval opening (3 inches by 2-1/2 inches) in the large rounded side of each potato.
4. Using a spoon, remove the hot potato pulp and place in a mixer bowl.
5. Add salt, pepper, butter and hot milk; beat on medium speed until light and fluffy. Gently stir in grated cheese.
6. Fill the potato shells with this mixture.
7. Using a spoon, make a depression in the center of each filled potato.
8. Place a heaping tablespoon of Welsh Rarebit in each depression.
9. Return potatoes to oven and bake 10 to 12 minutes until heated through.

POTATOES PARMESAN

(Serves 8)

4—11-1/2-ounce packages Frozen Potatoes au Gratin, defrosted*
1 cup bacon crumbs
1/2 teaspoon seasoned salt
1/4 cup grated Parmesan cheese

1. Place Potatoes au Gratin in a mixing bowl.
2. Add bacon crumbs and seasoned salt. Stir well to combine.
3. Pour mixture into a 1-1/2-quart casserole and sprinkle with Parmesan cheese.
4. Bake in a 400° F. oven for 30 to 35 minutes. Serve hot.

This is another one of those recipes that appeared early in our history and has remained on our menus ever since.

HOT DUTCH POTATO SALAD
(Serves 4)

1 pound potatoes
3/4 teaspoon salt
1/4 cup celery, cut in 1/4″ cubes
2 tablespoons finely chopped onion
6 slices bacon, cut in 3/8″ pieces, cooked crisp
3 tablespoons bacon fat

2 tablespoons all-purpose flour
1/2 teaspoon dry mustard
1/2 cup cider vinegar
1/2 cup water
1/4 cup granulated sugar
2-1/2 teaspoons salt
1/4 teaspoon pepper

1. Boil potatoes until tender; peel and cut into 1/8-inch slices. Place sliced potatoes in a 1-1/2-quart casserole dish. Sprinkle with salt.
2. Add celery, onion and crisp bacon pieces.
3. Melt bacon fat in a saucepan. Add flour and dry mustard; stir until smooth.
4. Add vinegar and water, stirring constantly. Simmer until thickened and flour taste has disappeared.
5. Add sugar, salt and pepper.
6. Pour sauce over potatoes in casserole and mix gently to distribute all ingredients evenly. Allow to stand at room temperature 1-1/2 to 2 hours so potatoes can absorb flavors.
7. Cover and bake in a 350° F. oven for 30 minutes.

POTATO PANCAKES
(Serves 6)

1—11-1/2-ounce package Frozen Potatoes au Gratin, defrosted*
1/3 cup all-purpose flour
1 egg, slightly beaten
1/4 teaspoon salt

1/2 teaspoon finely chopped chives or 1/2 teaspoon finely chopped green onion
3 tablespoons cooking oil or melted shortening

1. Place Potatoes au Gratin in a medium bowl. Add flour, slightly beaten egg, salt and chives or onion.

2. Stir to combine all ingredients.
3. Pour oil or shortening in a heavy skillet; heat for 1 to 2 minutes, until bubbly.
4. For each pancake drop 1/4 cup mixture into hot fat. With a spatula flatten to a 4-inch pancake. Fry 2 or 3 minutes on each side or until golden brown. Drain on absorbent paper. Serve hot.

HONEY GLAZED CARROTS

(Serves 4–6)

1 pound raw carrots
1 tablespoon butter, melted
3 tablespoons brown sugar
1 tablespoon honey
1/2 teaspoon salt

1. Peel carrots and cut in strips 1/2-inch by 1/2-inch by 2-1/2 inches long. Cook in boiling, salted water until barely tender. Drain well.
2. Combine butter, brown sugar, honey and salt in a heavy saucepan. Add drained carrots and simmer 4 to 6 minutes or until glazed, stirring occasionally.

CARROTS VICHY

(Serves 4)

1/4 cup butter
3-1/2 cups raw carrots, cut in strips 1/2″ by 1/2″ by 1-1/2″ long
2 teaspoons salt
1/4 cup granulated sugar
1/2 cup hot water
1 tablespoon freshly squeezed lemon juice
2 tablespoons finely chopped parsley

1. Melt butter in a heavy saucepan; add carrots, salt and sugar; stir to coat carrots with butter.
2. Add hot water and heat to boiling; reduce heat; cover, and cook 10 to 15 minutes or until most of the water has evaporated and the carrots have a rich glaze. Remove from heat.
3. Add lemon juice and parsley; mix gently. Serve at once.

Even a vegetable as familiar as a carrot can change its character when we change the way of making it. This recipe makes carrots seem sweeter, and it's certainly a way of pepping up a standard menu.

FRENCH-FRIED CARROTS

(Serves 4)

1-1/2 pounds raw carrots
1/4 cup all-purpose flour
1/2 teaspoon granulated sugar
1 teaspoon salt
1 egg, beaten
3 tablespoons milk
1 cup dry bread crumbs
Melted shortening or oil for deep frying

1. Peel carrots and cut into thin strips 1/2-inch by 1/2-inch by 2-1/2 inches long. Cook in boiling, salted water until barely tender; drain thoroughly and cool to room temperature.
2. Combine flour, sugar and salt; add beaten egg and blend smooth; add milk and mix well to make egg batter.
3. Dip carrots in egg batter and drain slightly on a wire rack; roll in dry bread crumbs.
4. Deep fry in 360° F. fat until golden brown. Drain on absorbent paper; sprinkle with salt and serve at once.

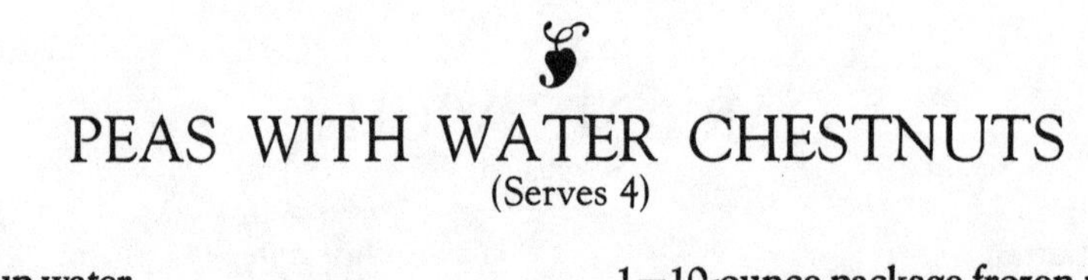

PEAS WITH WATER CHESTNUTS

(Serves 4)

1/4 cup water
3/4 teaspoon salt
1-1/2 teaspoons granulated sugar
1 tablespoon soft butter
1—10-ounce package frozen peas
6 water chestnuts, sliced
2 teaspoons butter, melted

1. Combine water, salt, sugar and soft butter; bring to a boil. Add peas and simmer until tender. Do not drain.
2. Sauté water chestnuts in melted butter until golden brown.
3. Combine peas and sautéed water chestnuts; stir gently before serving.

We designed this for the opening of Top of the Six's, *and guests liked it so much we included it in the menus for other cities, too.*

FRENCH STYLE GREEN PEAS

(Serves 4)

1-1/2—10-ounce packages frozen peas
1-1/4 cups lettuce strips, 1/4" by 1/4" by 1-1/2" long
1/3 cup canned tiny whole onions
2 tablespoons soft butter
3 parsley sprigs, tied in a cheesecloth bag
1-1/2 teaspoons granulated sugar
1 teaspoon salt
1/2 cup water
1 tablespoon soft butter
1/2 teaspoon all-purpose flour

1. Cook peas in boiling, salted water until tender; drain well.
2. Place lettuce in bottom of heavy saucepan.
3. Add onions, first amount of butter, parsley, sugar, salt and water; cover and heat to boiling. Reduce heat and simmer 2 minutes. Add cooked peas.
4. Blend second amount of butter with flour. Add to the peas and onion mixture. Cover and simmer 2 minutes. Remove parsley sprigs before serving.

STEWED TOMATOES WITH CROUTONS

(Serves 4)

1 slice bread
2 cups canned tomatoes, broken
1/4 teaspoon salt
1 tablespoon granulated sugar
Few grains pepper
1 tablespoon butter

1. Trim crusts from bread; cut bread into 1/2-inch cubes. Bake on a flat pan in 350°F. oven until golden brown.
2. Combine remaining ingredients and heat to boiling. Simmer 3 to 4 minutes.
3. When ready to serve, sprinkle croutons over tomatoes.

FRENCH-FRIED TOMATOES
(Serves 4–6)

4 firm tomatoes
1 teaspoon salt
1/2 cup all-purpose flour
3 eggs, beaten
1/3 cup water
1/2 teaspoon salt
Few grains pepper
1 cup dry bread crumbs
Melted shortening or oil for deep frying
Salt

1. Wash and stem tomatoes; cut into slices 1/2-inch thick.
2. Combine first amount of salt and flour.
3. Combine beaten eggs, water, second amount of salt and pepper; mix well to make egg batter.
4. Coat tomato slices in flour mixture; dip in egg batter and drain; dip in dry bread crumbs.
5. Place slices on wire rack and let stand 10 to 15 minutes before frying.
6. Preheat deep fat to 370° F. Fry tomato slices a few at a time for 1-1/2 to 2 minutes until golden brown.
7. Drain on absorbent paper; sprinkle lightly with salt and serve immediately.

SPINACH MUSHROOM CASSEROLE
(Serves 6)

2 tablespoons butter or margarine
1—4-ounce can mushrooms, drained
1/4 cup chopped onion
1/4 cup grated Cheddar cheese
2—12-ounce packages Frozen Spinach Soufflé, defrosted*

1. Preheat oven to 350° F.
2. Melt butter in small skillet; sauté mushrooms and onion 5 minutes.
3. Spoon defrosted Spinach Soufflé into a medium mixing bowl.
4. Add sautéed mushrooms and onions; combine thoroughly.
5. Pour mixture into a 1-quart casserole.
6. Sprinkle grated Cheddar cheese around edges.
7. Bake for 35 to 40 minutes or until a silver knife inserted in the center comes out clean.
8. Serve at once.

ESCALLOPED CABBAGE

(Serves 6)

1-1/4 cups water
1-1/4 teaspoons salt
1 medium head cabbage, cut in 1" squares (approximately 8 cups)
1 cup hot milk
1/3 cup hot coffee cream
3 tablespoons cooking broth from cabbage

Sauce:
1-1/2 tablespoons butter
3 tablespoons all-purpose flour
1/2 teaspoon salt

Topping:
2 tablespoons dry bread crumbs
1 teaspoon butter, melted

1. Heat water to boiling; add salt and cabbage; boil uncovered until cabbage is tender. Drain and save broth.
2. To make sauce, melt butter in a heavy saucepan; add flour, blend and simmer 2 minutes to partially cook flour.
3. Gradually add hot milk, cream and broth from cabbage, beating constantly. Cook over medium heat until thickened.
4. Add cabbage and blend. Pour into a 2-quart casserole.
5. Combine melted butter and bread crumbs; toss lightly. Sprinkle over cabbage.
6. Bake in a 350°F. oven for 20 minutes or until heated through.
7. Place under medium broiler to brown crumbs lightly.

HERB BUTTERED GREEN BEANS

(Serves 4)

1/4 teaspoon dill seed, crushed
1/8 teaspoon celery seed
1 tablespoon butter, melted
2 cups green beans, cut in 1" pieces

1. Combine crushed dill seed, celery seed and melted butter. Let stand several hours at room temperature.
2. Cook green beans in boiling, salted water until tender, drain well.
3. Pour herb butter mixture over beans and hold over low heat 10 minutes before serving.

FRENCH-FRIED CAULIFLOWER

(Serves 4–6)

1 medium head raw cauliflower
2 eggs, beaten
1/4 cup water
1/4 teaspoon salt
Few grains pepper
1/2 cup all-purpose flour
1 cup dry bread crumbs
Melted shortening or oil for deep frying
Salt

1. Wash cauliflower and separate into flowerettes; cook in boiling, salted water until barely tender. Drain thoroughly and cool to room temperature.
2. Combine beaten eggs, water, salt and pepper; blend to make egg batter.
3. Roll cooked cauliflower lightly in flour.
4. Dip floured cauliflower in egg batter and place on wire rack to drain.
5. Roll cauliflower in dry bread crumbs.
6. Deep fry cauliflower in 360° F. fat for 1 minute or until golden brown. Drain on absorbent paper and sprinkle lightly with salt. Serve at once.

This is one of our best "go-withs." It goes with chicken, beef, seafood.

RICE PILAF

(Serves 6)

2 tablespoons chicken fat
2 chicken bouillon cubes
1 tablespoon butter
3/4 cup diced fresh mushrooms
1/3 cup chopped onion
1/4 teaspoon seasoned salt
2-1/4 cups cooked rice, well drained

1. Melt chicken fat, bouillon cubes and butter in a heavy saucepan.
2. Add diced mushrooms, chopped onion and seasoned salt; sauté until vegetables are tender.
3. Fold rice and mushroom/onion mixture together. Place in a shallow casserole dish.
4. Cover and bake in 375° F. oven for 10 minutes; uncover, stir gently, and continue baking uncovered for 15 more minutes.

EGGPLANT MILANO

(Serves 6)

1 pound eggplant
1-1/2 teaspoons salt
2-1/2 tablespoons chopped onion
2 tablespoons margarine
1 cup canned tomatoes, broken
2 tablespoons tomato sauce
1/4 teaspoon salt
1/4 teaspoon granulated sugar
Few grains pepper
1/8 teaspoon sweet basil
1/2 cup finely grated Cheddar cheese

1. Peel eggplant and slice 1/4-inch thick; cut each slice in quarters. Place eggplant in serving casserole; sprinkle with first amount of salt and stir gently. Let stand for 15 minutes.
2. Sauté onion in margarine until golden brown.
3. Add tomatoes, tomato sauce, salt, sugar, pepper and sweet basil; heat to boiling. Reduce heat and simmer 10 minutes.
4. Pour sauce over eggplant and stir gently.
5. Sprinkle grated cheese over all. Cover and bake in 400° F. oven for 35 to 40 minutes until eggplant is tender.
6. Place under broiler to brown cheese lightly.

CORN-FILLED PEPPERS

(Serves 4)

4 green peppers
3 tablespoons margarine, melted
1—1-pound can stewed tomatoes
2—12-ounce packages Frozen Corn Soufflé, defrosted*

1. Preheat oven to 350° F.
2. Cut stem ends from peppers; remove seeds and membrane. Wash and dry thoroughly. Trim bottom of peppers, if necessary, so they will stand upright.
3. Brush outsides of peppers with melted margarine.
4. Pour stewed tomatoes into an 8-inch square casserole.
5. Spoon Corn Soufflé into peppers; place upright in casserole on top of tomatoes.
6. Bake 60 to 70 minutes or until a silver knife inserted in the center of soufflé comes out clean.

ORANGE GLAZED BEETS

(Serves 4)

2-3/4 teaspoons cornstarch
1/3 cup orange juice
1 tablespoon cider vinegar
1/4 cup granulated sugar
2/3 teaspoon salt
Dash cinnamon
Dash ground cloves
2 teaspoons lemon juice
1 tablespoon butter
2 cups cooked beets, cut into 1/2" cubes
2 tablespoons orange pieces, cut as directed below

1. Blend cornstarch with 2 tablespoons orange juice until smooth.
2. In a saucepan, heat remaining orange juice and vinegar to boiling.
3. Add sugar, salt and spices. Stir to mix well. Remove from heat.
4. Add cornstarch/orange juice mixture, while beating constantly with a wire whip. Return to the heat and cook until mixture thickens, stirring frequently.
5. Add lemon juice and butter; blend.
6. Add diced beets to sauce; stir gently with a rubber spatula and simmer for 2 to 3 minutes until beets are thoroughly heated.
7. Wash one orange. Cut off and discard end slice. Cut three to four very thin slices from the orange. Cut each slice in 10 to 12 wedge shaped pieces.
8. Add orange pieces to the heated beets and sauce. Stir just enough to distribute orange pieces evenly.

HARVARD BEETS

(Serves 4–6)

1 tablespoon cornstarch
1 cup cold water
1/2 cup cider vinegar
1/2 cup granulated sugar
1/2 teaspoon salt
1/2 bay leaf
1/4 teaspoon cinnamon
Dash ground cloves
3 tablespoons butter
3 cups cooked beets, cut in 1/2" cubes

1. Combine 1/4 cup of the water and cornstarch; blend smooth.
2. Heat remaining water and vinegar to boiling; add sugar, salt, bay leaf and spices; blend.

3. Gradually add cornstarch mixture, stirring constantly. Cook until mixture thickens and is clear. Remove bay leaf.
4. Add butter and stir. Add beet cubes and blend. Heat to boiling; reduce heat and simmer for 2 minutes.

CORN ZUCCHINI CASSEROLE

(Serves 6)

1 pound zucchini squash
1/3 cup chopped onion
2—12-ounce packages Frozen Corn Soufflé, defrosted*

1. Preheat oven to 350° F.
2. Wash and scrub squash with a vegetable brush; drain and cut into 1/2-inch chunks.
3. Fold squash and onion into Corn Soufflé; stir to combine.
4. Pour mixture into a 1-quart casserole. Bake 50 to 60 minutes. Serve at once.

ZUCCHINI MILANO

(Serves 4)

1-1/4 pounds zucchini squash
2 tablespoons margarine
2-1/2 tablespoons chopped onion
1 cup canned tomatoes, broken
2 tablespoons tomato sauce
1/4 teaspoon salt
1/4 teaspoon granulated sugar
Few grains pepper
1/8 teaspoon sweet basil

1. Wash and scrub squash with a vegetable brush. Slice into 1/2-inch thick rounds, leaving peel on.
2. Arrange squash overlapping, domino fashion, in serving casserole.
3. Sauté onions in margarine until golden brown. Add remaining ingredients and simmer 10 minutes.
4. Pour hot sauce over squash and shake casserole slightly so sauce will flow down between slices.
5. Cover and bake in 350° F. oven for 45 minutes. Uncover and bake 10 minutes longer to glaze surface.

BAKED CHILI ONIONS

(Serves 4)

1 pound small white onions
1 tablespoon salt
1 teaspoon chili powder
3 tablespoons butter, melted
3 tablespoons water

1. Peel onions; cook in boiling, salted water until tender. Drain thoroughly.
2. Place drained onions in a shallow 1-quart casserole. Sprinkle with salt and chili powder.
3. Pour melted butter over onions; pour water in bottom of dish.
4. Bake in 375° F. oven for 8 to 10 minutes or until onions are hot.

HARVEST ESCALLOPED APPLES

(Serves 4)

2 acorn squash
Salt
2 cups hot water
2—12-ounce packages Frozen Escalloped Apples, defrosted*
12 slices cooked bacon, crumbled
4 teaspoons brown sugar

1. Preheat oven to 375° F.
2. Scrub squash. Cut in half crosswise; scoop out seeds and stringy portion. Sprinkle cut sides of squash with salt.
3. Place squash, cut side down, in a shallow baking pan. Add hot water. Bake uncovered for 30 minutes or until squash is tender. Remove from oven and increase oven temperature to 400° F.
4. Combine Escalloped Apples and bacon. Fill each half of squash with apple mixture. Sprinkle each half with 1 teaspoon brown sugar. Place in baking pan and return to oven. Bake for 25 to 30 minutes.

NOTE: One-half pound cooked ground sausage meat may be substituted for bacon.

BRUSSELS SPROUTS AU GRATIN

(Serves 4)

2—10-ounce packages frozen Brussels sprouts
1— 10-ounce package Frozen Welsh Rarebit, defrosted*
1/2 cup dairy sour cream
2 tablespoons grated Parmesan cheese

1. Preheat oven to 400° F.
2. Cook Brussels sprouts in boiling, salted water for 5 minutes; drain well. Place in a 1-1/2-quart casserole.
3. Combine Welsh Rarebit and sour cream to make a sauce. Pour sauce over Brussels sprouts. Sprinkle with Parmesan cheese.
4. Bake 20 to 25 minutes or until piping hot.

APPLE-FILLED SWEET POTATO NESTS

(Serves 6)

1— 1-pound-6-ounce can yams or sweet potatoes
2 tablespoons margarine
2 eggs
1/4 teaspoon salt
1 tablespoon granulated sugar
1/4 teaspoon ground nutmeg
1/2 teaspoon vanilla extract
1— 12-ounce package Frozen Escalloped Apples, defrosted*

1. Preheat oven to 400° F.
2. In a large mixing bowl, whip potatoes until soft and smooth.
3. Add margarine, eggs, salt, sugar, nutmeg and vanilla extract. Continue beating until well combined.
4. On a lightly greased cookie sheet, spoon potato mixture to form 6 mounds, 2 inches apart.
5. With the back of a spoon make a depression in each mound, forming a shell.
6. Fill the center of each shell with Escalloped Apples. Bake for 30 minutes. Serve at once.

TANGY MACARONI AND CHEESE

(Serves 4–6)

2—10-ounce packages Frozen Welsh Rarebit, defrosted*
1 cup elbow macaroni
2 teaspoons salt
1 cup dairy sour cream
1/4 cup grated Cheddar cheese

1. Heat Welsh Rarebit in top of double boiler over rapidly boiling water for 15 to 20 minutes just until hot.
2. Cook macaroni following package directions. Drain well.
3. Pour Welsh Rarebit into a 2-quart casserole; add cooked macaroni, salt and sour cream. Stir to combine. Sprinkle with grated Cheddar cheese.
4. Bake in a 400°F. oven for 20 minutes.

. . . a
Salad?

We like to garnish salads well.

For chicken and turkey salads, we suggest fruit garnishes of fresh apricot, avocado, Bing cherries, blackberries, currant clusters, red grapes, frosted grapes, grapefruit, peaches, plums, pomegranate seeds, and blueberries; vegetable garnishes of chicory, endive, mint, parsley, radishes, watercress, fresh pimiento. For fish salads, garnish with ripe olives, sprigs of parsley, pimiento, shrimp, tomato, watercress, unsweetened whipped cream, avocado or capers.

Fruit salads can be garnished with fresh fruit or nutmeats, watercress, coconut.

And vegetable salads look most appetizing when garnished with fresh vegetables, hard-cooked eggs, ripe or stuffed olives.

We are always careful not to drown salads in their own dressing.

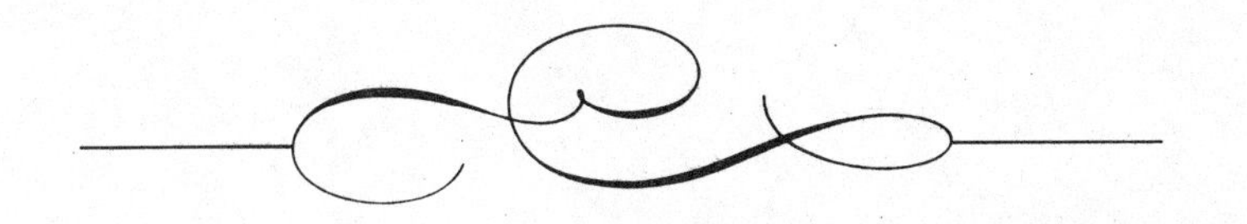

The secret of a good salad is fresh, crisped greens. And at Stouffer's, this is how we prepare our greens:

GREENS	PREPARATION DIRECTIONS (One day in advance)
Bibb or Boston Lettuce (for use in tossed salads or as cups)	1. Remove discolored or wilted outside leaves. 2. Cut out core from each head in a cone-shaped piece. 3. Spread and loosen cone-shaped opening gently, leaving head intact, to allow water to enter. 4. Wash thoroughly in cold water. Drain well. Chill.
Iceberg Lettuce	Warm Water Method: 1. Place cored, trimmed heads in warm water (approximately 110° F.); allow them to soak for 1 to 2 hours. (The longer time makes it easier to separate the leaves without tearing them.) 2. Remove heads from water and drain well, core end down. 3. Separate into leaves, cups, etc. and refrigerate for 30 minutes to 1 hour.
Chicory or Curly Endive Escarole Leaf Lettuce Romaine Spinach	1. Cut off stem ends and any discolored or rusted leaves. 2. Wash well, changing water 3 times. Each time, lift greens from cold water before discarding water. 3. Drain well and chill.

STORAGE OF GREENS
1. Place drained, washed greens standing up with core end down in: a) wire storage baskets or b) colanders 2. Do not lay greens on side or stand too closely together. 3. Place storage baskets or colanders on trays and refrigerate overnight to crisp and dry the greens.

DEVONSHIRE GREEN CABBAGE SLAW
(Serves 4)

1/2 cup dairy sour cream
2 tablespoons granulated sugar
1 teaspoon salt
1 tablespoon freshly squeezed lemon juice
2 teaspoons cider vinegar
5 cups finely shredded green cabbage, loosely packed

1. Combine sour cream, sugar, salt, lemon juice and vinegar; blend and chill.
2. Combine finely shredded cabbage and dressing; toss lightly to blend. Mixture will look frothy.
3. Chill for 30 minutes to blend flavors. Serve in crisp lettuce cups with parsley garnish.

NOTE: When serving, use tongs to keep slaw light and airy.

TOSSED SALAD DELUXE
(Serves 6)

3-1/2 cups lettuce hearts, cut in 1-1/2″ pieces
3-1/2 cups romaine, cut in 1-1/2″ pieces
1-3/4 cups Bibb or Boston lettuce, cut in 1-1/2″ pieces
3 cups fresh spinach, trimmed and cut in 1-1/2″ pieces
2 cups sliced mushrooms
1/3 cup red wine vinegar and oil dressing
1 teaspoon salt
2-1/2 tablespoons red wine vinegar and oil dressing
1 small Italian red onion

1. Prepare greens in advance and chill to crisp.
2. Combine sliced mushrooms with first amount of dressing and let stand 10 minutes; drain and chill.
3. When ready to serve, toss greens with salt and mushrooms. Add second amount of dressing and toss to coat greens. Garnish individual or large salad bowl with thinly sliced Italian red onion rings.

MARINATED THREE BEAN SALAD

(Serves 6)

1 cup canned green beans, cut in 1/2" lengths
1 cup canned wax beans, cut in 1/2" lengths
1 cup canned red kidney beans, drained and rinsed
1/4 cup chopped onion
1/4 cup salad oil
1/4 cup cider vinegar
5 tablespoons granulated sugar
1/2 teaspoon salt
1/4 teaspoon pepper

1. Combine beans and onion.
2. Combine remaining ingredients and blend thoroughly.
3. Pour dressing over bean mixture and toss lightly.
4. Cover and refrigerate overnight.

This salad was invented by the manager of our Shaker Square Tack Room *and one of our dietitians. We're not sure why they name it "Catalina" but we do serve it under different names at some of our restaurants. (It's sometimes called Tack Room or Gold Coast Salad.) The cauliflower seems to set this apart from all other salads.*

CATALINA SALAD BOWL

(Serves 8)

1-1/2 cups raw cauliflower flowerettes, 1/2" pieces
1-1/2 teaspoons salt
8 cups lettuce hearts, cut in 1-1/2" chunks
7 cups romaine, cut in strips 1" wide and 2" long
1-1/2 cups White French Dressing
1/3 cup Bleu cheese crumbs
1/3 cup bacon crumbs
16 half wedges of tomato

1. Combine cauliflower pieces, salt and chilled cut greens; toss together.
2. Add White French Dressing and toss to coat all greens.
3. Line a large salad serving bowl with lettuce leaves. Heap tossed greens into bowl. Sprinkle Bleu cheese and bacon crumbs over the top. Garnish with tomato wedges and watercress or parsley.

TARRAGON TOSSED SALAD WITH ARTICHOKE HEARTS

(Serves 6)

1—9-ounce package frozen artichoke hearts
3/4 cup Tarragon Dressing (below)
4-1/2 cups lettuce, cut in 3/4" pieces
1-1/2 cups romaine, cut in 1" pieces
2 cups fresh spinach, trimmed and cut in 1" pieces
2/3 cup Tarragon Dressing (below)
18 marinated artichoke hearts
2 tablespoons diced pimiento
6 ripe olives

1. Remove frozen artichoke hearts from package and thaw until they separate. Place in a deep container. Pour first amount of dressing over artichokes. Cover and refrigerate overnight. One hour before serving, drain thoroughly.
2. Combine greens and second amount of Tarragon Dressing; toss lightly.
3. Serve 1-1/2 cups salad per portion on chilled plates. Garnish each serving with 3 marinated artichoke hearts, 1 teaspoon diced pimiento and 1 ripe olive.

TARRAGON DRESSING

1-1/2 cups salad oil
1 cup tarragon vinegar
2 teaspoons salt
1/2 teaspoon pepper
1/4 teaspoon tarragon

1. Combine all ingredients; mix well and chill.
2. When ready to use, shake or mix well to form an emulsion.

FRONTIER SALAD BOWL

(Serves 4–6)

Salad Mixture:
5-1/2 cups finely shredded cabbage, well chilled
5 cups finely shredded lettuce, well chilled
1 teaspoon salt
1 cup Thousand Island Dressing (below)
1/4 cup julienne turkey, 1/4" by 1/4" by 2" pieces
3 tablespoons julienne ham, 1/4" by 1/4" by 2" pieces
1/4 cup julienne Swiss cheese, 1/4" by 1/4" by 2" pieces

Topping:
3/4 cup julienne turkey
2/3 cup julienne ham
1/2 cup julienne Swiss cheese

1. Place chilled, shredded cabbage and lettuce in a large mixing bowl. Add salt and toss lightly. Add dressing, 1/4 cup julienne turkey, 3 tablespoons ham and 1/4 cup Swiss cheese; gently toss ingredients to distribute them evenly throughout greens.
2. Line a large salad bowl with lettuce leaves. Heap the salad mixture into the bowl and arrange the additional julienne pieces on top. Garnish with ripe olives and watercress.

THOUSAND ISLAND DRESSING:

2/3 cup salad dressing
1 teaspoon chopped green pepper
2 teaspoons chopped hard-cooked egg
2 teaspoons chopped sweet pickles
3 tablespoons chili sauce
1/8 teaspoon salt

1. Mix all ingredients together thoroughly.

CHICKEN SALAD HAWAIIAN

(Serves 4)

2 whole fresh pineapples
2-1/2 cups diced cooked chicken
1 cup diced celery
3/4 teaspoon salt
1-2/3 cups seeded grapes, cut in half
3/4 cup Whipped Cream Dressing (page 201)
2-2/3 cups lettuce hearts, cut in 1/2" cubes
24 orange sections
20–24 Bing cherries or strawberries
Watercress
1/3 cup toasted slivered almonds

1. Split pineapple in half lengthwise through the leaves. Using a fruit knife, cut fruit from shell and save.
2. Combine diced chicken, celery, salt, grapes and Whipped Cream Dressing; blend and chill thoroughly.
3. For each salad: Place one pineapple shell on lettuce-lined plate. Put 2/3 cup of lettuce cubes in shell. Arrange 3/4 cup of chicken salad over lettuce cubes.
4. Cut reserved pineapple into sticks 3/4-inch by 3/4-inch by 2 inches. Arrange 5 pineapple sticks standing up around chicken salad. Place orange sections between pineapple sticks.
5. Garnish with Bing cherries or strawberries and a bouquet of watercress. Sprinkle top of chicken salad with toasted, slivered almonds.
6. Serve additional Whipped Cream Dressing, if desired.

BRANDIED BING CHERRY SALAD

(Serves 8)

2—3-ounce packages cherry gelatin
1-1/2 cups boiling water
1-1/2 cups Bing cherry juice and cold water
2 tablespoons lemon juice
1/2 cup brandy
1-1/3 cups pitted Bing cherries, halved
Whipped Cream Dressing (page 201)

1. Dissolve gelatin in boiling water.
2. Add cherry juice and water (use all of the cherry juice available and add water to make up the difference), lemon juice and brandy; stir. Chill to consistency of unbeaten egg whites, stirring occasionally.

3. Pour gelatin mixture into a lightly oiled 1-quart mold. Stir in cherry halves; chill overnight or until firm.
4. Unmold salad onto lettuce lined platter. Garnish with clusters of Bing cherries and frosted white grapes. Serve with Whipped Cream Dressing.

SUPREME CHICKEN SALAD

(Serves 8)

Jellied Wine Molds:

1—6-ounce (or 2—3-ounce) package red cherry gelatin
2-1/2 cups boiling water
1-1/2 cups sparkling Burgundy
2 teaspoons lemon juice
54 halves seeded black or red grapes

Chicken Salad:

4-1/2 cups cooked chicken breast, cut into julienne strips, 1/2" by 1/2" by 1-1/2" long
1/2 cup diced celery
1 teaspoon salt
1-1/2 cups Whipped Cream Dressing (page 201)
1-1/4 pounds seeded black or red grapes, cut in half

4 cups lettuce hearts, cut in 1/4" cubes
2/3 cup toasted julienne almonds

1. Thoroughly dissolve gelatin in the boiling water. Cool to lukewarm. Add sparkling Burgundy and lemon juice; mix well. Place 1/2 cup of gelatin mixture in each of eight individual molds. Chill until partially thickened. Add six grape halves to each mold and stir to distribute evenly. Chill overnight or for at least 6 hours until set.
2. Carefully combine chicken, celery and salt. Add dressing and mix lightly to combine. Chill thoroughly. Fold grapes into salad just before serving.
3. On chilled large luncheon plates, arrange crisp lettuce leaves. In the center of each plate, place 1/2 cup lettuce cubes and unmold one jellied wine mold on top of the cubes. Around each mold arrange 3/4 cup of chicken salad mixture. Sprinkle 2 teaspoons almonds over the chicken salad on each plate and garnish with bouquets of watercress.

FRESH FRUIT IN CANTALOUPE BOAT

(Serves 4)

2 medium cantaloupes
12 to 16 sprigs curly endive
3 cups mixed fresh fruit, well drained
1/4 cup Whipped Cream Dressing (page 201)
1/4 cup fresh blueberries
1—#2 can date-nut bread
3/4 cup Whipped Cream Cheese (page 203)

1. Peel cantaloupes to remove all rind; cut in half crosswise; remove seeds; trim ends so halves will sit flat on plates.
2. For each salad:
   Place one half cantaloupe on chilled plate; garnish with sprigs of curly endive. Place 3/4 cup of fresh fruit in center of cantaloupe; top with one tablespoon dressing. Sprinkle with 1 tablespoon fresh blueberries.
3. Cut date-nut bread into 12 slices; spread each of 6 slices with 2 tablespoons Whipped Cream Cheese. Cover with remaining slices; cut in half.
4. Arrange three half sandwiches on each salad plate.

...or
Not
Bread?

There are some people who believe you can judge a restaurant or a home dinner by the bread served. Hot breads are a Stouffer tradition, and we still think that one of the highlights of a dinner is home-baked breads and rolls. These recipes include both simple and more elaborate ways of adding that home-baked touch early in the dinner.

HERB BREAD
(Serves 6–8)

1—10-ounce loaf Frozen Garlic Bread*
2 tablespoons grated Parmesan cheese
1/2 teaspoon thyme
1/4 teaspoon sweet basil

1. Preheat oven to 400° F.
2. Place foil packaged bread in oven. Heat for 15 minutes.
3. Remove bread from package; pull apart along cut side.
4. Combine cheese, thyme and basil. Sprinkle evenly over cut sides of bread.
5. Place on a tray, cut side up. Bake for 10 minutes. Serve at once.

BLEU CHEESE BREAD
(Serves 6)

1—10-ounce loaf Frozen Garlic Bread, defrosted*
1/4 cup softened Bleu cheese

1. Preheat oven to 400° F.
2. Remove bread from aluminum foil wrapper; pull bread apart along cut side.
3. Spread or crumble Bleu cheese on buttered side and fold back together.
4. Place cheese/garlic bread back in aluminum foil wrapper. Heat 20 minutes. Serve warm.

HOT CHEESE BREAD
(Serves 8)

1—30″ loaf Italian or French bread

1—10-ounce package Frozen Welsh Rarebit, defrosted*

1. Preheat oven to 350° F.
2. Slice bread diagonally into 3/4-inch thick slices. Do not cut through bottom crust.
3. Spread defrosted Welsh Rarebit on both sides of each slice.
4. Place loaf on large piece of aluminum foil and tuck loosely around loaf—leave top of loaf uncovered. Heat in oven for 25 to 35 minutes or until hot and crusty.

PAN CINNAMON ROLLS
(Makes approximately 18)

Dough:
3/4 cup water (65°–70° F.)
1/4 cup non-fat dry milk
2 tablespoons butter or margarine
2 tablespoons shortening
2-1/3 tablespoons granulated sugar
1-3/4 teaspoons salt
1 egg
1 envelope activated, dry yeast
2-1/2 cups all-purpose flour

Filling:
1/4 cup butter, melted
1 cup brown sugar
1-1/2 teaspoons cinnamon
1/4 cup melted shortening

Glaze:
1 teaspoon butter, soft
1 cup confectioner's sugar
2 tablespoons hot coffee cream
1/4 teaspoon freshly squeezed lemon juice
1/4 teaspoon grated lemon rind

1. Pour water into mixing bowl; add remaining dough ingredients and blend thoroughly.
2. Turn out onto a lightly floured board and knead until dough is elastic, approximately 15 minutes. (If electric mixer with dough hook is available, steps #1 and #2 may be combined using mixer at low

speed for 10 to 15 minutes or until dough cleans the bowl and clings to dough hook.)
3. Place dough in bowl, cover and let rise until double in bulk; punch down and let stand 10 minutes.
4. Roll dough into a rectangle 6 inches wide and 1/2-inch thick.
5. Combine melted butter, brown sugar and cinnamon; blend well.
6. Spread over dough evenly.
7. Fold long side of dough nearest you toward center; fold opposite long side over first fold, envelope style, and seal securely.
8. Cut rolls into even slices 3/4-inch thick.
9. Place rolls 1/2-inch apart in a greased baking pan; brush tops lightly with melted shortening; cover and let rise until double in bulk.
10. Bake in 375° F. oven for 18 to 20 minutes or until golden brown.
11. Combine soft butter, confectioner's sugar and hot cream; beat until light and fluffy; add lemon juice and grated lemon rind; blend and spread over warm rolls.

CORN STICKS

(Makes approximately 18)

1/2 teaspoon salt
1/2 teaspoon granulated sugar
2 cups biscuit mix
1— 12-ounce package Frozen Corn Soufflé, defrosted*
6 tablespoons butter or margarine

1. Combine salt, sugar and biscuit mix in a medium bowl. Add defrosted Corn Soufflé. Stir until soft dough is formed.
2. Turn onto a well floured surface and knead about 12 strokes.
3. Roll dough to 6-inch by 10-inch rectangle. Cut into 1-inch by 3-inch strips.
4. Melt butter on a cookie sheet; roll cornsticks in the melted butter and arrange 1/2-inch apart. Bake at 450° F. for 15 minutes.

BUTTER CORN ROLLS

(Makes approximately 20)

2-1/2 tablespoons butter or margarine
2-1/2 tablespoons shortening
1-1/3 cups water (65°–70° F.)
2 tablespoons granulated sugar
1/2 teaspoon salt
7 tablespoons cornmeal
1/2 cup non-fat dry milk
2 envelopes activated, dry yeast
1 egg
2-1/8 cups all-purpose flour
1/4 cup cornmeal
1 teaspoon salt
2 tablespoons butter, melted

1. Melt butter or margarine and shortening in a heavy saucepan.
2. Add water, granulated sugar, salt and first amount of cornmeal; heat, stirring frequently. When mixture comes to a boil, remove from heat and cool to lukewarm.
3. Combine cooled cornmeal mixture, non-fat dry milk, yeast, egg, and flour in a large mixing bowl; blend thoroughly.
4. Turn out onto a lightly floured board and knead until dough is elastic, approximately 15 minutes. (If electric mixer with dough hook is available, steps #3 and #4 may be combined using mixer at low speed for 15 minutes or until dough cleans the sides of the bowl and clings to dough hook.)
5. Place dough in a bowl; cover and let rise until double in bulk.
6. Punch down to remove air bubbles. Let rise again to double volume. Punch down.
7. Combine 1/4 cup cornmeal and salt; toss lightly.
8. Roll dough into a rectangle 6 inches wide and 1/2-inch thick. Brush with melted butter; sprinkle with half of the cornmeal/salt mixture.
9. Fold the long side nearest you to center. Fold opposite long side over first fold, envelope style, and seal securely.
10. Cut roll into 3/4-inch slices. Holding slice at each end, twist at the center of roll and place in well-greased muffin pans, cut sides up. Sprinkle each roll with a small amount of remaining cornmeal/salt mixture; cover and let rise until double in bulk.
11. Bake in 400° F. oven for 20 minutes. Remove from oven and brush lightly with melted butter.

RUM RAISIN ROLLS

(Makes approximately 18)

Dough:
3/4 cup water (65°-70° F.)
1/4 cup non-fat dry milk
2 tablespoons butter or margarine
2 tablespoons shortening
2-1/3 tablespoons granulated sugar
1-3/4 teaspoons salt
1 egg
1 envelope activated, dry yeast
2-1/2 cups all-purpose flour

Filling:
3 tablespoons melted butter
1/3 cup brown sugar, lump free
1/2 teaspoon cinnamon
1/3 cup white raisins (or seedless raisins)

Glaze:
1-1/4 cups confectioner's sugar, sifted
Few grains salt
2 tablespoons coffee cream
1-3/4 teaspoons Jamaican rum

1. Pour water into mixing bowl; add remaining dough ingredients and blend thoroughly.
2. Turn out onto a lightly floured board and knead until dough is elastic, approximately 15 minutes. (If electric mixer with dough hook is available, steps #1 and #2 may be combined using mixer at low speed for 10 to 15 minutes or until dough cleans the bowl and clings to dough hook.)
3. Place dough in bowl; cover and let rise until double in bulk; punch down and let stand 10 minutes.
4. Roll dough into a rectangle 6 inches wide and 3/8-inch thick.
5. Brush with melted butter.
6. Combine brown sugar and cinnamon; sprinkle over dough; sprinkle white raisins over dough and press lightly.
7. Fold long side of dough nearest you toward the center; fold opposite long side over first fold, envelope style, and seal securely.
8. Cut into equal slices 3/4-inch thick; place in greased baking pans, cut side up with edges touching. Cover and let rise until double in bulk.
9. Bake in 375°F. oven for 18 to 20 minutes or until golden brown.
10. Combine sifted confectioner's sugar, salt, cream and rum; blend until smooth and drizzle over warm rolls.

SOUTHERN ORANGE ROLLS

(Makes approximately 24)

Dough:
1 cup water (65°–70° F.)
3-1/2 cups all-purpose flour
1/3 cup non-fat dry milk
1/3 cup butter, room temperature
1/3 cup granulated sugar
2 teaspoons salt
2 envelopes activated, dry yeast
2 eggs
Orange Filling (opposite)

1. In a large mixing bowl, combine all ingredients for dough and mix until smooth.
2. Turn out onto a lightly floured board and knead for 15 to 20 minutes or until dough no longer sticks to board. (If electric mixer with dough hook is available, steps #1 and #2 may be combined by mixing on low speed for 10 to 15 minutes or until dough cleans the sides of the bowl and clings to dough hook.)
3. Place dough in lightly buttered bowl; cover and set in a warm place (75°–80° F.) until doubled in bulk.
4. Punch down and divide dough into two equal parts. Let stand 8 to 10 minutes.
5. Roll each piece of dough into a rectangle 7 inches wide and 3/8-inch thick.
6. Spread each piece of dough with 1/3 of orange filling mixture, saving 1/3 for glazing.
7. Fold long side nearest you to center. Fold opposite long side toward the center, envelope style.
8. Seal edges securely and shape roll so it is even in thickness.
9. Slice each roll crosswise into 12 equal pieces.
10. Place rolls, cut side up, in well greased muffin pans. Cover and let rise until double in bulk.
11. Bake in a 350° F. oven for 15 to 20 minutes or until golden brown. Remove from oven and immediately brush tops lightly with remaining orange filling.
12. Sprinkle rolls with sifted confectioner's sugar just before serving.

ORANGE FILLING

1/2 cup granulated sugar
2 tablespoons all-purpose flour
1/2 cup orange juice
2 tablespoons grated orange rind
1 tablespoon butter

1. Sift granulated sugar and flour together.
2. Combine orange juice and finely grated orange rind in a heavy saucepan and heat to boiling point.
3. Gradually add sifted dry ingredients, beating constantly. Cook over medium heat for 10 minutes until the mixture thickens and the flour taste disappears.
4. Remove from heat and add butter; cool at room temperature, stirring occasionally.

DOUBLE CORN MUFFINS

(Makes approximately 12)

1/2 cup all-purpose flour
3 tablespoons granulated sugar
2-1/4 teaspoons baking powder
3/4 teaspoon salt
1 cup yellow cornmeal
1— 12-ounce package Frozen Corn Soufflé, defrosted*
3/4 cup milk
2 tablespoons melted butter

1. Preheat oven to 400°F.
2. Sift flour, sugar, baking powder and salt into a mixing bowl. Stir in cornmeal.
3. In small mixing bowl, blend Corn Soufflé, milk and melted butter.
4. Add Corn Soufflé mixture to dry ingredients. Stir with fork just until thoroughly moistened. *Do not beat.*
5. Fill greased muffin tins 2/3 full.
6. Bake for 25 minutes or until golden brown.

ORANGE NUT ROLLS

(Makes approximately 18)

Dough:
3/4 cup water (65°-70° F.)
1/4 cup non-fat dry milk
2 tablespoons butter or margarine
2 tablespoons shortening
2-1/3 tablespoons granulated sugar
1-3/4 teaspoons salt
1 egg
1 envelope activated, dry yeast
2-1/2 cups all-purpose flour

Pan Glaze:
1/3 cup butter, soft
3/4 cup firmly packed brown sugar
1-1/2 tablespoons honey
4 teaspoons grated orange rind
2 tablespoons broken pecan pieces

Filling:
1 tablespoon melted butter, cooled
1/2 cup lightly packed brown sugar
1 tablespoon grated orange rind
2 tablespoons orange juice

1. Pour water into mixing bowl; add remaining dough ingredients and blend thoroughly.
2. Turn out onto a lightly floured board and knead until dough is elastic, approximately 15 minutes. (If electric mixer with dough hook is available, steps #1 and #2 may be combined using mixer at low speed for 10 to 15 minutes or until dough cleans the bowl and clings to dough hook.)
3. Place dough in bowl; cover and let rise until double in bulk; punch down and let stand 10 minutes.
4. To prepare pan glaze: Cream soft butter and brown sugar together until fluffy; add honey, orange rind and pecans; blend. Place 1 tablespoon of the mixture in each greased muffin cup.
5. Roll dough into a rectangle 6 inches wide and 3/8-inch thick.
6. Brush dough with melted butter; sprinkle brown sugar, orange rind, and orange juice evenly over dough.
7. Fold long side nearest you toward center; fold opposite long side over first fold, envelope style, and seal securely.
8. Cut into slices 3/4-inch thick; place rolls, cut side up, into prepared muffin pans; cover and let rise until double in bulk.
9. Bake in 350° F. oven for 15 to 18 minutes or until golden brown.
10. Remove from oven; invert pans over trays and let stand 2 minutes to drain syrup over rolls. Remove pans from rolls and serve warm.

ORANGE CINNAMON BUNS

(Serves 6)

1 — 8-1/2-ounce package Frozen Danish Cinnamon Rolls, defrosted*
1/4 cup orange marmalade

1. Preheat oven to 350° F.
2. Spread orange marmalade on top of Danish Cinnamon Rolls. Heat for 10 to 12 minutes. Serve warm.

There isn't a week that goes by that someone doesn't ask for this recipe.

PUMPKIN MUFFINS

(Makes approximately 12)

1-1/2 cups all-purpose flour
2 teaspoons baking powder
1-1/2 teaspoons salt
1/2 cup granulated sugar
1/2 teaspoon cinnamon
1/2 teaspoon ground nutmeg
1 egg
1/2 cup milk
1/2 cup canned pumpkin
1/4 cup margarine, melted
3/4 cup raisins
1 tablespoon granulated sugar

1. Sift flour, baking powder, salt, first amount of sugar, cinnamon and nutmeg together into a bowl.
2. Beat egg slightly; add milk and mix thoroughly; add pumpkin and melted margarine; blend.
3. Add liquid to dry ingredients and stir to moisten. Add raisins and mix just until blended. *Do not beat.*
4. Spoon batter into well greased muffin tins. Sprinkle 1/4 teaspoon granulated sugar evenly over each muffin.
5. Bake at 400° F. for 18 to 20 minutes or until golden brown on top and bottom. Serve warm.

CRANBERRY MUFFINS

(Makes approximately 12)

1-1/8 cups fresh cranberries
1/4 cup granulated sugar
1-3/4 cups all-purpose flour
2-1/2 tablespoons granulated sugar
3 teaspoons baking powder
1 teaspoon salt
2 eggs, beaten
3/4 cup sweet fruit juice
1 teaspoon lemon juice
1/4 teaspoon grated orange rind
1/3 cup margarine, melted
1/3 cup chopped walnuts

1. Wash and drain cranberries; chop coarsely.
2. Add first amount of sugar; mix well and allow to stand 5 to 10 minutes.
3. Sift flour, second amount of sugar, baking powder and salt together.
4. Combine beaten eggs, fruit juice and lemon juice; beat to combine; add grated orange rind.
5. Add melted margarine.
6. Combine liquid and sifted dry ingredients; mix lightly but *do not beat.*
7. Gently stir in sugared cranberries and chopped nuts.
8. Fill greased muffin tins half full.
9. Bake in a 400° F. oven for 18 to 20 minutes or until golden brown.

DANISH CHEESE SANDWICH

(Serves 6)

1— 8-1/2-ounce package Frozen Danish Cinnamon Rolls, defrosted*
1— 3-ounce package cream cheese, room temperature
1 tablespoon granulated sugar
1/4 teaspoon vanilla extract

1. Preheat oven to 350° F.
2. In a small mixing bowl, combine cream cheese, sugar and vanilla extract until smooth and soft enough to spread.
3. Remove rolls from container. Save container. Split rolls; spread with cheese filling and put back together sandwich-fashion.
4. Place rolls back in aluminum container. Heat for 10 to 12 minutes. Serve warm or cool.

FRUIT-GLAZED DANISH COFFEE CAKE

(Serves 6)

1— 9-ounce package Frozen Danish Twisted Coffee Cake, defrosted*
1/2 cup apricot preserves
2 tablespoons shredded coconut

1. Preheat oven to 350° F.
2. Spread top of coffee cake with preserves. Sprinkle with coconut.
3. Heat 10 to 12 minutes or until coconut is lightly browned.

PEANUT DANISH

(Serves 6)

1— 9-ounce package Frozen Danish Twisted Coffee Cake, defrosted*
3 tablespoons peanut butter
1 tablespoon softened cream cheese
1 tablespoon milk

1. Preheat oven to 350° F.
2. Combine peanut butter, cream cheese and milk in a small bowl.
3. Spread mixture on top of coffee cake.
4. Heat for 8 to 10 minutes. Serve warm.

RUM-GLAZED DANISH

(Serves 6)

1— 11-ounce package Frozen Glazed Pecan Danish*
3 tablespoons rum

1. Preheat oven to 400° F.
2. Heat Glazed Pecan Danish for 10 minutes; pour rum evenly over rolls and heat 5 minutes longer. Serve warm.

CASHEW HONEY SQUARES

(Makes approximately 18)

Dough:

3/4 cup water (65°–70°F.)
1/4 cup non-fat dry milk
2 tablespoons butter or margarine
2 tablespoons shortening
2-1/3 tablespoons granulated sugar
1-3/4 teaspoons salt
1 egg
1 envelope activated, dry yeast
2-1/2 cups all-purpose flour

Pan glaze:

1/4 cup soft butter
1-1/4 cups lightly packed brown sugar
3 tablespoons honey
1/2 cup broken cashew nut pieces

1. Pour water into mixing bowl; add remaining dough ingredients and blend thoroughly.
2. Turn out onto a lightly floured board and knead until dough is elastic, approximately 15 minutes. (If electric mixer with dough hook is available, steps #1 and #2 may be combined using mixer at low speed for 10 to 15 minutes or until dough cleans the bowl and clings to dough hook.)
3. Place dough in bowl; cover and let rise until double in bulk; punch down and let stand 10 minutes.
4. To prepare pan glaze: Cream butter and brown sugar until fluffy; blend in honey; spread over bottom of oblong cake pan.
5. Sprinkle cashew pieces over sugar mixture.
6. Pinch off pieces of dough to form balls 1-1/2 inches in diameter; arrange rolls in prepared pan; cover and let rise until double in bulk.
7. Bake in a 375°F. oven for 20 minutes or until golden brown.
8. Remove from oven and let stand 2 minutes; invert pan over tray to drain syrup over rolls; remove pan and serve warm.

HOT CROSS BUNS

(Makes approximately 24)

7/8 cup water (65°–70°F.)
2 envelopes activated, dry yeast
1/3 cup non-fat dry milk
3 tablespoons butter or margarine
3 tablespoons shortening
1/4 cup granulated sugar
1 teaspoon salt
1 egg
3 cups all-purpose flour
1/2 teaspoon cinnamon
1/3 cup seeded raisins
1/3 cup brown sugar
2-2/3 tablespoons hot coffee cream

1. Combine all ingredients, except raisins, brown sugar and cream, in a large mixing bowl and blend thoroughly.
2. Turn out onto a lightly floured board and knead until dough is elastic, approximately 15 minutes. (If electric mixer with dough hook is available, steps #1 and #2 may be combined using mixer at low speed for 15 minutes or until dough leaves sides of the bowl clean and clings to dough hook.)
3. Knead raisins into dough so raisins are covered.
4. Place dough in bowl, cover and let rise until double in bulk; punch down and let stand 10 minutes.
5. Pinch off pieces of dough and form balls approximately 1-1/2-inches in diameter.
6. Place rolls 1 inch apart on a lightly greased baking sheet. With a pair of sharp scissors make 2 snips in the top of each roll to form cross indentations.
7. Cover and let rise until double in bulk.
8. Bake in 375°F. oven for 20 to 25 minutes or until golden brown.
9. Combine brown sugar and hot cream; heat until sugar is dissolved.
10. Brush each hot roll lightly with glaze.
11. Prepare a firm butter cream frosting; using a pastry tube with a small opening, form a cross of frosting in indentations on top of rolls.

With the emphasis on natural foods and bread baking, men and women of all ages now make their own bread regularly. The recipe we have included is one of our oldest, one of our most frequently used. And when our baked bread is a few days old, it makes super toast.

STOUFFER'S HOMEMADE BREAD

(Makes 3–9″ loaves)

3 cups milk
3 tablespoons shortening, melted
2-1/3 tablespoons salt
1-1/2 tablespoons granulated sugar
1 cup lukewarm water
2 envelopes activated, dry yeast or 1—1-ounce cake yeast
10 cups all-purpose flour, sifted
Melted shortening
Melted butter

1. Pour milk into a medium saucepan, and scald over a high heat. Add shortening, salt and sugar; mix well. Remove from heat and let stand until lukewarm.
2. Dissolve yeast in water; add to milk mixture. Add half of the flour; beat until smooth. Stir in remaining flour.
3. Turn dough out onto a lightly floured board and knead until smooth.
4. Place into a greased bowl; brush with melted shortening; cover and let rise until double in bulk. Punch down once and let stand for 30 minutes.
5. Divide dough evenly in three sections. Knead each section and shape into smooth loaves. Place each loaf into a greased 9-inch by 5-inch by 3-inch bread pan. Cover and let stand until double in bulk.
6. Brush each loaf with melted butter and bake in a 375° F. oven for 50 to 60 minutes. Remove from pans at once and cool on racks.

NOTE: This recipe will also make six, 6-inch by 3-1/4-inch by 3-1/4-inch loaves. Bake the small loaves in a 350° F. oven for 25 to 35 minutes.

For Dessert We Have...

Lots and lots of suggestions. We began with Dutch Apple Pie, and that reputation for good desserts has stayed with us all our life. In putting together this section of the book we took the absolute all-time dessert favorites and carefully reconstructed them for the home cook. Again we caution you to follow directions precisely or you will be disappointed with the results. Baking is really chemistry, and tampering with the ingredients means less successful desserts.

Now for a few of our own kitchen tricks:

1. *When beating eggs, you will find that egg whites at room temperature beat to a greater volume than cold egg whites. And we call room temperature 60–65° F.*

2. *When whipping cream, our dietitians have found that day-old heavy cream will whip better than very fresh cream. And a chilled bowl and beater will increase the volume.*

3. *When making piecrust, we suggest the use of lard instead of shortening to insure the flakiest crust possible.*

4. *If you use our homemade piecrust recipe (opposite) and you need a baked pie shell, prick bottom and sides of shell at 1-inch intervals and bake in a 410° F. oven for 18 to 20 minutes until a rich, golden brown.*

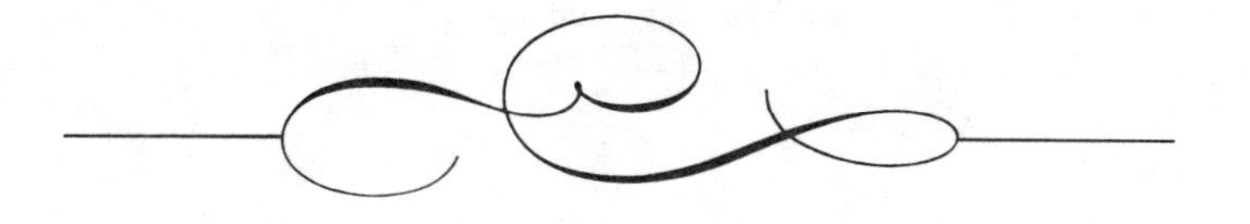

PIES

We have probably baked and served two hundred different kinds of pies, but our all-time favorite is still the very first pie ever served at Stouffer's: Dutch Apple Pie. This is Mother Stouffer's original recipe, and we never have found a better recipe!

DUTCH APPLE PIE

(Makes 1—9″ pie)

Stouffer's Homemade Crust:
1 cup all-purpose flour
1/2 teaspoon salt
1/3 cup cold lard (or shortening)
2-1/2 to 3 tablespoons ice water

Filling:
4 cups apples (Jonathan, Winesap or McIntosh apples only), peeled, cored and cut in 3/4″ cubes
1/8 teaspoon cinnamon
1-3/4 cups granulated sugar
1/4 cup all-purpose flour
1/2 teaspoon salt
3 tablespoons milk
6 tablespoons coffee cream

1. To make crust: Combine flour and salt in mixing bowl. Cut lard into mixture with a pastry blender (or by using two knives) until pieces are the size of large beans.
2. Add ice water and mix lightly with a fork. Pastry should be just moist enough to hold together; *not sticky*. Chill thoroughly.
3. Roll chilled dough to 1/8-inch thickness and line pie pan, lifting and smoothing so as to remove air bubbles. *Do not stretch dough.* Flute edge, then trim pastry even to pan.
4. Spread cubed apples evenly in pie shell; sprinkle with cinnamon.
5. Mix sugar, flour and salt together; add milk and cream. Beat mixture 8 to 10 minutes at medium speed with an electric mixer. Pour evenly over apples.
6. Bake in a 375°F. oven for 1 to 1-1/4 hours. Serve warm.

NOTE: This pie is very juicy. If juice runs over during baking, clean rim and loosen crust while juice is still hot. Use the point of a silver knife wrapped in a clean wet cloth.

BLACK BOTTOM PIE

(Makes 1—10″ pie)

1— 10″ baked pie shell

Chocolate Filling:
1/3 cup granulated sugar
1 tablespoon cornstarch
1-1/4 cups milk
2 egg yolks, slightly beaten
1-1/4 unsweetened chocolate squares, melted
1-1/2 teaspoons vanilla extract

Rum Chiffon Filling:
1 teaspoon unflavored gelatin
3 tablespoons cold water
2 egg yolks, room temperature
3 tablespoons granulated sugar
3 tablespoons light rum
2 egg whites, room temperature
1/8 teaspoon salt
1/4 cup granulated sugar
1 cup heavy cream or whipping cream

Sweetened whipped cream and semi-sweet chocolate curls for garnish

1. To make chocolate filling: Combine sugar and cornstarch.
2. Heat milk in a heavy saucepan (do not boil); slowly add cornstarch/sugar mixture, beating constantly. Heat to boiling; reduce heat and cook 8 to 10 minutes or until starch taste disappears.
3. Pour a small amount of hot mixture into beaten egg yolks stirring constantly; return mixture to saucepan, beating constantly. Remove from heat and let stand 10 minutes.
4. Add melted chocolate to hot mixture and beat to combine. Add vanilla and blend thoroughly.
5. Cool to 80°F. stirring occasionally. Pour cooled filling into baked pie shell and spread evenly. Chill for 1/2 hour or until set.
6. To make rum chiffon filling: Soften gelatin in cold water for 5 minutes.
7. Beat egg yolks with first amount of sugar until lemon colored; gradually add rum. Cook in the top of a double boiler over rapidly boiling water until mixture thickens slightly.
8. Add softened gelatin and beat until dissolved. Remove from heat and chill until mixture has consistency of unbeaten egg whites.
9. Beat room-temperature egg whites until frothy; add salt and second amount of sugar; continue beating until egg whites form stiff moist peaks.

10. Fold gelatin mixture into egg whites.
11. Whip cream until soft peaks form. Fold into gelatin mixture and combine thoroughly.
12. Pour over chocolate filling in pie shell. Chill several hours. Top with swirls of sweetened whipped cream and semisweet chocolate curls.

There was a time when Key Lime Pie was a Florida delicacy. Now it's enjoyed all over the United States . . . and it should be.

KEY LIME PIE

(Makes 1—9″ pie)

1— 9″ baked pie shell
1/3 cup egg yolks, room temperature
2 teaspoons granulated sugar
1— 15-ounce can sweetened condensed milk
1/2 teaspoon finely grated lime rind (omit rind if frozen lime juice is used)
1/2 cup freshly squeezed Persian lime juice or 1/2 cup reconstituted frozen lime juice
3 egg whites, room temperature
1/4 teaspoon cream of tartar
1/4 cup granulated sugar

1. Beat egg yolks 2 or 3 minutes; add first amount of sugar and the sweetened condensed milk; continue beating until foamy. Blend in grated lime rind.
2. Gradually add lime juice, beating constantly.
3. Beat room-temperature egg whites until frothy; add cream of tartar and beat; gradually add second amount of sugar and continue beating until peaks form.
4. Pour lime filling into baked pie shell.
5. Swirl meringue over filling to edges of pie crust (not over rim).
6. Bake in 325° F. oven until meringue is light golden brown.
7. Cool 45 minutes before serving; pie should be slightly warm when served.

LEMON ANGEL PIE

(Makes 1—10″ pie)

Crust:
4 egg whites, room temperature
1/3 teaspoon cream of tartar
1 cup plus 1-1/2 tablespoons granulated sugar, sifted
1 teaspoon vanilla extract

Filling:
1 cup granulated sugar
1/4 teaspoon salt
3-1/2 tablespoons cornstarch
1 cup water
2 egg yolks, beaten
1/4 cup freshly squeezed lemon juice

1-1/2 cups sweetened whipped cream

1. Generously butter bottom and sides of a 10-inch pie pan.
2. To make crust: Beat room-temperature egg whites until frothy; gradually add cream of tartar and sifted sugar and beat until soft peaks are formed; fold in vanilla extract.
3. Place egg white mixture in buttered pie pan; using a spatula, spread mixture across bottom of pan (not up the sides) leaving a mound of mixture in the center which is 2 to 2-1/2 inches high. During baking, meringue will rise on sides of pan to complete the crust and when removed from oven, will fall into a natural pie-crust shape.
4. Bake in a 300° F. oven for 50 to 60 minutes or until light golden brown and dry. Cool.
5. Meanwhile make filling: Blend sugar, salt and cornstarch together.
6. Heat water to boiling in a heavy saucepan; gradually add sugar mixture, stirring constantly. Simmer until thickened and clear. Remove from heat.
7. Add a small amount of hot mixture to beaten egg yolks, stirring vigorously; return mixture to saucepan, stirring constantly. Remove from heat and let stand 5 minutes to cook eggs.
8. Blend in lemon juice. Cool at room temperature.
9. Pour cool filling over meringue crust.
10. When ready to serve, garnish with mounds of sweetened whipped cream; sprinkle lightly with nutmeg or grated lemon rind, if desired.

FROSTED DAIQUIRI PIE

(Makes 1—9" pie)

Vanilla Crumb Crust:
1-1/2 cups finely ground vanilla wafers
1/4 cup granulated sugar
1/4 cup melted butter

Filling:
1 envelope unflavored gelatin
1/4 cup cold water
3 egg yolks, room temperature
1 cup granulated sugar
1/2 teaspoon salt
6-2/3 tablespoons freshly squeezed lime juice
1 to 2 drops green food coloring
5 tablespoons light rum
3 egg whites, room temperature
1/3 cup granulated sugar

1-1/4 cups sweetened whipped cream

1. To make crust: Blend wafer crumbs and sugar; add slightly cooled butter and mix thoroughly.
2. Pat crumbs onto bottom and sides of a 9-inch pie pan, making sides slightly thicker than bottom. Crust should not overlap rim of pie pan.
3. Bake in 350° F. oven for 12 to 14 minutes or until golden brown. Cool thoroughly.
4. Meanwhile make filling: Soften gelatin in cold water for 5 minutes.
5. Beat egg yolks with first amount of sugar and salt until light in color; gradually add lime juice and beat thoroughly.
6. Place egg yolk mixture in top of double boiler; cook over rapidly boiling water, beating constantly with a wire whip until thickened slightly; remove from heat.
7. Add softened gelatin and beat until gelatin is dissolved; add green food coloring and blend; cool mixture slightly and blend in rum. Chill until mixture thickens to consistency of unbeaten egg whites.
8. Beat egg whites until frothy; gradually add second amount of sugar and continue beating until stiff shiny peaks are formed.
9. Fold chilled gelatin mixture into beaten egg whites using a wire whip.
10. Pour into cooled vanilla crumb crust; chill several hours until set.
11. When ready to serve, spread top of pie with sweetened whipped cream; garnish with half slices of lime, if desired.

PEACH MELBA 'N CREAM PIE

(Makes 1—9″ pie)

1—9″ baked pie shell
1-2/3 cups cooked Raspberry Danish Dessert
1—8-ounce package soft cream cheese
2 tablespoons granulated sugar
1/8 teaspoon salt
1/2 teaspoon vanilla extract
4 teaspoons coffee cream
3-1/2 cups peeled, sliced fresh peaches
1-1/2 cups sweetened whipped cream

1. Prepare Raspberry Danish Dessert according to package directions, reducing liquid slightly. Cool until partially set.
2. Beat cream cheese until soft and smooth; add sugar, salt, vanilla extract and cream; beat smooth. Spread into the bottom of baked pie shell.
3. Fold peaches into Danish Dessert and pour over cheese mixture in pie shell.
4. Chill for several hours or until firm.
5. Spread with sweetened whipped cream. Garnish with fresh raspberries or peach slices, if desired.

APPLE WALNUT UPSIDE-DOWN PIE

(Makes 1—10″ pie)

5 tablespoons butter
1/2 cup brown sugar
1/3 cup chopped walnuts
Pastry for a 2-crust pie
4 cups apples, peeled, cored and cut in 3/4″ cubes
1-1/8 cups granulated sugar
3 tablespoons all-purpose flour
3/4 teaspoon cinnamon
1/8 teaspoon ground nutmeg
1/4 teaspoon salt

1. Melt butter and add brown sugar; beat to combine.
2. Spread butter/sugar mixture in the bottom of a 10-inch pie pan.
3. Sprinkle chopped walnuts over butter/sugar mixture.
4. Divide pie pastry in half; roll each half to 1/8-inch thick. Carefully line prepared pie pan with dough so as not to make holes in dough with nuts. Trim even with edge of the pan.

5. Fill pan with cubed apples.
6. Combine granulated sugar, flour, cinnamon, nutmeg and salt; blend thoroughly; sprinkle evenly over apples.
7. Place top crust on pie and trim even with edge of pan. Prick top with tines of a fork (do not slash with a knife). Seal crust edges and *roll edges toward the center of pie*. There should be no crust touching the rim of the pan.
8. Bake at 375°F. for 50 to 55 minutes. Remove from oven. Carefully run a knife around edge of pan to loosen pie; invert on a serving plate. Let stand 2 minutes. Remove pan.
9. Serve warm, garnished with sweetened whipped cream or ice cream.

In addition to our baked-from-scratch apple pies, we have some apple pie ideas using our Frozen Escalloped Apples:

APPLE-RHUBARB PIE

(Makes 1—9″ pie)

Pastry for a 2-crust pie
2 cups fresh rhubarb, cut in 1″ pieces
2 eggs, beaten
1-1/2 cups granulated sugar
2 tablespoons quick-cooking tapioca
1/8 teaspoon salt
1 tablespoon grated orange rind
1— 12-ounce package Frozen Escalloped Apples, defrosted*

1. Preheat oven to 425°F.
2. Prepare pie crust and roll out half of dough to fit a 9-inch pie plate.
3. Wash fresh rhubarb; drain well.
4. In a large mixing bowl, combine eggs, sugar, tapioca, salt and orange rind. Stir in rhubarb making sure all pieces are coated. Add defrosted Escalloped Apples and mix well; spoon mixture into pastry shell.
5. Roll out remaining pastry; cut slashes in it to let steam escape. Cover pie; seal, trim and flute edges.
6. Brush top crust lightly with milk and sprinkle with granulated sugar.
7. Place in oven and bake for 50 minutes or until crust is golden brown.

APPLE DELIGHT

(Serves 8)

Crust:
1-1/2 cups finely crushed graham crackers
1/4 cup butter or margarine, melted

Filling:
1/4 cup butter or margarine
1 cup confectioner's sugar
1 whole egg
2— 12-ounce packages Frozen Escalloped Apples, defrosted*
1 cup whipped cream
1 tablespoon granulated sugar
1/4 teaspoon cinnamon

1. Combine graham cracker crumbs and melted butter. Mix well. Set aside 1/4 cup of crumb mixture for topping.
2. Place remaining crumb mixture in an 8-inch square baking dish.
3. Press firmly to form the bottom crust. Place in refrigerator and chill for 45 minutes.
4. Cream butter or margarine and confectioner's sugar.
5. Add egg and beat until thick and foamy. Spread over the chilled crumb crust.
6. Gently combine Escalloped Apples, whipped cream, granulated sugar, and cinnamon. Spoon over egg mixture.
7. Sprinkle with the reserved 1/4 cup of graham cracker crumbs. Chill for approximately two hours before serving.

APPLE CRUMB PIE

(Makes 1—9″ pie)

1— 9″ unbaked pie shell
2— 12-ounce packages Frozen Escalloped Apples, defrosted*
1/4 teaspoon cinnamon
3/4 cup all-purpose flour
1/2 cup granulated sugar
1/3 cup butter, room temperature

1. Combine Escalloped Apples and cinnamon. Pour into a 9-inch unbaked pie shell.
2. Combine flour, sugar, and butter; mix together with a fork until crumbly. Sprinkle evenly over top of apples.
3. Bake at 400° F. for 40 to 50 minutes or until filling is hot and bubbly and crumbs are golden brown.

EASY APPLE PIE

(Makes 1—9″ pie)

Pastry for a 2-crust pie
2— 12-ounce packages Frozen Escalloped Apples, defrosted*
1/4 cup granulated sugar
1/4 teaspoon cinnamon
1/8 teaspoon ground nutmeg

1. Preheat oven to 425°F.
2. Prepare pie crust and roll out half of dough to fit 9-inch pie plate.
3. Combine defrosted Escalloped Apples, sugar, cinnamon and nutmeg. Pour into pie shell.
4. Roll out remaining pastry, cut slashes in it to let steam escape. Cover pie; seal, trim and flute edges. Brush top lightly with milk and sprinkle with granulated sugar.
5. Bake in oven for 50 minutes or until crust is golden brown.

APPLE PEARADISE PIE

(Makes 1—9″ pie)

2 cups shredded coconut
1/4 cup margarine, melted
2— 12-ounce packages Frozen Escalloped Apples*
1— 10-ounce package frozen strawberries, defrosted and drained slightly
1— 1-pound can Bartlett pear halves, cut into 1/2″ slices
1 cup sweetened whipped cream

1. Combine coconut and margarine. Press firmly into an ungreased 9-inch pie plate. Bake at 300°F. for 20 to 30 minutes, or until lightly browned. Cool.
2. Bake Escalloped Apples following package directions. Cool. Combine apples with strawberries.
3. Arrange pear slices in coconut crust. Spoon apple/berry mixture over all. Chill for 2 hours or overnight.
4. Top with whipped cream before serving.

SIMPLY DELICIOUS APPLE PIE

(Makes 1 – 9″ pie)

Pastry for a 2-crust pie
1/4 cup brown sugar
2 tablespoons all-purpose flour
1/2 teaspoon cinnamon
1/4 teaspoon ground nutmeg
1/4 teaspoon salt
2— 12-ounce packages Frozen Escalloped Apples, defrosted*
3 tablespoons butter
1/4 cup coffee cream

1. Preheat oven to 425° F.
2. Prepare pie crust and roll out half of dough to fill 9-inch pie plate.
3. In a small bowl, combine brown sugar, flour, cinnamon, nutmeg and salt with a fork.
4. Spoon contents of one package Escalloped Apples in bottom of pastry shell, spread evenly. Sprinkle one half sugar mixture over top of apples. Spoon contents of the other package of Escalloped Apples over first layer and cover with remaining sugar mixture. Dot with butter. Pour cream in center of mixture.
5. Roll out remaining pastry; cut slashes in it to let steam escape. Cover pie. Seal, trim and flute edges. Brush top lightly with milk and sprinkle with granulated sugar.
6. Bake in oven for 50 minutes or until crust is golden brown.

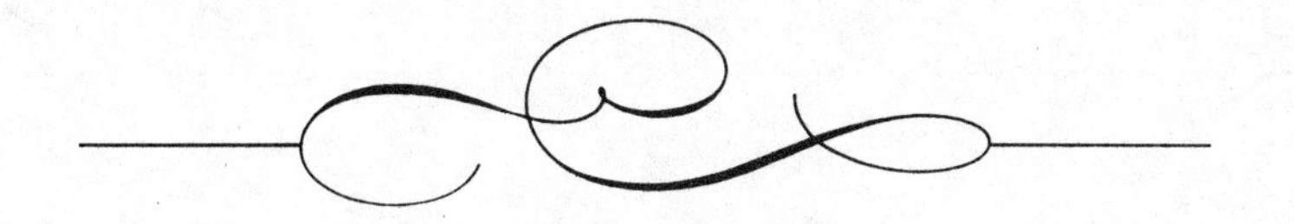

CAKES

During the Second World War, sugar rationing put a real crimp in our dessert menus, so we asked our dietitians to come up with a new sugarless dessert. They invented Plantation Cake, and it proved so popular that we have kept it on our menus all these years.

PLANTATION CAKE

(Serves 8)

1/2 cup butter or margarine
6 tablespoons shortening
3/4 cup lightly packed brown sugar
1/4 teaspoon salt
2-1/2 cups all-purpose flour, sifted
2/3 cup water
2/3 teaspoon baking soda
2/3 cup molasses
Whipped Cream Cheese (page 203)
Lemon Sauce (page 202)

1. Cream butter or margarine and shortening until very light and fluffy; gradually add brown sugar and salt; cream well.
2. Stir in sifted flour and mix until mixture resembles dry crumbs.
3. Blend water with soda and molasses; set aside.
4. Grease and flour a 9-inch square pan.
5. Measure 2 cups of crumb mixture into pan; pat evenly to 1/4-inch thickness.
6. Sprinkle 3/4 cup of soda/molasses mixture over crumb layer.
7. Spread 1/2 cup crumb mixture over liquid.
8. Cover evenly with remaining liquid and top with remaining crumbs.
9. Bake in 350° F. oven for 45 to 50 minutes. Serve warm with Whipped Cream Cheese and warm Lemon Sauce.

Stouffer cooks refer to this as the smart cake, but we have no idea whether Wellesley alumnae ever ate this cake. We do know millions of others have eaten it, and it is our most requested recipe. When making the cake, be sure you follow the direction to flour the nuts so they will not sink to the bottom of the batter.

WELLESLEY FUDGE CAKE

(Makes 1–2 layer cake)

2 squares unsweetened chocolate
2/3 cup margarine, room temperature
1-1/3 cups granulated sugar
1/2 teaspoon baking soda
1/2 teaspoon salt
1 teaspoon vanilla extract
3 egg yolks
2 cups cake flour
3/4 teaspoon baking powder
1 cup chopped walnuts
2/3 cup buttermilk
3 egg whites, room temperature
Wellesley Fudge Icing (opposite)

1. Melt chocolate and set aside to cool.
2. Beat margarine on high speed of mixer until smooth and creamy. Add sugar, baking soda, salt and vanilla extract; beat until light and fluffy.
3. Add egg yolks and beat until well blended. Add cooled, melted chocolate and beat until well blended.
4. Sift flour and baking powder together once. Mix approximately 1/3 of this flour with the walnuts to coat them.
5. Using low speed, add the remaining 2/3 flour mixture to chocolate mixture alternately with the buttermilk, beginning and ending with flour mixture.
6. Stir in floured walnuts.
7. Beat egg whites on high speed until stiff but not dry. Fold beaten egg whites into cake batter by hand just until combined.
8. Grease and flour two 9-inch cake pans. Divide batter between pans and spread evenly. Bake in a 350° F. oven for 25 to 30 minutes or until cake springs back when lightly touched.
9. Cool layers for 10 minutes. Remove from pans and cool on wire racks.
10. Frost cake with Wellesley Fudge Icing. For an extra flourish, finely chopped walnuts may be pressed around sides of cake and sprinkled lightly over the top.

WELLESLEY FUDGE ICING

2 squares unsweetened chocolate
3 tablespoons butter
3 tablespoons margarine
3 cups confectioner's sugar, sifted
1/4 cup hot coffee cream
1/2 cup chopped walnuts

1. Melt chocolate and set aside to cool.
2. Cream butter and margarine until smooth.
3. Add sifted confectioner's sugar alternately with hot cream and beat on low speed until smooth.
4. Add cooled, melted chocolate and beat on high speed until well combined and fluffy.
5. Add walnuts and stir just until nuts are well distributed.

LEMON ANGEL CREAM CAKE

(Serves 6)

3/4 teaspoon unflavored gelatin
4 teaspoons cold water
2 egg yolks
3 tablespoons granulated sugar
1/4 cup freshly squeezed lemon juice
2 egg whites, room temperature
1/3 cup granulated sugar
2-1/4 cups angel food cake, crust trimmed and cut in 1-1/2" cubes
3/4 cup sweetened sliced strawberries

1. Soften gelatin in cold water for 5 minutes.
2. Beat egg yolks and first amount of sugar together until light and creamy; add lemon juice gradually and continue beating until all the juice has been added and mixture is smooth.
3. Cook egg yolk mixture in top of double boiler over rapidly boiling water until slightly thickened, stirring constantly. Remove from heat.
4. Add softened gelatin and stir until gelatin is dissolved. Chill until mixture has consistency of unbeaten egg whites.
5. Beat egg whites until frothy; add second amount of sugar and continue beating until stiff, shiny peaks are formed.
6. Fold thickened gelatin mixture into beaten egg whites.
7. Fold in trimmed cake cubes and mix gently to distribute evenly.
8. Pour into an 8-inch square pan and chill several hours or until set.
9. Cut into squares and serve with sweetened sliced strawberries. Garnish with sweetened whipped cream, if desired.

SUNSHINE PEACH CREAM CAKE

(Serves 12)

Cake:
1-1/4 cups cake flour
3/4 cup granulated sugar
1-1/2 teaspoons baking powder
1/2 teaspoon salt
6 tablespoons salad oil
4 egg yolks, unbeaten
1/2 cup pineapple juice
1-1/4 teaspoons vanilla extract
1 teaspoon fresh lemon juice
3/4 cup (5 to 6) egg whites, room temperature
1/2 teaspoon cream of tartar
5 tablespoons granulated sugar

Filling:
1/2 cup butter
1-1/2 cups confectioner's sugar
2 whole eggs
2 cups fresh peaches, cut in 1/4" slices
1-1/2 cups sweetened whipped cream

1. Sift cake flour, first amount of sugar, baking powder and salt into mixing bowl.
2. Make an indentation in the center of the flour mixture and add (in order) salad oil, egg yolks, pineapple juice, vanilla extract and lemon juice. Beat just until ingredients are smoothly combined.
3. Beat egg whites until frothy; add cream of tartar and beat; gradually add second amount of sugar and beat until egg whites stand in very stiff peaks.
4. Fold beaten egg whites into batter mixture by hand and mix just until combined.
5. Pour batter into a 10-inch tube pan. Cut through batter several times with a table knife to break up air bubbles.
6. Bake in 325° F. oven for 45 to 55 minutes. Cake should appear dry around center of the tube.
7. Invert pan and cool thoroughly.
8. Trim brown crust from cake and cut cake into 1/2-inch slices.
9. Cover bottom of a 9-inch by 13-inch casserole or cake pan with cake slices.
10. Cream butter until soft; add confectioner's sugar and whole eggs; beat until light and fluffy.
11. Spread half of the filling over cake slices.
12. Arrange half of peach slices in a single layer over filling. Make a second layer of cake slices, filling and peaches over the first layer. Chill several hours.

13. Spread with sweetened whipped cream and garnish with toasted, slivered almonds, if desired.

WILLIAMSBURG ORANGE WINE CAKE

(Serves 8–10)

1/2 cup soft butter
1 cup granulated sugar
2 eggs
1 teaspoon vanilla extract
2 tablespoons grated orange rind
1 cup seedless raisins
1/2 cup chopped walnuts
1-1/2 cups all-purpose flour
1 teaspoon baking soda
1/2 teaspoon salt
1 cup buttermilk
2 teaspoons cream sherry
Sherry Butter Cream Frosting (below)

1. Cream butter 15 minutes.
2. Gradually add sugar and continue creaming 20 minutes longer until light and fluffy.
3. Add eggs and beat 5 minutes longer.
4. Add vanilla extract, orange rind, raisins, and nuts. Mix thoroughly.
5. Sift flour, soda and salt together; add alternately with buttermilk, beginning and ending with flour. Beat for 1 minute after final flour addition.
6. Line a 9-inch by 13-inch oblong pan with brown paper; grease well.
7. Pour batter into pan and spread evenly.
8. Bake at 350°F. for 25 minutes.
9. Cool cake; brush cake with cream sherry and frost with Sherry Butter Cream Frosting.

SHERRY BUTTER CREAM FROSTING

1/2 cup soft butter
1-1/2 cups confectioner's sugar
4 teaspoons cream sherry

1. Cream butter until fluffy.
2. Add confectioner's sugar and continue beating.
3. Add sherry and beat until smooth and creamy. Spread on cooled cake.

MINTED CHOCOLATE CAKE

(Serves 8–10)

1—14-1/2-ounce package Frozen Chocolate Chip Cake, defrosted*
1-1/4 cups confectioner's sugar
2 tablespoons butter or margarine
4 teaspoons heavy cream
2 tablespoons crème de menthe

1. Remove Chocolate Chip Cake from aluminum container and place on a serving dish.
2. In a small bowl, combine sugar, butter, cream and crème de menthe. Beat until smooth and creamy.
3. Frost top and sides of cake.

To speed dessert making, we have found new ways of using Stouffer's frozen desserts, making it possible to add individual touches:

FRENCH CRUMB SHORTCAKE

(Serves 6)

1—10-ounce package Frozen French Crumb Cakes, defrosted*
1 pint vanilla ice cream
1—10-ounce package frozen raspberries, defrosted

1. Split crumb cakes. Spoon ice cream between layers. Spoon fruit over ice cream filled cakes. Serve immediately. Garnish with sweetened whipped cream, if desired.

GLAZED RUM RAISIN CAKE

(Serves 8)

1—15-1/2-ounce package Frozen Raisin Tea Cake, defrosted*
3 tablespoons rum
1/3 cup confectioner's sugar

1. Leave cake in pan and drizzle 2 tablespoons of rum over cake; allow to stand one hour.

2. In a small mixing bowl, combine sugar and 1 tablespoon rum; beat until smooth.
3. Transfer cake from pan to serving platter.
4. Pour glaze over cake and allow to set 15 minutes before serving.

FRESH BANANA CREAM CAKE

(Serves 6)

1— 10-ounce package Frozen French Crumb Cakes, defrosted*
2 bananas, thinly sliced
2 cups vanilla pudding, canned or cooked
3/4 cup milk
1/2 cup toasted coconut

1. Split crumb cakes in half. Place a single layer of cake halves, cut side up, in the bottom of a 12-inch by 7-inch oblong baking dish. Top with banana slices.
2. In a small bowl, combine prepared pudding and milk to make a smooth sauce. Pour sauce completely over banana cake.
3. Refrigerate 2 to 4 hours or overnight. Garnish with toasted coconut.

ALMOND RUM CAKE

(Serves 8–10)

1—14-ounce package Frozen Almond Crunch Cake, defrosted*
1/4 cup water
2 tablespoons granulated sugar
2 tablespoons orange juice concentrate
1/4 cup rum
1-1/2 cups sweetened whipped cream

1. Remove Almond Crunch Cake from container; place on serving plate.
2. Using a skewer or a two-pronged fork, prick holes in entire top of cake.
3. In a small saucepan, bring water and sugar to a boil, simmer for 5 minutes. Remove from heat. Stir in orange concentrate and rum.
4. Pour sauce over top of cake. Allow to stand 30 minutes.
5. Frost top and sides of cake with whipped cream. Refrigerate for 1 to 2 hours.

CHEESE FILLED RAISIN CAKE
(Serves 10–12)

1—15-1/2-ounce package Frozen Raisin Tea Cake*
1—3-ounce package cream cheese, room temperature
1 tablespoon coffee cream
2 tablespoons chopped, toasted pecans

1. Cut cake into 1/4-inch slices; let stand at room temperature for 30 minutes.
2. In a small mixing bowl, combine cream cheese and coffee cream and blend smooth. Add pecans and mix well. Spread one slice of cake with cheese filling and top with another slice, sandwich-fashion.
3. Cut sandwiches in 3 strips crosswise; arrange on plates; garnish with sugar frosted grape clusters, if desired.

ALMOND CHOCOLATE SHORTCAKE
(Serves 8)

1—14-ounce package Frozen Almond Crunch Cake, defrosted*
1/2 cup softened butter
1 quart vanilla ice cream
1 cup warm fudge sauce
2 cups sweetened whipped cream

1. Preheat oven to 450° F.
2. Cut cake into 1/2-inch slices. Butter each slice lightly and place on a baking sheet. Toast until lightly browned.
3. Serve with a scoop of ice cream; top with fudge sauce and sweetened whipped cream.

NOTE: For added interest, 2 tablespoons of coffee liqueur may be blended into warm fudge sauce.

APPLE HOLIDAY CAKE

(Serves 8)

1/2 cup soft butter or margarine
1 cup firmly packed brown sugar
2 eggs, beaten
2 cups all-purpose flour
2 teaspoons baking soda
1 teaspoon cinnamon
1/2 teaspoon ground allspice
1/4 teaspoon ground cloves
1/4 teaspoon salt
2— 12-ounce packages Frozen Escalloped Apples, defrosted*
1 cup coarsely chopped dates
3/4 cup chopped walnuts
Cream Cheese Frosting (below)

1. Preheat oven to 350°F.
2. Grease a 9-inch square baking pan.
3. In a medium bowl, cream butter or margarine until light and fluffy. Gradually add the brown sugar and continue beating until smooth.
4. Add beaten eggs; blend well.
5. Sift all dry ingredients together and add, stirring just until all ingredients are combined.
6. Fold in defrosted Escalloped Apples, dates and nuts.
7. Pour batter into prepared pan.
8. Bake 50 minutes or until cake tester inserted in center comes out clean. Let cool on a wire rack.
9. Frost top of cooled cake with Cream Cheese Frosting.

CREAM CHEESE FROSTING

1—3 ounce package cream cheese, room temperature
1 tablespoon margarine
1 teaspoon vanilla extract
2 cups sifted confectioner's sugar

1. In a small bowl, combine cream cheese, margarine and vanilla extract. Beat until smooth and fluffy.
2. Gradually add sugar and beat until fluffy.

APPLE CAKE

(Serves 8–10)

1—16-ounce box spice cake mix
3/4 cup milk
2 eggs
1/4 teaspoon cinnamon
1—12-ounce package Frozen Escalloped Apples, defrosted*
Nut Cinnamon Topping (below)

1. Preheat oven to 350°F.
2. Place cake mix in a medium bowl; add milk, eggs and cinnamon. Beat 1 to 2 minutes.
3. Fold apples into cake batter with a spoon.
4. Pour mixture into a buttered and floured 9-inch by 12-inch baking pan.
5. Sprinkle with Nut Cinnamon Topping.
6. Bake for 40 minutes.

NUT CINNAMON TOPPING

1/2 cup chopped pecans
1/8 teaspoon cinnamon
1/4 cup brown sugar
1 teaspoon melted butter

1. Combine all ingredients in a small bowl; toss with a fork to combine.

DANISH ICE CREAM CAKE

(Serves 6)

1— 11-ounce package Frozen Glazed Pecan Danish, defrosted*
1 pint vanilla ice cream
1/2 cup caramel sauce

1. Preheat oven to 350°F.
2. Heat Glazed Pecan Danish 15 minutes. Remove from oven and separate rolls with a fork.
3. Serve with a scoop of ice cream and top with caramel sauce.

DANISH APPLE CAKE
(Serves 8-10)

2— 12-ounce packages Frozen Escalloped Apples*
1/4 cup butter
1—6-ounce box zwieback, coarsely crushed
3 tablespoons granulated sugar
1/2 teaspoon cinnamon
1/2 cup currant jelly, melted
1-1/2 cups sweetened whipped cream

1. Bake Escalloped Apples following package directions.
2. Melt butter in a large frying pan; add zwieback crumbs, sugar and cinnamon; cook, stirring until lightly toasted.
3. Pour toasted crumbs into a shallow 2-quart serving container; press into an even layer.
4. Spread apples evenly over crumb mixture; drizzle jelly evenly over apples. Top with sweetened whipped cream. Cover and chill thoroughly.

STRAWBERRY SHORTCAKE
(Serves 6)

1—14-ounce package Frozen Almond Crunch Cake, defrosted*
2—10-ounce packages frozen sliced strawberries
1 cup sweetened whipped cream

1. Cut cake into 1/2-inch slices.
2. Place one slice of cake on each dessert plate and spoon 2 tablespoons of strawberries over cake.
3. Top with another slice of cake and cover with more strawberries.
4. Garnish with sweetened whipped cream.

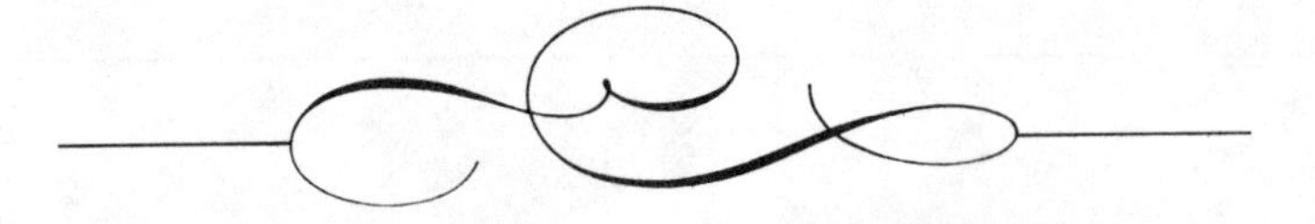

FROZEN THINGS

Nobody in the world loves frozen desserts more than Americans. Here are some of the things we do to make ice cream more than ice cream in the restaurants. You'll see that we, too, use the frozen short cut even with ice-cream desserts.

BAKED ALASKA
(Serves 6–8)

1—14-ounce package Frozen Almond Crunch Cake, defrosted*
1 pint vanilla ice cream, softened
3 egg whites, room temperature
1/4 teaspoon cream of tartar
1/2 cup granulated sugar

1. Remove cake from container, set container aside. Cut cake in half horizontally.
2. Press softened ice cream into bottom of aluminum cake container; return to freezer until firm.
3. Whip egg whites and cream of tartar until frothy. Gradually beat in sugar. Continue to beat until stiff and glossy.
4. Place bottom half of cake on baking tray, top with the prepared slab of ice cream. Cover ice cream with top half of cake. Completely cover cake and ice cream with meringue. Freeze firm.

NOTE: After freezing, if cake will not be used at once, wrap in aluminum foil and store in freezer.

5. At serving time preheat oven to 500° F.
6. Bake 3 to 5 minutes or until lightly browned.
7. Using a spatula, transfer cake from baking sheet onto a serving platter. Slice and serve immediately.

GRASSHOPPER PARFAIT
(Serves 6)

1-1/2 pints vanilla ice cream
1/2 cup white crème de cacao
1/2 cup green crème de menthe
1/2 cup sweetened whipped cream
6 fresh mint sprigs

1. Place six parfait glasses in the freezer until frosty.
2. Assemble each parfait as follows:
   1 small dip ice cream
   1 teaspoon crème de cacao
   1 teaspoon crème de menthe
   1 small dip ice cream
   1 teaspoon crème de cacao
   1 teaspoon crème de menthe
   1 small dip ice cream
   1 teaspoon crème de cacao
   1 teaspoon crème de menthe
3. Freeze firm; allow to stand at room temperature 5 minutes before serving.
4. Garnish each parfait with sweetened whipped cream and a fresh mint sprig.

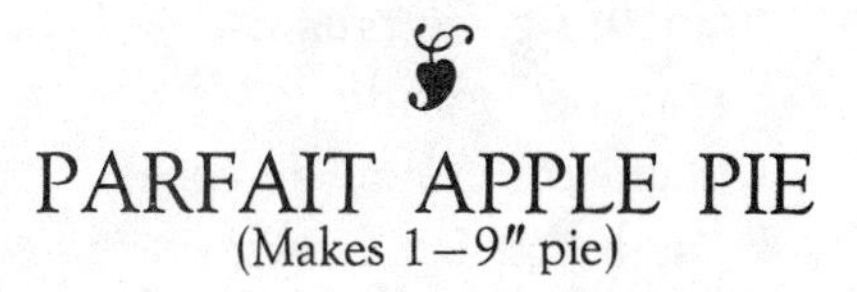

PARFAIT APPLE PIE
(Makes 1—9″ pie)

1—9″ baked pie shell
2—12-ounce packages Frozen Escalloped Apples*
2 tablespoons rum
1 quart vanilla ice cream

1. Bake Escalloped Apples following package directions; cool for 1/2 hour.
2. Combine apples and rum.
3. Spoon ice cream into pie shell; top with apples. Serve at once.

NUTTY-COCONUT BALLS

(Serves 6)

3/4 to 1 cup currant jelly (or desired flavor)
1—10-ounce package Frozen French Crumb Cakes, defrosted*
1/2 cup toasted coconut
1/2 cup untoasted coconut
1/2 cup chopped, toasted pecans

1. Heat jelly until it turns to liquid; remove from heat. Using a pair of tongs, dip each crumb cake into jelly, coating the entire surface.
2. Roll two cakes in toasted coconut, two in plain coconut and two in pecans. Place on a serving plate.

BRANDY ALEXANDER PARFAIT

(Serves 6)

1-1/2 pints vanilla ice cream
1/2 cup brandy
1/2 cup brown crème de cacao
1/2 cup sweetened whipped cream
Nutmeg

1. Place six parfait glasses in the freezer until frosty.
2. Assemble each parfait as follows:
   1 small dip ice cream
   1 teaspon brandy
   1 teaspoon crème de cacao
   1 small dip ice cream
   1 teaspoon brandy
   1 teaspoon crème de cacao
   1 small dip ice cream
   1 teaspoon brandy
   1 teaspoon crème de cacao
3. Freeze firm; allow to stand at room temperature 5 minutes before serving.
4. Garnish each parfait with sweetened whipped cream and sprinkle with nutmeg.

BABA AU RHUM PARFAIT

(Serves 6)

1—10-ounce package Frozen French Crumb Cakes, defrosted*
1/4 cup rum
1/4 cup strawberry preserves
1 pint vanilla ice cream, softened
Sweetened whipped cream or fresh strawberries for garnish

1. Break each crumb cake into six pieces.
2. For each parfait, place three broken pieces of cake in the bottom of a parfait or sherbet glass. Pour 1/2 teaspoon of rum over cake. Spoon 1 teaspoon of preserves over rum-soaked cake. Top with 2 tablespoons of softened ice cream. Repeat layer, ending with ice cream. Freeze firm.
3. Just before serving, garnish with a dollop of sweetened whipped cream or fresh strawberries. Serve immediately.

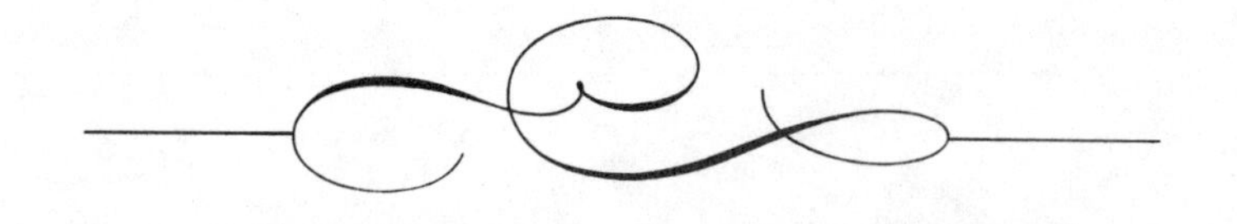

ET CETERA

There are some things that defy categorizing. What do you call a Fresh Strawberry Bavarian, other than delicious? How do you classify Prune Whip? So here for your et cetera file are some of our finest etc's.

FRESH STRAWBERRY BAVARIAN

(Serves 8)

2 cups fresh sliced strawberries
2/3 cup granulated sugar
1 tablespoon unflavored gelatin
1/4 cup cold water
1/2 cup boiling water
1 tablespoon lemon juice
2 egg whites
2 tablespoons granulated sugar
Dash salt
3/4 cup heavy cream
Sweetened whipped cream and whole strawberries for garnish

1. Combine sliced strawberries and first amount of sugar; blend well and let stand 30 minutes.
2. Soften gelatin in cold water for 5 minutes.
3. Pour boiling water over softened gelatin and stir until gelatin is dissolved.
4. Add gelatin mixture and lemon juice to strawberry mixture and chill until slightly thickened.
5. Beat egg whites until frothy; gradually add second amount of sugar and salt and continue beating until egg whites form soft peaks; fold into berry mixture and chill again, stirring occasionally so berries won't settle to the bottom.
6. Whip cream until stiff; fold into berry mixture.
7. Pour into a lightly oiled 1-1/2-quart mold; chill overnight.
8. Unmold onto chilled serving platter; garnish with sweetened whole strawberries and sweetened whipped cream.

ORANGE BAVARIAN

(Serves 8)

4 teaspoons unflavored gelatin
1/3 cup cold orange juice
2-1/4 cups orange juice
3 tablespoons lemon juice
1/4 teaspoon grated orange rind
1 cup granulated sugar
2 cups heavy cream
1/3 cup fresh orange sections
Sweetened whipped cream for garnish

1. Soften gelatin in cold orange juice for 5 minutes.
2. Combine second amount of orange juice, lemon juice, orange rind, and sugar. Stir and cook over low heat until sugar is dissolved. Remove from heat.
3. Add softened gelatin to hot juice mixture and beat until dissolved. Chill to the consistency of unbeaten egg whites.
4. Whip gelatin mixture for 2 to 3 minutes until light and fluffy.
5. Whip heavy cream until soft peaks form. Fold whipped cream into gelatin mixture. Pour into a lightly oiled 1-1/2-quart mold and chill overnight.
6. Unmold on chilled serving plate. Garnish with rosettes of sweetened whipped cream and fresh orange sections.

FRENCH CRUMB TRIFLE

(Serves 6)

1—10-ounce package Frozen French Crumb Cakes, defrosted*
1/4 cup strawberry preserves
2 cups vanilla pudding, canned or cooked
1/2 cup cream sherry
2 tablespoons toasted, slivered almonds
1-1/2 cups sweetened whipped cream

1. Split crumb cakes in half, and spread each half with 1 teaspoon of preserves. Place cake halves in a 12-inch by 7-inch oblong baking dish, filled side up, in a single layer. Drizzle sherry over preserves.
2. Pour pudding over cake halves. Cover and refrigerate overnight.
3. For festive service top with sweetened whipped cream and toasted, slivered almonds.

People love it; they absolutely love it. We even have one customer in New York who looks for Prune Whip on the menu, then settles back and orders it twice: once as an appetizer and once for dessert.

PRUNE WHIP WITH CREAM CUSTARD SAUCE

(Serves 4)

1 cup cooked, strained prunes, cooled
1/4 teaspoon salt
1/3 cup granulated sugar
3 egg whites, room temperature
1/4 cup chopped nuts
1 tablespoon lemon juice
Cream Custard Sauce (below)

1. Combine cooled, strained prunes, salt, sugar and egg whites. Whip until stiff enough to hold its shape.
2. Fold in nuts and lemon juice and blend.
3. Rinse a 1-quart shallow baking dish with cold water. Pour mixture into dish; set in pan containing 1/2-inch of hot water.
4. Set pan in oven and bake at 325° F. for 40 to 45 minutes or until mixture is puffed up and has formed a thin crust.
5. Remove from oven and cool slowly. Serve with Cream Custard Sauce.

CREAM CUSTARD SAUCE

4 teaspoons granulated sugar
1 teaspoon cornstarch
Dash salt
1/3 cup milk
1/4 cup coffee cream
1 egg yolk, beaten
3/4 teaspoon vanilla extract
1/4 cup heavy cream

1. Blend sugar, cornstarch and salt together.
2. Combine milk and coffee cream in the top of a double boiler and heat over rapidly boiling water but do not boil.
3. Gradually add sugar mixture, beating constantly. Cook until thickened, stirring occasionally.
4. Pour a small amount of the hot mixture into beaten egg yolk, beating constantly. Return mixture to pan, beating rapidly. Cook 1 to 2 minutes longer. Remove from heat.

5. Cool sauce at room temperature, stirring frequently; add vanilla extract and blend.
6. Whip heavy cream until stiff; fold into custard and refrigerate at once.

CHERRY BLOSSOM CAKES

(Serves 6)

1—8-3/4-ounce package Frozen Macaroon Crumb Cakes*
1 pint vanilla ice cream
1/2 cup sweetened whipped cream
Red Cherry Sauce (below)

1. Remove Macaroon Crumb Cakes from freezer. While still frozen, slice each cake in half horizontally. (Cake will crumble less if sliced while frozen.)
2. Cover sliced cakes and defrost at room temperature for 45 minutes.
3. When ready to serve, place bottom half of each cake (cut side up) on dessert plates. Pour 1 tablespoon of Red Cherry Sauce (without cherries) over cut surface of each cake. Top with vanilla ice cream which has been spooned (ice cream should be flat rather than rounded scoops). Cover with cake tops (cut side down) and gently press to secure cake to the ice cream.
4. Spoon a dollop of sweetened whipped cream on top of each cake and pour 2 tablespoons of Red Cherry Sauce (with cherries) over whipped cream.

RED CHERRY SAUCE

1 cup canned cherry pie filling
1/3 cup water
1/3 cup granulated sugar
Dash salt
3/4 teaspoon butter
1-1/2 teaspoons freshly squeezed lemon juice

1. Stir pie filling before measuring to insure even distribution of the cherries.
2. Combine cherry pie filling, water, sugar and salt. Heat to boiling.
3. Add butter and lemon juice; mix to combine ingredients. Remove from heat and cool to room temperature.

This is such a favorite that people forsake their diets on the days we serve it.

CHOCOLATE SOUFFLÉ WITH ICE CREAM SAUCE

(Serves 6)

5 tablespoons cake flour
3/4 cup granulated sugar
1/2 teaspoon salt
1/2 cup less 1-1/2 teaspoons cocoa
1 cup less 1 tablespoon water
3 egg yolks, beaten
1 teaspoon vanilla extract
9 egg whites, room temperature
Ice Cream Sauce (below)

1. Sift cake flour, sugar, salt and cocoa together.
2. Heat water to boiling in a heavy saucepan.
3. Gradually add sifted dry ingredients to boiling water, beating constantly with a wire whip. Heat to boiling; reduce heat and simmer 3 to 5 minutes or until mixture thickens and flour taste disappears. Remove from heat.
4. Pour hot mixture into beaten egg yolks, beating constantly until well blended; add vanilla extract and blend.
5. Cool to room temperature, stirring frequently to prevent film from forming on top.
6. Beat room-temperature egg whites in a large bowl until stiff and dry.
7. Fold cooled chocolate mixture into beaten egg whites by hand using a wire whip.
8. Pour mixture into a lightly buttered 1-1/2-quart oblong baking dish and spread so mixture is mounded slightly in the center.
9. Set baking dish in a pan containing 1/2-inch of hot water; set pan in oven and bake at 315°F. for 1-1/4 to 1-1/2 hours or until a silver knife inserted in the center comes out clean.
10. Cool for 30 minutes. Serve with Ice Cream Sauce.

ICE CREAM SAUCE

1 egg white, room temperature
2 tablespoons granulated sugar
1 egg yolk, room temperature
3/4 teaspoon vanilla extract
1/3 cup heavy cream

1. Beat room-temperature egg white until frothy; gradually add sugar and continue beating until stiff peaks form.
2. Beat room-temperature egg yolk until thick and lemon colored; add vanilla extract and blend.
3. Fold egg yolk into beaten egg white by hand using a wire whip.
4. Whip heavy cream until peaks form; fold into sauce; chill thoroughly.

Variation:

Try the Chocolate Soufflé with Coffee Liqueur and Whipped Cream: Serve each portion of Chocolate Soufflé topped with 1 tablespoon coffee liqueur and sweetened whipped cream.

MOCHA BAVARIAN CRÈME

(Serves 8)

4 teaspoons unflavored gelatin
1/4 cup cold milk
3/4 cup hot coffee
2-1/2 teaspoons instant coffee
3-1/4 teaspoons boiling water
2/3 cup milk
7 tablespoons granulated sugar
1/4 teaspoon salt
2 egg whites, room temperature
2 tablespoons granulated sugar
1 cup heavy cream
Sweetened whipped cream and chocolate curls for garnish

1. Soften gelatin in cold milk for 5 minutes.
2. Add hot coffee and stir until gelatin is dissolved.
3. Blend instant coffee and boiling water; add to gelatin mixture.
4. Add milk, first amount of sugar and salt. Stir until sugar and salt are dissolved. Chill mixture, stirring occasionally, until it is the consistency of unbeaten egg whites.
5. Beat room-temperature egg whites until frothy; gradually add remaining sugar and beat until soft peaks are formed.
6. Beat gelatin mixture 2 to 3 mintues until light and fluffy; fold in beaten egg whites.
7. Whip cream until stiff; fold into coffee mixture.
8. Pour into a lightly oiled 1-1/2-quart mold. Chill overnight.
9. Unmold onto a chilled serving platter. Garnish with sweetened whipped cream and chocolate curls.

DUTCH APPLE PUFFS

(Serves 8)

5 eggs
1 cup all-purpose flour
1 cup milk
8—5" foil or glass pie pans
1 cup melted butter
1/2 cup freshly squeezed lemon juice
2—12-ounce packages Frozen Escalloped Apples*
1/2 cup sifted confectioner's sugar

1. Preheat oven to 500° F.
2. In a medium bowl, combine eggs, flour and milk. Beat until batter is smooth and has a thin consistency.
3. Put 2 tablespoons butter into each pie pan.
4. Pour 1/2 cup batter into each pan.
5. Lower oven temperature to 400° F. Bake puffs for 15 to 20 minutes.
6. Bake Escalloped Apples following package directions.
7. When puff shells are baked, immediately slide them onto plates.
8. Drizzle with lemon juice and sprinkle with confectioner's sugar.
9. Fill with Escalloped Apples. Sprinkle again with confectioner's sugar and serve at once. A dollop of sour cream may be added as a garnish, if desired.

SOUR CREAM APPLE SOUFFLÉ

(Serves 4–6)

3 eggs, separated
1/3 cup granulated sugar
1 teaspoon vanilla extract
1 teaspoon finely grated lemon rind
1/2 cup dairy sour cream
1—12-ounce package Frozen Escalloped Apples, defrosted*
Confectioner's sugar

1. Preheat oven to 350° F.
2. Beat egg whites until frothy; add granulated sugar gradually and continue beating until stiff. Set aside.
3. Beat egg yolks until thick; add vanilla extract and lemon rind.
4. Stir in sour cream and Escalloped Apples; fold in beaten egg whites. Pour into a 1-quart baking dish.

5. Bake for 40 to 50 minutes, until soufflé is puffed and brown or until a silver knife inserted in the center comes out clean.
6. Dust with confectioner's sugar when ready to serve.
7. Garnish with sweetened whipped cream or grenadine syrup, if desired.

APPLE SNOW SOUFFLÉ

(Serves 4)

1—12-ounce package Frozen Escalloped Apples*
2 tablespoons butter or margarine
3 tablespoons all-purpose flour
1/8 teaspoon salt
2/3 cup milk
1/2 teaspoon vanilla extract
3 eggs, separated
3 tablespoons granulated sugar
1/4 teaspoon cinnamon

1. Bake Escalloped Apples following package directions.
2. Coat a 1-quart mold or baking dish with butter or margarine. Dust lightly with granulated sugar, tapping out any excess.
3. Melt butter or margarine over low heat in a small saucepan. Stir in flour and salt. Cook, stirring constantly, for 1 minute until well blended.
4. Slowly stir in milk. Add vanilla extract and continue stirring until sauce thickens and is smooth. Cook 1 minute (sauce will be very thick). Cool.
5. Beat egg yolks well in a large bowl, gradually beating in sugar.
6. Blend egg yolks and cooled sauce together. Add Escalloped Apples.
7. Beat egg whites until stiff and dry. Fold into sauce.
8. Pour into mold. Sprinkle top of soufflé with cinnamon. Place mold in a pan containing 1 inch of hot water.
9. Set pan in oven and bake at 325° F. for 1 hour and 10 minutes.
10. Remove mold from pan of water and let stand for 15 minutes.
11. Loosen edge of mold with a knife; cover with a serving plate and invert to unmold.
12. Spoon grenadine syrup over or sprinkle with confectioner's sugar, if desired.

MACAROON CAKE À LA MODE WITH STRAWBERRY SAUCE

(Serves 6)

1—8-3/4-ounce package Frozen Macaroon Crumb Cakes*
1—10-ounce package frozen strawberries, defrosted
1 pint vanilla ice cream

1. Defrost Macaroon Crumb Cakes at room temperature. Heat in a 350° F. oven just until warm.
2. Place defrosted strawberries in a bowl and stir gently to mix.
3. Place 1 warm Macaroon Crumb Cake in each dessert dish (preferably shallow ones). Top each with a scoop of vanilla ice cream and ladle 2 tablespoons of strawberries over each serving. Serve at once.

COCONUT ANGEL PUDDING

(Serves 6)

2/3 cup hot milk
1/3 cup cold milk
3 tablespoons cornstarch
3 tablespoons granulated sugar
1/4 teaspoon salt
5 egg whites, room temperature
1/2 teaspoon cream of tartar
3 tablespoons granulated sugar
1 cup shredded coconut
3/4 teaspoon vanilla extract
Sweetened sliced strawberries or raspberries

1. Scald milk in a heavy saucepan.
2. Blend cold milk and cornstarch together until smooth.
3. Whip cornstarch mixture into hot milk; cook over low heat until thickened and the starch taste disappears.
4. Add first amount of sugar and salt; blend. Cool to room temperature.
5. Beat egg whites and cream of tartar together until frothy; gradually add second amount of sugar and continue beating until soft peaks are formed.
6. Gently fold room-temperature sauce into egg whites; fold in shredded coconut and vanilla extract.

7. Pour mixture into an 8-inch square baking dish which has been rinsed with cold water. Spread evenly.
8. Set dish in a pan containing 1/2-inch of hot water.
9. Set pan in oven and bake at 325° F. for 30 to 35 minutes or until a silver knife inserted in the center comes out clean. Cool to room temperature.
10. Cut into squares and serve with sweetened, sliced strawberries or raspberries.

APPLE POPOVER DESSERT

(Serves 4)

1—12-ounce package Frozen Escalloped Apples, defrosted*
1/8 teaspoon cinnamon
1/2 teaspoon lemon juice
1 tablespoon maple syrup
1/8 teaspoon ground allspice
4 Basic Popovers (below)
2 cups sweetened whipped cream

1. Place Escalloped Apples in top of double boiler; heat over rapidly boiling water.
2. Add cinnamon, lemon juice, maple syrup and allspice; stir to combine. Continue to heat for 15 minutes.
3. Slice popovers in half lengthwise. Spoon apple filling into sliced popovers and top with sweetened whipped cream. Serve warm.

BASIC POPOVERS

(Makes 4)

1 cup milk
7/8 cup all-purpose flour
1 tablespoon cooking oil
1/2 teaspoon salt
2 eggs

1. Combine milk, flour, cooking oil and salt. Beat with an electric beater on high speed for 1 minute.
2. Add eggs one at a time, beating 20 seconds after each addition. Fill *well greased* muffin-tin cups 2/3 full.
3. Place in a cold oven; set at 425° F. and bake for 35 minutes. Remove popovers from pan.

PENNSYLVANIA DUTCH CAKE

(Serves 6)

1—15-1/2-ounce package Frozen Raisin Tea Cake*
1 cup Whipped Cream Cheese (page 203)
1-1/2 cups warm Lemon Sauce (page 202)

1. Remove lid and liner from Raisin Tea Cake; invert cake onto a cutting board and allow to partially defrost.
2. Cut cake into 12 equal slices with a warm, damp knife. Rearrange slices into cake shape and wrap with aluminum foil. Place in a 325°F. oven for 10 minutes until warm.
3. When ready to serve, place 2 slices of warm cake, slightly overlapping, on each dessert plate.
4. Place 1 rounded tablespoon of Whipped Cream Cheese in the center of the cake slices.
5. Pour 2 tablespoons of warm Lemon Sauce over the cheese and cake.

CHOCOLATE RUM TRIFLE

(Serves 6)

1/2 cup dairy sour cream
1 teaspoon granulated sugar
1 tablespoon grated orange rind
1—10-ounce package Frozen French Crumb Cakes, defrosted*
2 cups chocolate pudding, canned or cooked
1/4 cup rum
1-1/2 cups sweetened whipped cream
2 tablespoons toasted, slivered almonds

1. In a small mixing bowl, combine sour cream, sugar and orange rind.
2. Split crumb cakes in half. Spread each half with sour cream mixture. Place cake halves in an oblong baking dish, filled side up, in a single layer.
3. Combine pudding and rum to make a smooth sauce. Pour over the cakes.
4. Refrigerate overnight. Garnish with sweetened whipped cream and toasted, slivered almonds.

MARMALADE MERINGUE TORTE
(Serves 8–10)

1—14-ounce package Frozen Almond Crunch Cake, defrosted*
3 tablespoons pineapple marmalade
1—3-ounce package cream cheese, room temperature
2 egg whites, room temperature
1/8 teaspoon salt
1/3 cup brown sugar

1. Preheat oven to 400° F.
2. Remove cake from container, cut cake in 3 layers, horizontally, and place on an ovenproof serving plate.
3. In a small bowl, combine marmalade and cream cheese; blend well. Spread center and bottom layers of cake with cheese mixture. Put layers back together.
4. Whip egg whites and salt until frothy. Gradually add sugar; continue beating until stiff and glossy.
5. Completely cover cake with meringue. Bake 5 minutes or until lightly browned.

APPLE CRISP
(Serves 4)

1/2 cup bread crumbs
1 tablespoon granulated sugar
1/4 cup firmly packed brown sugar
1/4 teaspoon cinnamon
1-1/2 teaspoons all-purpose flour
1 tablespoon butter or margarine, melted
2—12-ounce packages Frozen Escalloped Apples*

1. Preheat oven to 400° F.
2. Combine all dry ingredients and mix thoroughly; pour melted butter or margarine over mix; toss lightly with a fork.
3. Remove lids from the packages of Escalloped Apples and sprinkle 1/4 cup of the topping over each pan.
4. Place the pans in the oven, and bake 30 to 35 minutes until lightly browned and bubbly.
5. Serve plain, with a scoop of ice cream or with "pouring cream."

HOT APPLE AMBROSIA

(Serves 8)

2—12-ounce packages Frozen Escalloped Apples, defrosted*
2 tablespoons grated orange peel
2 cups orange sections
1 cup shredded coconut

1. In a medium bowl, combine Escalloped Apples, orange peel and orange sections.
2. Pour into a 1-1/2-quart baking dish and sprinkle with coconut. Bake at 400°F. for 25 to 30 minutes or until coconut is golden brown. Serve hot.

And Other Good Things
Cal Sacks

Here are some recipes we couldn't resist adding.

CUCUMBERS IN SOUR CREAM
(Serves 4)

1/4 cup thinly sliced onion
1/3 cup cider vinegar
2 tablespoons cold water
1-1/4 teaspoons salt
2 medium cucumbers, peeled and sliced (approximately 2 cups)

Dressing:
1/2 teaspoon cider vinegar
1/3 cup dairy sour cream
1/4 teaspoon salt
3/4 teaspoon granulated sugar
1 tablespoon salad dressing

1. Combine onion, vinegar and water and let stand 30 minutes. Strain and discard onion.
2. Add first amount of salt to vinegar solution and pour over sliced cucumbers. Cover with a thin layer of crushed ice and let stand 15 minutes. Drain well.
3. Combine dressing ingredients and blend smooth. Add drained cucumbers and mix well. Chill thoroughly.

Variations:

Cucumbers and Onions in Sour Cream: Add 1/4 cup thinly sliced Bermuda onions to cucumber sour cream mixture.

Dill Cucumbers in Sour Cream: Add 1/2 teaspoon fresh or dried chopped dill weed to sour cream mixture and blend well.

SOUR CREAM CHEESE SAUCE
(Makes 1-3/4 cups)

1— 10-ounce package Frozen Welsh Rarebit*
1/2 cup dairy sour cream

1. Heat frozen Welsh Rarebit in top of double boiler over hot water for 25 to 30 minutes or until hot.
2. Add sour cream; stir well to combine and continue heating for 5 more minutes.
3. Serve hot over vegetables, such as broccoli, asparagus or artichoke hearts.

ESCALLOPED APPLE-BERRY RELISH
(Makes 1-1/2 cups)

1—12-ounce package Frozen Escalloped Apples*
1/2 cup whole cranberry sauce
1/4 teaspoon cinnamon

1. Bake Frozen Escalloped Apples following package directions.
2. Place contents in saucepan and gently stir in whole cranberry sauce and cinnamon; simmer 5 minutes; chill.
3. Relish may be served in lemon or orange baskets on beds of curly endive, if desired.

QUICK APPLE CHUTNEY
(Serves 8)

2 medium oranges
2— 12-ounce packages Frozen Escalloped Apples, defrosted*
1/3 cup raisins
1/4 teaspoon ground allspice

1. Cut oranges in half; scoop out center and cut sections from the membranes. Cut edges of orange shells into saw-tooth points.
2. Combine Escalloped Apples, raisins, allspice and orange sections.
3. Fill orange shells with mixture; place in baking dish and bake at 400°F. for 20 to 25 minutes.

APPLE CHUTNEY
(Serves 4–6)

1— 12-ounce package Frozen Escalloped Apples, defrosted*
1/3 cup raisins
1/3 cup crushed pineapple
1/8 teaspoon ground cloves
2 tablespoons granulated sugar
2 tablespoons grated orange peel
1 teaspoon cider vinegar
1/8 teaspoon ground ginger
Pinch ground allspice

1. Combine all ingredients in a medium mixing bowl and pour into a 1-quart baking dish. Cover loosely.
2. Bake at 350°F. for 40 to 45 minutes. May be served warm or cool.

From Atlanta to New York they ask for this recipe. And this is the first time we have ever given it.

BLEU CHEESE DRESSING

(Makes 2 cups)

6 ounces Bleu cheese
1/4 cup cream cheese
1 cup salad oil
2 tablespoons cider vinegar
1 teaspoon granulated sugar
1/2 teaspoon paprika

1. Combine Bleu cheese and cream cheese and mix well.
2. Add oil and vinegar alternately, beating constantly.
3. Add sugar and paprika; beat until well blended.
4. Cover and store in refrigerator.
5. Mix well before serving.

CELERY DRESSING

(Makes 4 cups)

4 tablespoons chicken fat
2/3 cup chopped onion
2 cups diced celery
6 tablespoons chicken broth
10 slices white bread
1 teaspoon salt
1/8 teaspoon pepper
1/8 teaspoon sage

1. Melt chicken fat in a heavy skillet. Add onion, celery and chicken broth; simmer 10 minutes or until vegetables are tender.
2. Cut bread into flakes 1/8-inch by 1/4-inch; add seasonings.
3. Combine vegetable/broth mixture with seasoned bread flakes and toss lightly.
4. Place dressing in a buttered casserole and bake for 20 minutes at 350°F. or use as turkey stuffing.

NOTE: If this dressing is used to stuff fish, substitute butter for chicken fat and water for chicken broth.

GOLDEN CORN FRITTERS

(Makes approximately 24)

3/4 cup all-purpose flour
1/2 teaspoon baking powder
1/2 teaspoon salt
1 egg
1— 12-ounce package Frozen Corn Soufflé, defrosted*
Melted shortening or oil for deep frying
Maple syrup

1. Sift flour with baking powder and salt.
2. Beat egg; stir flour mixture into egg.
3. Add defrosted Corn Soufflé. Blend lightly.
4. Drop by teaspoonfuls into 350° F. deep fat and fry until golden brown; about 4 minutes.
5. Serve hot with warm maple syrup.

APPLE FRITTERS

(Makes approximately 20)

1-1/3 cups all-purpose flour
2 teaspoons baking powder
3/4 teaspoon salt
1/2 cup milk
1— 12-ounce package Frozen Escalloped Apples, defrosted*
2 eggs, slightly beaten
Melted shortening or oil for deep frying

1. Sift flour, baking powder and salt; add milk and blend.
2. Stir in defrosted Escalloped Apples and slightly beaten eggs.
3. Drop by tablespoonfuls into 350° F. deep fat. Brown on all sides; drain on absorbent paper.
4. For festive service, serve warm with syrup, or sprinkle with plain confectioner's sugar, or cinnamon sugar (1 teaspoon cinnamon to 1 cup confectioner's sugar).

BLUEBERRY FRITTERS

(Makes approximately 24)

Sauce:
1 cup fresh blueberries
2/3 cup water
1/4 cup granulated sugar
1/2 teaspoon cornstarch
Dash salt
1/2 teaspoon lemon juice

Fritters:
2 egg yolks
2/3 cup milk
1 tablespoon butter, melted
2 egg whites, room temperature
1-1/4 cups all-purpose flour
2-1/4 teaspoons baking powder
1 teaspoon salt
3 tablespoons granulated sugar
1 cup fresh blueberries
Melted shortening or oil for deep frying

1. To make sauce: Combine blueberries and water in a heavy saucepan. Heat to boiling; reduce heat and simmer 2 to 4 minutes or until blueberries are soft. Beat with a wire whip to break up berries.
2. Strain mixture through a food mill and discard pulp.
3. Combine sugar, cornstarch and salt; add to hot blueberry mixture, stirring constantly with a wire whip. Simmer, stirring frequently, for 3 to 5 minutes or until cornstarch taste disappears. Remove from heat and add lemon juice. Keep warm.
4. To make fritters: Beat egg yolks until thick. Add milk and melted butter; mix thoroughly.
5. In a separate bowl, whip egg whites until they form rounded peaks, but are not dry.
6. Sift flour, baking powder, salt and sugar together once. Add egg yolk/milk mixture and blend. Partially fold in beaten egg whites.
7. Fold in whole fresh blueberries to evenly distribute.
8. Drop by rounded teaspoonfuls into 350° F. deep fat. Fry until fritters are a rich golden brown and are cooked through. Drain on absorbent paper.
9. Serve warm, sprinkled with confectioner's sugar. Pass bowl of warm blueberry sauce, too.

SWISS APPLE FRITTERS

(Makes 12)

3 apples
Melted shortening or oil for deep frying
1 cup cake flour
1 tablespoon granulated sugar
1 teaspoon baking powder
1/4 teaspoon salt
2 eggs, beaten
1/3 cup milk
2 teaspoons shortening, melted
1/4 cup confectioner's sugar
3/4 teaspoon cinnamon

1. Peel and core apples. Cut crosswise into rings 1/4-inch to 3/8-inch thick.
2. Preheat deep fat to 375°F.
3. Sift cake flour, granulated sugar, baking powder and salt together once.
4. Combine beaten eggs, milk and melted shortening; add to dry ingredients and stir only until mixture is smooth.
5. Dip each apple ring into batter and drain on wire rack. Place rings in fat a few at a time. Fry for 1-1/2 minutes on each side or until browned and cooked through. Drain on absorbent paper.
6. Sift confectioner's sugar and cinnamon together; sprinkle over warm fritters.

CHEESE MELBA TOAST

(Makes approximately 3 dozen)

1 loaf unsliced day old bread
1/2 cup soft butter
2 tablespoons grated Parmesan cheese

1. Cut bread into 1/4-inch slices. Cut slices in half and place close together on a flat baking pan.
2. Blend softened butter with grated Parmesan cheese; spread each half slice with 1/2 teaspoon cheese butter.
3. Bake in 375°F. oven for 12 to 15 minutes or until golden brown and crisp. Remove from oven; cool slightly before removing from pan.
4. Store in a tightly covered container in a dry, warm place.

Of all the toasts and breads we serve, this is our most popular.

SESAME MELBA TOAST

(Makes approximately 3 dozen)

1 loaf unsliced day old bread
1/4 cup sesame seeds
1/4 pound soft butter

1. Cut bread in 1/4-inch slices.
2. Spread sesame seeds on a baking tray and toast in a 375° F. oven for 10 minutes. Cool.
3. Cut bread slices in half and place close together on a baking sheet.
4. Cream butter until smooth; add cool toasted sesame seeds and blend.
5. Spread each half slice of bread with 1/2 teaspoon butter mixture.
6. Bake in 375° F. oven for 12 to 15 minutes or until lightly browned and crisp. Cool slightly before removing from trays.
7. Store in a tightly covered container in a dry, warm place.

HERB MELBA TOAST

(Makes approximately 3 dozen)

1 loaf unsliced day old bread
6 tablespoons soft butter
1/4 teaspoon leaf tarragon
1/8 teaspoon marjoram
3/4 teaspoon finely chopped parsley
3/4 teaspoon sweet basil

1. Cut bread into 1/4-inch slices. Cut slices in half and place close together on a flat baking pan.
2. Blend butter and herbs together; spread 3/4 teaspoon herb butter on each half slice of bread.
3. Bake in 375° F. oven for 12 to 15 minutes or until golden brown and crisp. Remove from oven; cool slightly before removing from pan.
4. Store in tightly covered container in a dry, warm place.

No one ever seems to get the same French Toast flavor at home that we get at Stouffer's Restaurants. The secret is the Clarified Butter; only Clarified Butter will keep toast from burning and will give it a golden brown, crusty appearance.

FRENCH TOAST

(Serves 6)

1 loaf unsliced day old white bread
6 eggs
3/4 cup milk
1/2 teaspoon salt
1/2 cup Clarified Butter (below)

1. Cut day old bread into 5/8-inch slices and cut slices in half diagonally.
2. Beat eggs and milk together; add salt and blend to make egg batter.
3. Heat Clarified Butter in a heavy skillet until bubbling.
4. Dip bread triangles into egg batter and place in hot butter. Fry until golden brown; drain well. Serve with whipped butter and warm syrup.

Variations:

Sesame French Toast: Before turning bread in the skillet, sprinkle each triangle with 1 teaspoon sesame seeds. Turn and fry until golden brown. Serve seed-side up.

Orange French Toast: Prepare as for regular French Toast substituting orange juice for the milk; add 2-1/2 teaspoons finely grated orange rind to egg batter.

CLARIFIED BUTTER

(Makes 1 cup)

1. Melt 1 pound of butter over low heat.
2. Skim off froth.
3. Strain clear liquid through a fine cheesecloth to keep out sediment of milk solids.
4. Refrigerate until needed for use.

RYE CHIPS

1. Trim bottom crust from loaves of sliced cocktail rye bread.
2. Spread slices out flat on trays and allow to dry in the air for one hour or longer.
3. Bake in a 375°F. oven for 5 to 6 minutes until slices curl and are light brown.

NOTE: Rye Chips can be served at room temperature for "dunking" or can be drizzled with melted butter (plain or garlic), reheated in a 375°F. oven for 2 minutes, and served hot.

WHIPPED CREAM DRESSING

(Makes 1-1/2 cups)

1/2 cup heavy cream
1 teaspoon granulated sugar
1/2 cup salad dressing

1. Whip heavy cream and sugar until soft peaks form.
2. Fold into salad dressing just to blend.

RED DIPPING SAUCE

(Makes 2-1/2 cups)

1 cup salad oil
1/2 cup ketchup
1/3 cup honey
2 tablespoons cider vinegar
1 tablespoon freshly squeezed lemon juice
2 tablespoons Japanese soy sauce
2 teaspoons Worcestershire sauce
2 teaspoons salt
2 tablespoons finely grated onion

1. Combine all ingredients and mix thoroughly.
2. Serve at room temperature.

NOTE: This sauce must be made the day of use and will not keep overnight.

We serve this with ham and other cold meats, and we recommend it to you for adding new flavor to leftovers.

CUMBERLAND SAUCE

(Makes 1 cup)

1 cup red currant jelly
1/4 cup prepared mustard

1. Melt jelly in a heavy saucepan, beating with a wire whip until smooth.
2. Blend in mustard and beat smooth. Remove from heat and cool to room temperature.

LEMON SAUCE

(Makes 2-1/2 cups)

1 cup granulated sugar
2 tablespoons cornstarch
1/4 teaspoon salt
1-1/2 cups water
2 egg yolks, beaten
3 tablespoons freshly squeezed lemon juice
1-1/2 teaspoons finely grated lemon rind
4 teaspoons butter

1. Blend sugar, cornstarch and salt together in a bowl.
2. Place water in top of double boiler and heat over rapidly boiling water while gradually adding dry ingredients; beat constantly; cook until mixture is thickened and starch taste disappears.
3. Beat a small amount of hot liquid into beaten egg yolks. Return to mixture in top of double boiler, beating constantly. Cook 2 to 3 minutes longer. Remove from heat.
4. Add lemon juice, grated lemon rind and butter and blend well. Serve warm.

WHIPPED CREAM CHEESE

(Makes 1-1/2 cups)

2—3-ounce packages cream cheese, room temperature
1/4 teaspoon salt
1 teaspoon granulated sugar
2-1/2 tablespoons coffee cream

1. Beat cream cheese until smooth; blend in salt and sugar.
2. Gradually add cream and continue beating until fluffy as whipped cream.

MUSTARD SAUCE

(Makes 1 cup)

1/2 cup granulated sugar
1 tablespoon dry mustard
1-1/4 teaspoons cornstarch
1/4 teaspoon salt
1 egg yolk
1/2 cup hot coffee cream
2-1/4 teaspoons cider vinegar

1. Mix sugar, dry mustard, cornstarch and salt together in a heavy saucepan.
2. Beat egg yolk slightly; add to dry ingredients and mix until thoroughly combined.
3. Gradually add hot cream to egg mixture, beating until smooth.
4. Place over medium heat and cook, stirring frequently, until sauce thickens and starch taste disappears.
5. Slowly add vinegar, beating constantly.
6. Remove sauce from heat and cool at room temperature, stirring frequently to prevent formation of a crust.

CAUTION: This recipe has a large amount of salt and we find it most delicious when used on unsalted greens. You may prefer less salt, and can make it effectively with a reduced amount. Take your own tastes into account when preparing, and add more salt later if desired.

WHITE FRENCH DRESSING

(Makes 1 quart)

3 tablespoons cornstarch
1/4 cup cold water
1/2 cup boiling water
1/4 teaspoon paprika
1/4 cup hot water
1/2 cup granulated sugar
3 tablespoons salt
1 teaspoon dry mustard
2-3/4 cups salad oil
1 cup cider vinegar
1/2 teaspoon onion juice
1 clove garlic

1. Dissolve cornstarch in cold water. Add boiling water and cook 3–5 minutes over medium heat until thick; stirring constantly.
2. Dissolve paprika in hot water; add to cornstarch mixture and cook one minute longer.
3. Add sugar, salt and mustard; mix well. Strain mixture to eliminate lumps.
4. Whip hot mixture on medium speed of an electric mixer, while gradually adding salad oil *alternately* with vinegar. Add onion juice.

NOTE: To make onion juice, chop onion finely and place in a cheesecloth bag. Squeeze to obtain the quantity of juice required.

5. Add garlic clove (which has been tied in a cheesecloth bag); cover and refrigerate for 24 hours to blend flavors.
6. Remove garlic clove after the 24-hour period. Store in the refrigerator in a covered container. Stir well before each use.

When
Company
Comes

It's a lunch or a brunch or a sit-down dinner.

It's a party on the patio, Thanksgiving dinner, and a Fourth of July picnic.

It's all those occasions when you want to do your best for those you care about most.

In other words, it's party time. Time to find some recipes that give you a chance to show what you can do in the kitchen without spending too much time in the kitchen.

So here are some tried and true menu ideas, and when the specific recipes are included in the book, we italicize the recipe title.

Have a good time.

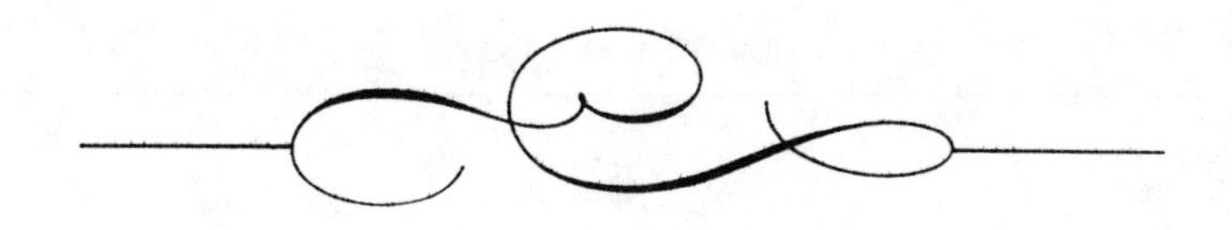

FOR PARTIES

BUFFETS FOR THE COCKTAIL HOUR

King Crab Newburg
Swiss-Cheese Balls
Barbecued Vienna Sausages
Fried Egg Rolls with Hot Mustard and Plum Sauce
Creamy Clam Dip with Chips
Stuffed Cucumber Slices on Party Rye
Deviled Pickled Eggs
Tangy Cheddar Cheese Spread with *Sesame Melba Toast*

Sherried Chicken Livers
Lobster Stuffed Jumbo Shrimp
Sauerkraut Balls
Tiny Hot Ham Biscuits with *Cumberland Sauce*
Medley of Fresh Vegetable Relishes with *Onion Cheese Dip*
Wee Cream Puffs Filled with Curried Chicken Salad
Bacon Tomato Rarebit Dip with Crisp Crouton Sticks
Wedge of Bleu Cheese with Assorted Wafers
Platter of Red Grapes, Pineapple Fingers, Pear and Apple Wedges

AN INFORMAL COCKTAIL PARTY

Meat Balls Stroganoff
Crab Stuffed Mushrooms
Bacon Wrapped Olives
Radish Roses
Green Goddess Dip with Crisp *Rye Chips*

FOR BRUNCH

Crabmeat Crêpes Supreme with Artichokes
Butter Corn Rolls
Tray of Melon Wedges
Pan Cinnamon Rolls
Coffee

Bloody Marys
Herb Scrambled Eggs with Canadian Bacon
Orange French Toast Triangles
Coffee

PATIO BRUNCH FOR A CROWD

Whiskey Milk Punch
Whole Fresh Strawberries and Fresh Pineapple Wedges
with Powdered Sugar and Sour Cream
Baked Avocado Stuffed with Crabmeat
Potato Pancakes
French-Fried Tomatoes
Devonshire Green Cabbage Slaw
Bleu Cheese Bread
Danish Cheese Sandwiches
Butter Balls
Iced Coffee

FOR THE KAFFEE KLATSCH

Rum-Glazed Danish Rolls
Corn Sticks
Butter Balls
Orange Marmalade
Café au Lait

LUNCHEONS

Consommé Madrilène
Cheese Soufflé with Mushrooms
Buttered Broccoli Spears
Brandied Bing Cherry Salad
Crisp Hard Rolls with Butter
Nutty-Coconut Balls with Fudge Sauce

Iced *Crème Vichyssoise*
Ham Loaf with Fresh Rhubarb Sauce
French-Fried Carrots
Sliced Tomato Salad with Avocado and Watercress
Herb Bread
Lemon Angel Cream Cake

Salmon Loaf with Fresh Cucumber Sauce
Buttered Asparagus Spears
Sliced Pear and Crabapple Salad
Hot Cheese Bread
Watermelon Pickle Slices
Key Lime Pie

LUNCHEONS ON THE TERRACE

Chilled Fresh Tomato Bisque
Chicken Salad Hawaiian
Double Corn Muffins
Grasshopper Parfait with Chocolate Petit Fours
Iced Tea with Fresh Lime

Viennese Chicken Soup
Fresh Fruit in Cantaloupe Boat with Whipped Cream Dressing
Cashew Honey Squares and Butter
Chocolate Soufflé with Ice Cream Sauce

LUNCHEON BUFFET

Cold Sliced Baked Ham
Escalloped Apple-Berry Relish
Supreme Chicken Salad
Crabmeat Stuffed Shrimp
Spinach Ring with Noodles Romanoff
Tray of Ripe and Stuffed Olives
Buttered Biscuits
Marinated Three Bean Salad
Cucumbers in Sour Cream
Jellied Fruit Salad
Coconut Angel Pudding with Fresh Strawberries

BUFFET DINNERS

Fresh Fruit Supreme Laced with Champagne and Served from a Punch Bowl
Chicken Filled Crêpes
Thin Slices of *London Broil*
Sautéed Fresh Mushroom Caps
Corn Filled Peppers
Harvard Beets
Tray of Marinated Vegetables with Curried Mayonnaise
Assorted Hot Breads
Mocha Bavarian Crème

Orange Cocktail au Rhum
Hot Oysters en Ramekin
Turkey Stuffed Ham Rolls
Polynesian Pepper Steak
Rice Pilaf
Brussels Sprouts with Nutmeg
Carrots Vichy
Garden Green Salad
with Assorted Dressings,
Garlic Croutons and Crumbled Bacon
Cranberry Muffins
Crisp *Herb Melba Toast*
Butter
Chocolate Rum Trifle with Whipped Cream

DINNERS AT EIGHT

Compote of *Fresh Fruit Supreme* with Lime
Fresh Mushroom Bisque
Tenderloin of Beef Madeira
Zesty Cheese Potatoes
French Style Green Peas
Tarragon Tossed Salad with Artichoke Hearts
Assorted Hot Breads—Butter Balls
Brandy Alexander Parfait
Demitasse

Compote of *Sherried Fresh Fruit*
Lobster Thermidor
Buttered Green Peas with Water Chestnuts
Catalina Salad Bowl with White French Dressing
Crusty *Buttered French Bread*
Minted Chocolate Cake

Kemma Curry of Lobster
Fluffy Rice
Apple Chutney
Shredded Coconut
Chopped Peanuts
Bacon Crumbles
Chopped Chives
White Raisins
Diced Hard-Cooked Egg
Sour Cream Slaw with Shredded Onions
Cardamom Bread
Sugared Fresh Pineapple Slices
Toasted Almond Cookies
Darjeeling Tea

Quiche Lorraine
Short Ribs of Beef in Yorkshire Pudding
Spinach Soufflé
Baked Chili Onions
Hearts of Lettuce with *Bleu Cheese Dressing*
Orange Nut Rolls
French Crumb Trifle

French Onion Soup au Gratin
Baked Stuffed Trout with Lemon
Potatoes Hashed in Cream
Herb Broiled Tomatoes
Mixed Green Salad
Parker House Rolls
Frosted Daiquiri Pie
Demitasse

LATE SUPPERS

Beef Hash Rounds with Tomato Slices and Mushroom Caps
Bibb Lettuce with White French Dressing
Fresh Fruit Grenadine

Polynesian Sweet Sour Pork
Fluffy Rice
Broiled Tomato Halves
Herb Buttered Bread
Champagne Sherbet

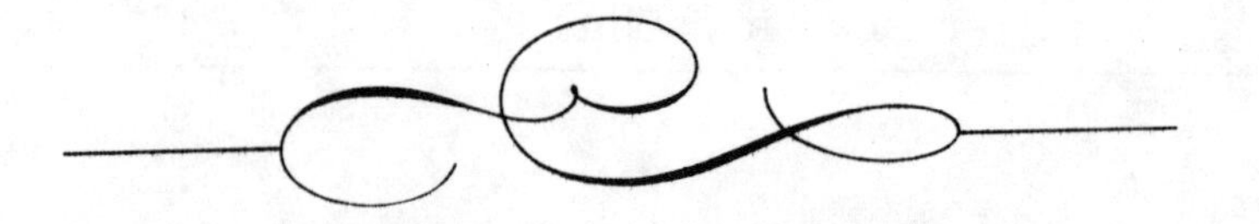

FOR FAMILY OCCASIONS AND HOLIDAYS

HEARTY LUNCHEONS

Lancaster Chicken Corn Soup
Heidelberg Open Club Sandwich
Crisp Potato Chips
Dutch Apple Pie
Coffee

A Mug of Steaming *Old-Fashioned Navy Bean Soup*
Monaco Grill Sandwich
Dill Pickle Spears
Black Bottom Pie
Coffee

SATURDAY LUNCH

Cream of Tomato Soup
Reuben Grill Sandwich
Hot Dutch Potato Salad
Fresh Fruit

A FAMILY DINNER

Frosted Cranberry Shrub
Baked Chicken and Biscuit
Herb Buttered Green Beans
Pumpkin Muffins
Wellesley Fudge Cake

AN EASTER BRUNCH

Minted Grapefruit Cocktail
Eggs à la Goldenrod with Fresh Asparagus Spears
Frizzled Ham
Southern Orange Rolls
Coffee

MOTHER'S DAY DINNER

Frosty Vegetable Juice
Baked Breast of Chicken and Grape Casserole
Bouquet of Buttered Fresh Vegetables
Green Salad with Russian Dressing
Nut Muffins with Whipped Butter
Lemon Angel Pie

A FALL FAMILY DINNER

Harvest Macaroni and Beef
Buttered Green Beans
Escalloped Apples
Tossed Salad Deluxe
Sesame Bread Sticks
Apple Walnut Upside-Down Pie

THE FOURTH OF JULY

Bouillon on the Rocks with Lime Wedge
Sesame Fried Chicken
Fresh Corn on the Cob
Spinach Mushroom Casserole
Thick Slices of Tomato, Green Pepper Strips and Cucumber Wedges
Buttermilk Biscuits with Honey Butter
Peach Melba 'n Cream Pie

LABOR DAY

Turkey Chowder
Charcoal Broiled Beef Tenderloin en Brochettes
Rice Pilaf
Zucchini Milano
Garden Relishes and Pickled Beets
Bleu Cheese Bread
Sunshine Peach Cream Cake

FOR THANKSGIVING DAY

Orange Tomato Bouillon
Roast Tom Turkey with *Celery Dressing* and Gravy
Creamy Whipped Potatoes
Brussels Sprouts au Gratin
Harvest Escalloped Apples
Bread and Butter Pickles
Individual Jellied Cranberry Salads on Beds of Leaf Lettuce
Rum Raisin Rolls
Sweet Butter
Williamsburg Orange Wine Cake
Demitasse
Mint Wafers
Salted Nuts

A CHRISTMAS FEAST

Herring in Sour Cream
Hot Sherried Consommé
Roast Goose with Chestnut Stuffing
Apple-Filled Sweet Potato Nests
Creamed Pearl Onions
Spinach Soufflé
Orange Baskets Filled with Fresh Fruit
Celery Seed Dressing
Watermelon Pickles, Marinated Artichoke Hearts and Tomato Conserve
Hot Buttered Rolls
Ice Cream Snowballs with Brandied Mincemeat Sauce Flambé
Demitasse

IT'S NEW YEAR'S EVE

Sparkling Burgundy Punch
Sliced Baked Ham Served with Parker House Rolls
Individual *Spinach Quiches*
Burgundy Beef Balls
Mushroom Rarebit with *Melba Toast*
Smoked Oysters on Party Rye
Chicken Liver Pâté with Crackers
Horseradish Cream Cheese Dip
Chips for Dipping
Cheddar Cheese Nut Ball with Port Wine
Assorted Wafers
Tray of Nibbles (olives, pickles, fresh
cauliflower bits, radishes, cherry tomatoes)
Warm Brandied Fruit Cake
Coffee

LATE SUPPERS FOR THE TWO OF YOU

Eggs Benedict
Broiled Peaches with Toasted Almonds
Baba au Rhum Parfait
Coffee

Sherried Rarebit Open Face Sandwich
Herb Buttered Zucchini
Escalloped Apple-Berry Relish
Coconut Lemon Cake

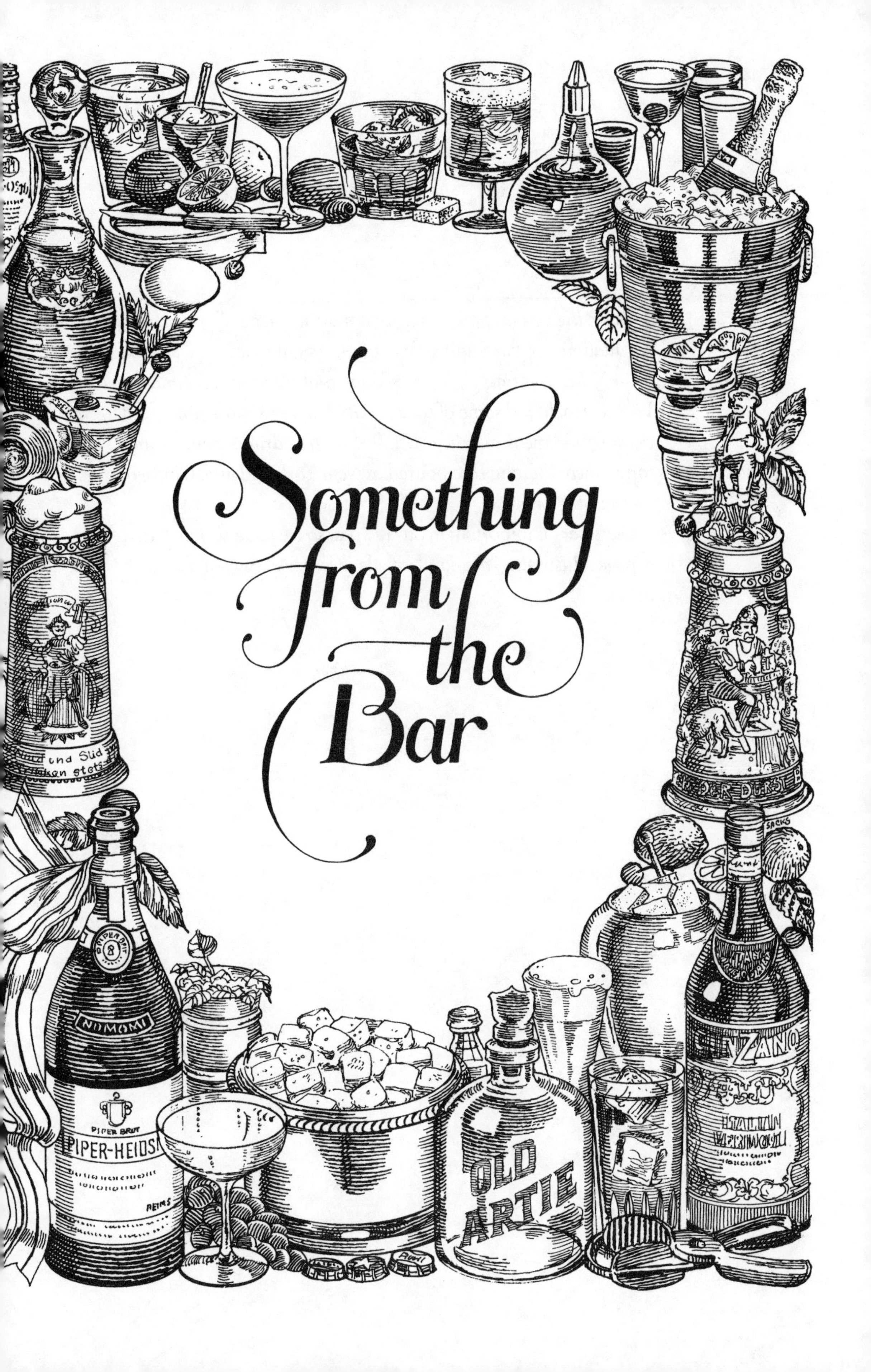

Something from the Bar

From the day we poured our first martini we developed a reputation for bartending. We think anyone can mix a good drink if he uses fine ingredients and combines them accurately. We have included some of the best tips from our bartenders, and because we measure every drink, Stouffer drinks have a uniformity whether they are poured in New York, Atlanta, Chicago, or any other town.

Glassware is important in our recipes, so we have also included a page illustrating the kind of glassware we suggest for each drink.

GLASSWARE

Mariner's Grog
Shot
Old Fashioned
Brandy Inhaler
Cloud
Whiskey Sour
Cocktail
Cordial
Claret Wine
Ramos Fizz
Hollow Stem Champagne
Saucer Champagne
Hurricane Sting
Metal Julip Cup
Hot Whiskey
Champagne Cocktail
Collins
Highball
Chimney or Zombie
Glacier Gold

TIPS ON MIXING A GOOD DRINK

CHILL OR HEAT GLASSES: Chill all glasses for iced drinks; heat all glasses or cups for hot drinks. This ensures that proper temperature for drink will be maintained.

USE FINEST INGREDIENTS: Liquor should be the best available. Good drinks demand good ingredients; use only fresh fruit and fruit juices.

MEASURE EXACTLY: Exactness of your blending is essential for a good drink every time.

ORDER OF INGREDIENTS: Ice, sugar or Simple Syrup, fresh fruit juices, spirits and flavoring.

ICE: Be sure that the ice used in the drink is made from distilled water. If ice has certain inpurities or has taken the taste of foods from the refrigerator, it will affect the flavor of the drink. Stouffer's drinks have specially processed ice.

SHAKING OR STIRRING: Shaking makes drinks cloudy; stirring keeps drinks clear.

MIXING A FROZEN DRINK: Use same care as used in mixing a regular drink, but be sure ice is finely shaved (about the size of rice granules). If available, use a blender. Or shake drink slowly 30 seconds and then rapidly for 20 seconds. When straining a drink, do not hold strainer tightly against lip of cup.

Standard Bar Measurements:

1 dash. . . . . 1/6 teaspoon (1/32-ounce)
1 teaspoon (barspoon) . . . . . . 1/8 ounce
1 pony . . . . 1 ounce
1 jigger (barglass) . . . . 1-1/2 ounces
1 wineglass . . . . 4 ounces
1 split. . . . . 6 ounces
1 cup . . . . 8 ounces

SIMPLE SYRUP

Stir 1 pound of granulated sugar into 1 pint of water until sugar dissolves. Bring solution to a boil and continue boiling for 3 minutes. Cool and use as needed. Can be stored in glass jar in refrigerator.

EGG WHITE MIXTURE
(for cocktails)

Combine 1 egg white with 2-1/2 ounces Simple Syrup and beat vigorously.

ACAPULCO

1/2 oz. grenadine
3/4 oz. lemon juice
1/2 oz. curaçao
1/2 oz. brandy
1/2 oz. light rum

Combine above ingredients and shake with cracked ice; strain into a cocktail glass.

ALABAMA

1 level barspoon powdered sugar
1/2 oz. lemon juice
1 oz. brandy
1/8 oz. curaçao

Combine above ingredients and shake with cracked ice; strain into a cocktail glass.

ALEXANDER BRANDY

1 oz. heavy cream
1 oz. brown crème de cacao
1 oz. brandy

Combine above ingredients and shake well with ice cubes and small amount of shaved ice. Strain into a pre-chilled claret glass.

ALEXANDER GIN

Prepare the same as an Alexander Brandy Cocktail, substituting gin for the brandy and using white crème de cacao.

ANGEL'S TIP
(an after-dinner drink)

1/3 cordial glass brown crème de cacao
1/3 cordial glass maraschino liqueur
1/3 cordial glass heavy cream

Hold barspoon close to surface of drink, and in the order given above, pour off back of barspoon so ingredients float on each other.

APRICOT COBBLER

1 level barspoon powdered sugar
3/4 oz. orange juice
3/4 oz. lime juice
1-1/2 oz. apricot brandy

Combine above ingredients and shake with cracked ice. Strain into an 8-ounce highball glass 1/3 full of shaved ice. Finish by filling glass with crushed ice to within 1/2" of top. Decorate with stemmed cherry, 1/2 slice of orange and thin stick of fresh pineapple. Serve with a straw.

APRICOT DELIGHT

1/2 barspoon powdered sugar
1/4 oz. lime juice
1/2 oz. lemon juice
1-1/4 oz. apricot brandy

Combine above ingredients and shake with cracked ice; strain into a whiskey sour glass. Decorate with a stemmed cherry and 1/2 slice of orange.

ARTIST

1/4 oz. Simple Syrup
1/2 oz. lemon juice
1 oz. sherry
1 oz. rye whiskey

Combine above ingredients and shake with cracked ice; strain into a whiskey sour glass.

B & B
(an after-dinner drink)

1/2 cordial glass brandy
1/2 cordial glass Benedictine

Float ingredients off back of barspoon into a cordial glass.

BACARDI

1/3 oz. grenadine
1/2 oz. lime juice
1-1/2 oz. Bacardi Silver Label Rum

Combine above ingredients and shake with cracked ice; strain into a cocktail glass.

BACARDI COLLINS

1 heaping barspoon powdered sugar
1/4 oz. lime juice
1/2 oz. lemon juice
2 oz. Bacardi Amber Rum

Combine above ingredients and shake with cracked ice; strain into a 12-ounce highball glass. Fill with ice cubes and top with soda water. Decorate with a stemmed cherry and 1/2 lime slice.

BACARDI PUNCH

2/3 oz. grenadine
2/3 oz. lemon juice
1 oz. pineapple juice
2 oz. Bacardi Silver Label Rum

Combine above ingredients and shake with cracked ice; strain into a 12-ounce highball glass. Fill glass with crushed ice. Decorate with a stemmed cherry and a lime wedge. Serve with straws.

BALI BALI PUNCH

1 heaping barspoon brown sugar
1 oz. orange juice
1/2 oz. lemon juice
3/4 oz. light rum
3/4 oz. Jamaican rum
1 dash Benedictine

Combine above ingredients and shake with cracked ice; strain into a chimney glass. Fill glass with shaved ice. Slit 1/4 slice of pineapple and hang on glass rim; 1/4" from each side of the pineapple, hang lime slices. Serve with straws.

BANANA DAIQUIRI

1 level barspoon powdered sugar
1/4 oz. lime juice
1/2 oz. crème de bananes
1-1/4 oz. light rum

Combine above ingredients and shake with cracked ice; strain into a cocktail glass.

BANSHEE

1 oz. heavy cream
1 oz. crème de bananes
1 oz. white crème de cacao

Combine above ingredients and shake with cracked ice; strain into a claret glass.

BARKING DOG

2 dashes curaçao
2/3 oz. dry vermouth
2/3 oz. sweet vermouth
2/3 oz. gin

Combine above ingredients and stir with cracked ice; strain into a cocktail glass.

BEE BITE

1 level barspoon granulated sugar
1/2 oz. orange juice
3/8 oz. lime juice
1-1/4 oz. light rum

Combine above ingredients and shake with cracked ice; strain into a cocktail glass.

BERMUDA ROSE

1/4 oz. grenadine
1/3 oz. lemon juice
1/8 oz. apricot brandy
1-1/4 oz. gin

Combine above ingredients and shake with cracked ice; strain into a cocktail glass.

BETWEEN THE SHEETS

1/4 oz. lemon juice
5/8 oz. Cointreau
5/8 oz. brandy
5/8 oz. light rum

Combine above ingredients and shake with cracked ice; strain into a cocktail glass.

BIMINI

3/4 oz. grenadine
1/2 oz. lime juice
1-1/4 oz. Jamaican rum

Combine above ingredients and shake with cracked ice; strain into a cocktail glass.

BLACK ORCHID

1 oz. heavy cream
2/3 oz. white crème de cacao
1 oz. blackberry brandy

Combine above ingredients and shake with cracked ice; strain into a claret glass.

BLACK RUSSIAN

1 oz. Kahlúa
1 oz. vodka

Pour ingredients over ice cubes in an old-fashioned glass. Stir slightly to blend.

BRANDY EGGNOG

1 rounded barspoon powdered sugar
1 whole egg
3 oz. milk
1-1/2 oz. brandy

Combine above ingredients and shake with cracked ice; strain into a Ramos Fizz glass.

BRONX

1 oz. orange juice
1/4 oz. dry vermouth
1/4 oz. sweet vermouth
1/2 oz. gin
1 dash orange flower water

Combine above ingredients and shake with cracked ice; strain into a claret glass.

CARLOTA

1/2 oz. heavy cream
1/4 oz. Kahlúa
1 oz. tequila

Combine above ingredients and shake with cracked ice; strain into a cocktail glass. Sprinkle with nutmeg.

CARLTON COCKTAIL

1/3 oz. lime juice
1/3 oz. curaçao
1-1/4 oz. apricot brandy

Combine above ingredients and shake with cracked ice; strain into a cocktail glass.

CHAMPAGNE COCKTAIL

1 sugar cube
Peychaud bitters (if not available, use Angostura)
4 oz. chilled champagne

Saturate sugar cube with bitters; place in saucer champagne glass and add champagne. Place 1/2 slice of orange against side of glass and directly opposite one thin stick of fresh pineapple for decoration.

CHERRY BLOSSOM

1/4 oz. maraschino cherry juice
1/4 oz. lemon juice
1/2 oz. orange juice
1-1/2 oz. sloe gin

Combine above ingredients and shake with cracked ice; strain into a cocktail glass.

CLARET COBBLER

1 slightly rounded barspoon powdered sugar
2 oz. claret wine

Combine above ingredients and shake with cracked ice; strain into an 8-ounce highball glass which is immersed in shaved ice. Fill glass with shaved ice and stir until outside is well frosted. Remove and decorate with a stemmed cherry, 1/2 slice of orange and one fresh pineapple stick. Add two straws.

NOTE: All cobblers are made the same, substituting desired liquor or wine for the claret.

CLARET LEMONADE

1 oz. Simple Syrup (page 223)
1-1/2 oz. lemon juice
3/4 oz. claret or Burgundy wine

Shake syrup and lemon juice with ice; strain into a 12-ounce highball glass. Fill glass 1/2 full with medium cracked ice, then add plain water to fill to within 3/4″ of the top. Float claret or Burgundy by pouring over back of barspoon held close to surface. Add a lime wedge to drink for decoration.

CLARIDGE PUNCH

1/4 oz. Simple Syrup (page 223)
1/2 oz. lemon juice
1-1/2 oz. orange juice
1/4 oz. light rum
1/4 oz. Jamaican rum
1-1/2 oz. brandy

Combine above ingredients and shake with cracked ice; strain into a 12-ounce highball glass. Fill with finely cracked ice; serve with straws.

CLIPPER

1 level barspoon granulated sugar
1/3 oz. lime juice
1/2 oz. orange juice
1 oz. light rum

Combine above ingredients and shake with cracked ice; strain into a cocktail glass. Garnish with four sprigs of fresh mint.

CLOUD 666

1 heaping barspoon sugar (extra fine)
3/8 oz. coffee cream
1/4 oz. lime juice
1/2 oz. lemon juice
1-1/4 oz. gin
1-1/2 oz. light rum

Combine above ingredients and shake well with ice cubes only. Strain into a Cloud 666 glass or saucer champagne glass. Mix only one drink at a time and pour fully.

CLOVER CLUB

2/3 oz. grenadine
1/2 oz. lemon juice
1/4 oz. heavy cream
1/2 egg white
1 oz. gin
1 small dash orange flower water

Combine above ingredients and shake well with cracked ice; strain into a claret glass.

CLOVER LEAF

Prepare the same as a Clover Club Cocktail and then place a small spring of mint on top of the drink.

COFFEE COCKTAIL

1 small rounded barspoon powdered sugar
1 whole egg
1/2 oz. brandy
1 oz. port wine

Combine above ingredients and shake well with cracked ice; strain into a Hot Whiskey glass.

COLTON PUNCH

1/2 oz. lime juice
1 oz. curaçao
1 oz. apricot brandy

Combine above ingredients and shake with cracked ice; strain into a Hot Whiskey glass. Decorate with 1/2 slice orange, one cube pineapple and one stemmed cherry.

CONTINENTAL

1/4 oz. grenadine
5/8 oz. dry vermouth
1-1/4 oz. light rum

Combine above ingredients and stir with cracked ice; strain into a cocktail glass. Decorate with a lemon peel.

CUBA LIBRE

1/2 oz. lime juice
1-1/4 oz. light rum

Fill a highball glass 2/3 full with shaved ice and pour ingredients over ice. Fill with cola and garnish with a lime wedge.

DAIQUIRI

1 level barspoon powdered sugar
1/2 oz. lime juice
1-1/2 oz. light rum

Combine above ingredients and shake with cracked ice; strain into a cocktail glass.

DARBY SOUR

1 rounded barspoon powdered sugar
1/2 oz. lime juice
1/2 oz. grapefruit juice
1-1/2 oz. gin

Combine above ingredients and shake with cracked ice; strain into a whiskey sour glass. Top with small amount of soda water and decorate with red or green cherry.

DIXIE SOUR

1/2 oz. raspberry syrup
1/4 oz. lime juice
1/2 oz. lemon juice
1-1/4 oz. whiskey

Combine above ingredients and shake with cracked ice; strain into a whiskey sour glass. Top with small amount of soda water and decorate with a stemmed cherry.

NOTE: Brandy, gin, rum, or vodka may be substituted for the whiskey.

DORSET

1/3 oz. lemon juice
1/3 oz. cherry brandy
1/4 oz. Benedictine
1-1/4 oz. gin

Combine above ingredients and shake with cracked ice; strain into a cocktail glass.

DUBONNET COCKTAIL

1 oz. Dubonnet **1 oz. gin**

Combine above ingredients and stir with cracked ice in mixing glass; strain into a cocktail glass. Twist lemon peel and drop into glass for decoration.

EGGNOG

1 rounded barspoon powdered sugar
1 whole egg
3 oz. milk
1-1/2 oz. bourbon whiskey

Start with sugar and egg in mixing glass; mix well. Next, put in milk, and 3 or 4 cubes of ice; finally add whiskey. Shake and strain into a Ramos Fizz glass. Dust with fresh nutmeg.

NOTE: Variations of this drink can be made substituting brandy, liqueurs, rum, Scotch or wines for the bourbon whiskey.

FLAMINGO PUNCH

1/2 oz. grenadine
3/4 oz. orange juice
1/4 oz. lime juice
1/2 oz. lemon juice
1/2 oz. curaçao
2 oz. light rum

Combine above ingredients and shake with cracked ice; strain into a 12-ounce highball glass. Frost glass, add shaved ice and decorate with 1/2 slice orange, a stemmed cherry, and a fresh pineapple stick. Serve with straws.

FLEETWOOD

1/3 oz. raspberry syrup
1/3 oz. lime juice
2/3 oz. light rum
2/3 oz. apple jack
4 or 5 drops anisette

Combine about ingredients and shake with cracked ice; strain into a cocktail glass.

FLORADORA

1/2 oz. strawberry syrup
1/2 oz. lemon juice
1-1/2 oz. bourbon whiskey

Combine above ingredients and shake with cracked ice; strain into a cocktail glass.

FRENCH "75"

1 heaping barspoon powdered sugar
2/3 oz. lemon juice
1-1/2 oz. gin
3 oz. chilled champagne

Combine above ingredients *except* the champagne, and shake with cracked ice; strain into a 12-ounce highball glass in which a few ice cubes have been placed. Fill glass with the chilled champagne. Gently force ice cubes down once or twice to aid in blending the champagne. *Do not stir*, or the champagne will lose its effervescence.

FRISCO COLLINS

1 rounded barspoon powdered sugar
1 oz. raspberry syrup
1 oz. lemon juice
1-1/2 oz. gin

Combine above ingredients and shake with cracked ice; strain into a 12-ounce highball glass. Add a few ice cubes; fill with soda water. Decorate with a stemmed cherry and a lime slice.

GANDY

1/4 oz. grenadine
1/4 oz. lemon juice
1/4 oz. orange juice
1/2 oz. triple sec
1 oz. light rum

Combine above ingredients and shake with cracked ice for a few seconds; strain into a cocktail glass.

GEORGIA

2/3 oz. lemon juice
2/3 oz. peach brandy
2/3 oz. rye whiskey

Combine above ingredients and shake with cracked ice; strain into a cocktail glass.

GIBSON

1/3 oz. dry vermouth
1-2/3 oz. gin
1/2 dash Scotch whisky

Pour ingredients into a mixing glass containing ice cubes. Stir to blend; strain into a pre-chilled cocktail glass. Twist a lemon peel for oil on surface of drink and decorate with three large size pickled onions. Be sure to rinse onions in clear water before placing them in the drink.

GILFORD

5/8 oz. dry vermouth
1/3 oz. triple sec
1-1/8 oz. brandy

Combine above ingredients and stir with cracked ice; strain into a cocktail glass. Decorate with a stemmed cherry.

GIMLET

1/3 oz. lime juice
1-1/2 oz. gin or vodka

Combine above ingredients and shake with cracked ice. Place 3 or 4 pieces of ice (about 1/3 the size of an ice cube) into a saucer champagne glass; strain liquid into glass and float a full slice of lime on top.

NOTE: See page 256 for Rose's Gimlet recipe.

GIN DAISY

1/2 barspoon powdered sugar
1/4 oz. raspberry syrup
1/2 oz. lime juice
1/3 oz. blackberry brandy
1-1/4 oz. gin

Combine above ingredients and shake with cracked ice; strain into a Ramos Fizz glass. Add cubed or cracked ice, and decorate with 1/2 slice orange and a stemmed cherry.

NOTE: You can use whiskey, sherry, port, madeira, apple jack, brandy or rum as substitutes for the gin.

GIN FIZZ

1 rounded barspoon powdered sugar
1 oz. lemon juice
2 oz. gin

Combine above ingredients and shake thoroughly with cracked ice; strain into a Ramos Fizz glass. Fill with chilled soda water.

GIN RICKEY

1/2 oz. lime juice
2 oz. gin

Pour ingredients into a 12-ounce highball glass. Add enough fine ice to cover the bottom of the glass. Put in 3 medium ice cubes, fill to within 1/2″ of rim with soda water. Push barspoon up and down several times to mix; *do not stir*. Decorate with 1/4 lime, slightly squeezed.

NOTE: You can use whiskey, brandy, rum, Scotch or sloe gin as substitutes for the gin.

GIN AND TONIC

1-1/2 oz. gin
3 to 3-1/3 oz. tonic water

Fill a 10-ounce highball glass with ice cubes. Add gin and fill the remainder of the glass with tonic water. Squeeze gently 1/4 small lime, then drop it into glass to decorate. Gently agitate the ice cubes to mix. If drink is stirred too vigorously, the effervescence will be lost.

GLACIER GOLD

1/4 oz. Simple Syrup (page 223)
1/2 oz. triple sec
1/3 oz. lemon juice
1/4 oz. lime juice
1/4 oz. orange juice
1-1/8 oz. amber rum

Mound shaved ice up on one side of a saucer champagne glass. Gently press an orange against the mound of ice, compressing and forcing the ice up the side of the glass to form a crescent shape which will extend 1-1/2 inches above the rim of the glass. Remove orange. Combine above ingredients and shake with cracked ice; strain into prepared glass.

GOLDEN CADILLAC

1 oz. heavy cream
1 oz. white crème de cacao
1 oz. Galliano

Combine above ingredients and shake with cracked ice; strain into a saucer champagne glass.

GOLDEN DREAM

1/2 oz. orange juice
1/2 oz. heavy cream
1/2 oz. Cointreau
1 oz. Galliano

Combine above ingredients and shake with ice cubes; strain into a claret glass.

GOLDEN FIZZ

Prepare the same as a Gin Fizz (see page 240), but add one egg yolk.

GRASSHOPPER

1 oz. heavy cream
1 oz. white crème de cacao
1 oz. green crème de menthe

Combine above ingredients and shake well with ice cubes and small amount of shaved ice; strain into a claret glass.

GREEN DRAGON

1/2 barspoon powdered sugar
1 oz. lemon juice
1 oz. O-Cha
1 oz. vodka

Combine above ingredients and shake with cracked ice; strain into a Zombie glass filled with shaved ice. Garnish with a lime slice and a paper parasol. Serve with straws.

NOTE: O-Cha is a green Japanese liqueur with the aroma and taste of fresh green tea.

HARVEY WALLBANGER

1 oz. vodka
3/4 oz. Galliano

Fill a highball glass 3/4 full with orange juice and ice cubes. Add the vodka and stir. Float Galliano on top.

HILTY DILTY

1/4 oz. grenadine
1/2 oz. lime juice
1-1/2 oz. apricot brandy

Combine above ingredients and shake with cracked ice; strain into a cocktail glass.

HORNET

1 oz. white crême de menthe
1 oz. Scotch whisky

Combine above ingredients and shake with cracked ice; strain into a cocktail glass.

HOT BUTTERED RUM

1/2 oz. maple syrup
1/3 oz. lemon juice
1 oz. Jamaican rum
1/2 teaspoon butter

Pour boiling water into a Hot Whiskey glass, and rinse to heat glass thoroughly. Pour in ingredients, and fill balance of glass with hot water. Put 1/2 teaspoon butter on top.

HURRICANE PUNCH

1 barspoon powdered sugar
1/2 oz. lime juice
3/4 oz. Pa-Pi-A Nectar
3/4 oz. fresh pineapple juice
1/3 oz. apricot brandy
3 oz. amber rum

Combine above ingredients into a blender or shake vigorously with cracked ice. Pour into a chimney glass. Decorate with slice of lime and a stemmed cherry through which 3 colored picks have been placed making a spoke effect. Place on top of drink with several picks sticking into the ice. Serve with straws.

HURRICANE SLING

1 level barspoon powdered sugar
1/2 oz. lime juice
1/2 oz. lemon juice
1/2 oz. pineapple juice (sweetened)
1/4 oz. apricot brandy
1/2 oz. amber rum
1-1/2 oz. light rum
6 drops almond extract

Combine above ingredients and shake with cracked ice; strain into a Hurricane Sling glass. Insert a large straw decorated with 3 cherries and 2 squares of fresh pineapple.

IRISH COFFEE

3/4 glass hot coffee
3 sugar cubes
3/4 oz. Irish whiskey

Preheat the Hot Whiskey glass in very hot water and let stand for a few seconds, then empty. Immediately fill the glass with coffee, drop in sugar and stir until dissolved. Add the whiskey and top with slightly whipped heavy cream poured over a spoon.

IRISH ROSE

2/3 oz. grenadine
1/2 oz. lemon juice
1/2 egg white
1/8 oz. heavy cream
1/4 oz. apple jack
3/4 oz. gin

Fill the stem of a hollow-stem champagne glass with green crème de menthe. Stop stem with red or green cherry. Combine the above ingredients and shake vigorously with cracked ice; strain into the prepared glass.

JACK ROSE

1/4 oz. grenadine
1/2 oz. lemon juice
1-1/4 oz. apple jack

Combine above ingredients and shake with cracked ice; strain into a cocktail glass.

JACK ROSE (frozen)

1/2 oz. grenadine
1/2 oz. lemon juice
1-1/4 oz. apple jack

Combine ingredients as shown on page 222 for making frozen drinks. Serve in a saucer champagne glass.

JAMAICA COLLINS

1 heaping barspoon powdered sugar
1/4 oz. lime juice
1/2 oz. lemon juice
2 oz. Jamaican rum

Combine above ingredients and shake with cracked ice; strain into a 12-ounce highball glass with ice cubes. Fill with soda water. Decorate with a stemmed cherry and a lime wedge.

KENTUCKY LADY

1 oz. grenadine
1/4 oz. lemon juice
2 oz. orange juice
1 oz. bourbon whiskey

Combine above ingredients and shake with cracked ice; strain into a Ramos Fizz glass filled with shaved ice. Serve with short straws.

KING GEORGE

3/4 oz. Kahlúa
Dash of heavy cream

Pour Kahlúa into a cordial glass and float a small amount of cream on top. Garnish with a stemmed cherry.

MAI TAI

1/2 oz. Simple Syrup (page 223)
1 oz. lime juice
1/2 oz. curaçao
1 oz. light rum
1 oz. amber rum

Pack a Mariner's Grog glass with shaved ice and add above ingredients. Do not mix. Top with: 1/4 oz. Jamaican rum and 1/4 oz. 151-proof rum. Garnish with a lime wedge, stick of fresh pineapple, and a stemmed cherry.

MAJOR BAILEY COBBLER

Mint leaves and sprigs
5/8 oz. Simple Syrup (page 223)
1/4 oz. lime juice
1/3 oz. lemon juice
2 oz. gin

Start with an 8-ounce old-fashioned glass. Put in 12 mint leaves and all the other ingredients. Muddle, then strain into a 12-ounce highball glass which has been set in crushed ice for frosting. After drink has been poured, stir until outside is frosted with ice particles. Place one sprig of mint in center of glass; fill glass with shaved ice. Place another sprig of mint, whose leaves have been touched in powdered sugar, in glass next to rim as the decoration. Place glass on a plate along with two straws.

MANHATTAN

5/8 oz. sweet vermouth
1-1/4 oz. bourbon whiskey
1 or 2 drops Angostura bitters

Combine above ingredients in mixing glass containing several ice cubes. Stir to blend and strain into a cocktail glass. Decorate with a stemmed cherry.

MANHATTAN CANADIAN

3/4 oz. sweet vermouth
1-1/2 oz. 90.4-proof Canadian whiskey
3 to 7 drops Angostura bitters

Follow the same instructions as for a regular Manhattan.

NOTE: For a sweet Manhattan, add a dash of Simple Syrup to either recipe.

MANHATTAN (dry)

5/8 oz. dry vermouth
1-1/4 oz. bourbon whiskey
1/2 dash (or about 6 drops) orange bitters

Combine above ingredients and stir with cracked ice; strain into a cocktail glass. Add twist of lemon peel or large olive.

MARGARITA

1-1/2 oz. Simple Syrup/Egg White Mixture (page 223)
1/2 oz. lime juice
1/4 oz. triple sec
1-1/4 oz. tequila

Prepare a brandy snifter by rubbing rim of the glass with a lime wedge, then dipping rim into salt. Do not allow more than 1/16″ of salt to form on rim. Combine above ingredients and shake with cracked ice; strain into the prepared glass.

MARIETTA

1/5 oz. Simple Syrup (page 223)
1/5 oz. cherry brandy
1/4 oz. dry vermouth
1-1/4 oz. rye whiskey
1 drop pernod or anisette

Combine above ingredients and stir with cracked ice; strain into a cocktail glass.

MARINER'S GROG

1-1/2 oz. grenadine
1/2 oz. lime juice
1-1/2 oz. lemon juice
1 oz. orange juice
1-1/2 oz. Jamaican rum
1-1/2 oz. amber rum

Prepare a Mariner's Grog or double old-fashioned glass by rubbing the rim of the glass with a lime wedge and dipping rim into powdered sugar. Fill glass with ice cubes. Combine above ingredients and shake with cracked ice; strain into the prepared glass. Skewer 2 cherries on a straw and place in glass.

MARTINI

1/3 oz. dry vermouth
1-2/3 oz. gin
1/2 dash Scotch whisky

Combine above ingredients in mixing glass containing ice cubes. Stir to blend; strain into a prechilled cocktail glass. Gently twist lemon peel for oil on surface of drink. Decorate with large olive.

MARTINI (4 to 1)

3/8 oz. dry vermouth
1-1/2 oz. gin
1/2 dash Scotch whisky

Follow the same instructions as for a regular Martini.

MARTINI (3 to 1)

1/2 oz. dry vermouth
1-1/2 oz. gin
1/2 dash Scotch whisky

Follow the same instructions as for a regular Martini (page 249).

MINT FREEZE

1 heaping barspoon powdered sugar
1/2 oz. lime juice
1/2 oz. green crème de menthe
1-1/4 oz. light rum
Mint leaves

Use a blender and add whole mint leaves. Follow directions for preparing a frozen drink on page 222. Serve in a saucer champagne glass.

MINT JULEP

Mint leaves and sprigs
3/4 oz. Simple Syrup (page 223)
3 oz. bourbon whiskey

Muddle 10 mint leaves in the bottom of a julep cup; add shaved ice until cup is half full. Add another layer of 10 muddled mint leaves and fill remainder of cup with shaved ice. Take 5 or 6 sprigs of mint (cut ends so they will bend) and form into a bouquet. Dip tip of bouquet in powdered sugar, and place at one side of cup. Mound shaved ice over top of cup. Put two straws on opposite sides. Cut straws to stick 1″ above the cup. Pour ingredients into a mixing glass; stir until thoroughly blended, then pour slowly into the prepared julep cup. Complete mounding of ice over the top.

MORNING ROSE

1/2 oz. grenadine
1/2 oz. lemon juice
3/4 oz. light rum
3/4 oz. triple sec

Combine above ingredients and shake with cracked ice; strain into a claret glass.

NEW ORLEANS FIZZ

1-1/2 heaping barspoons powdered sugar
1 oz. lemon juice
1 oz. heavy cream
1 egg white
1-1/2 oz. gin
1 small dash vanilla extract
3 dashes orange flower water

Combine above ingredients. Wrap shaker in a towel and shake with a few ice cubes and a small amount of shaved ice for a full 3 minutes in long easy shakes. Take a Ramos Fizz glass which has been prechilled and drop in one dash of orange flower water. Roll it around inside the glass and drain out the surplus. Strain drink into the prepared glass.

NEW ORLEANS WHISKEY COCKTAIL

1/4 oz. pernod or anisette
1/4 oz. Simple Syrup (page 223)
1/4 oz. water
1/4 oz. Jamaican rum
1-1/2 oz. rye whiskey
2 dashes Peychaud bitters

Put pernod or anisette into an 8-ounce old-fashioned glass, roll, pour out. Add above ingredients, one ice cube, one twisted lemon peel and stir.

OH JOHNNY

1/4 oz. maple syrup
1/4 oz. lime juice
3/4 oz. grapefruit juice
1-1/4 oz. apple jack

Combine above ingredients and shake with cracked ice; strain into a cocktail glass.

OLD-FASHIONED

1 piece of lump sugar
1 small dash orange bitters
1 small dash Angostura bitters
1 small dash Peychaud bitters
1 oz. water
1-1/2 oz. bourbon whiskey

Muddle together all the ingredients *except* the whiskey, in an 8-ounce old-fashioned glass with ice cubes. Decorate with one stick of fresh pineapple, 1/2 slice of orange, one piece lemon peel, one stemmed cherry and add one dash curaçao. Then add the whiskey.

ORANGE BLOSSOM

1 oz. orange juice
1 oz. gin
1 dash orange flower water

Moisten rim of a claret glass by rubbing with a piece of orange, then dip rim into powdered sugar to get frosted effect. Combine ingredients and shake with ice; strain into the specially prepared glass.

PINEAPPLE DREAM

1 level barspoon powdered sugar
1/2 oz. lime juice
1/2 oz. pineapple juice
1 oz. light rum

Combine above ingredients and shake with cracked ice; strain into a cocktail glass.

PINE VALLEY

1/3 oz. Simple Syrup (page 223)
1/3 oz. lime juice
1-1/2 oz. gin
4 mint leaves

Combine above ingredients and shake with cracked ice for 10 seconds; just long enough to bruise mint, not cut it up. Strain into a cocktail glass.

PINK LADY

1/2 oz. grenadine
1/2 oz. lemon juice
1/2 egg white
1/4 oz. apple jack
3/4 oz. gin

Combine above ingredients and shake well with cracked ice; strain into a claret glass.

PINK SQUIRREL

1 oz. heavy cream
1 oz. crème de noyaux (almond liqueur)
1 oz. white crème de cacao

Combine above ingredients and shake with ice cubes; strain into a saucer champagne glass.

PLANTATION COCKTAIL

1 level barspoon powdered sugar
1/2 oz. lime juice
1/2 oz. pineapple juice
1 oz. light rum
1 dash curaçao

Combine above ingredients and shake with cracked ice; strain into a cocktail glass. Decorate with a stemmed cherry and a stick of pineapple long enough to come to the rim of glass.

PLANTER'S PUNCH

1 rounded barspoon powdered sugar
1/3 oz. grenadine
1 oz. lemon juice
1/2 oz. port wine
1/4 oz. brandy
1-1/2 oz. Jamaican rum

Combine above ingredients and shake with cracked ice; strain into a 12-ounce highball glass which is filled with shaved ice and is immersed in a bed of finely shaved ice. Leave it there for several minutes after has been poured; stir until the outside is frosted with ice particles. Decorate with pineapple stick, 1/2 slice orange, 1/2 slice lime, and two stemmed cherries. Serve with straws.

PLAYHOUSE SQUARE COCKTAIL

2/3 oz. grenadine
1/2 oz. lemon juice
1/2 egg white
1/4 oz. heavy cream
1/2 oz. apple jack
1 oz. gin

Combine above ingredients and shake with a few ice cubes and small amount of shaved ice; strain into a cocktail glass.

POUSSE CAFÉ
(an after-dinner drink)

Into a cordial glass, pour five different cordials in layers off the back of a barspoon. Start with the heaviest cordials on the bottom and float brandy on top. Suggested cordials to use in order of density: brown crème de cacao, green crème de menthe, crème de noyaux, triple sec, brandy.

ROB ROY

5/8 oz. sweet vermouth
1-1/4 oz. Scotch whisky
1/2 dash Angostura bitters

Combine above ingredients and stir with ice cubes; strain into a cocktail glass. Decorate with a stemmed cherry.

ROB ROY (dry)

5/8 oz. dry vermouth
1-1/4 oz. Scotch whisky
1/2 dash Angostura bitters

Combine above ingredients and stir with ice cubes; strain into a cocktail glass. Garnish with a lemon twist.

ROSE'S GIMLET

1/2 oz. Rose's lime juice
1-1/2 oz. gin or vodka

Combine above ingredients and shake with cracked ice; strain into a saucer champagne glass filled with small pieces of ice. Float a full slice of lime on top.

ROYAL FIZZ

Prepare the same as a Gin Fizz (see page 240), but add one whole egg.

RUM COLLINS

Prepare the same as a Tom Collins (see page 263), substituting amber rum for the gin.

RUSTY NAIL

1 oz. Scotch whisky
1 oz. Drambuie

Combine above ingredients and stir to blend. Pour over ice cubes into an old-fashioned glass.

SAKÉ MARTINI

1/3 oz. saké
1-2/3 oz. gin
1/2 dash Scotch whisky

Combine above ingredients and stir with ice cubes; strain into a cocktail glass. Twist lemon peel for oil on surface of drink and add an olive or lemon twist for decoration.

SARATOGA

3/4 oz. sweet vermouth
3/4 oz. gin
3/4 oz. brandy
1 dash orange bitters

Combine above ingredients and stir with cracked ice; strain into a cocktail glass.

SARATOGA FIZZ

1 heaping barspoon powdered sugar
1/4 oz. lime juice
1/2 oz. lemon juice
1 egg white
1-1/4 oz. bourbon whiskey

Combine above ingredients and shake with cracked ice; pour without straining into a Ramos Fizz glass. Top with small amount of soda water; decorate with a stemmed cherry.

SARATOGA SOUR

1 heaping barspoon powdered sugar
1/4 oz. lime juice
1/2 oz. lemon juice
1 egg white
1-1/4 oz. bourbon whiskey

Combine above ingredients and shake with cracked ice; strain into a whiskey sour glass. Decorate with a stemmed cherry. Top with a small amount of soda water.

SATELLITE

2 oz. gin
1 oz. Galliano

Pour ingredients over ice cubes directly into an old-fashioned glass. Squeeze lime wedge directly into the glass and place in glass as garnish.

SAZARAC

Few drops pernod or anisette
1/2 oz. Simple Syrup (page 223)
1 oz. water
1-1/2 oz. bourbon whiskey
5 drops Peychaud or Angostura bitters

Put pernod or anisette in thoroughly chilled old-fashioned glass. Swirl about in the glass so that the whole interior of glass has been covered with a film. Pour excess out and add other ingredients; place large ice cubes in drink and stir to blend. Squeeze oil of lemon peel on surface and drop peel into the drink.

SCORPION PUNCH

1 barspoon powdered sugar
1/2 oz. lemon juice
1-1/2 oz. orange juice
6 drops almond extract
1 slice fresh pineapple
1 oz. Jamaican rum
1-1/4 oz. light rum

Combine above ingredients and shake vigorously with cracked ice long enough to break the slice of pineapple into small shreds. Pour without straining into a 14-ounce highball glass. Finish filling glass with ice cubes; decorate with fresh pineapple stick, stemmed cherry and a slice of lime.

SCOTCH COCKTAIL (frozen)

1 slightly rounded barspoon powdered sugar
1/2 oz. lime juice
1-1/2 oz. Scotch whisky

Prepare as indicated on page 222 for frozen drinks, and serve in a saucer champagne glass.

SCOTCH MIST

1-1/2 oz. Scotch whisky

Fill a Hot Whiskey glass with finely shaved ice and with the handle of the barspoon create a channel in the ice. Pour in Scotch and insert a short straw.

SCOTCH-ON-THE-ROCKS

1-1/2 oz. Scotch whisky **1/2 to 1 oz. water**

Put three ice cubes into an 8-ounce old-fashioned glass, and pour Scotch over the ice; add water. Fill with cracked ice and add a twist of lemon peel for decoration.

SCOTCH SOUR

Prepare the same as a Whiskey Sour (see page 266), substituting Scotch whisky for the bourbon whiskey.

SHERRY COBBLER

Prepare the same as a Claret Cobbler (see page 231), substituting sherry for the claret.

SHERRY FLIP

1 rounded barspoon powdered sugar **1-1/2 oz. sherry**
1 whole egg

Combine above ingredients and shake very well with cracked ice; strain into a Hot Whiskey glass.

NOTE: Wine, brandy, or other liquor can be substituted for the sherry.

SIDE CAR

1/8 oz. lemon juice
1 oz. triple sec
1 oz. brandy

Rub a piece of lemon around the rim of a cocktail glass. Insert rim in powdered sugar to gain frosted effect. Combine ingredients and shake with ice; strain into the specially prepared glass.

SILVER FIZZ

Prepare the same as a Gin Fizz (see page 240), but add one egg white.

SLOE GIN FIZZ

3/4 oz. Simple Syrup (page 223)
2 oz. lemon juice
2 oz. sloe gin

Combine above ingredients and shake with cracked ice; strain into a Ramos Fizz glass, and top with a small amount of soda water.

SMITHFIELD COCKTAIL

3/8 oz. Simple Syrup (page 223)
1/2 oz. lime juice
3/8 oz. lemon juice
3/8 oz. Cointreau
1-1/4 oz. light rum

Combine above ingredients and shake with cracked ice; strain into a cocktail glass.

SOUTH SEA DIPPER

1 barspoon granulated sugar
1/4 oz. lime juice
1/4 oz. pineapple juice
1-1/2 oz. light rum

Combine above ingredients and shake with medium-size pieces of cracked ice. Pour ingredients, without straining, into an 8-ounce old-fashioned glass. Fill glass with cracked ice. Decorate with slice of lime placed over edge of glass, one pineapple stick, and a stemmed cherry.

SPHINX

1 scant barspoon powdered sugar
1/2 oz. maraschino cherry juice
1/2 oz. lemon juice
1/2 oz. grapefruit juice
1-1/2 oz. light rum

Combine above ingredients and shake with cracked ice; strain into a cocktail glass.

STINGER

1 oz. white crème de menthe
1 oz. brandy

Combine above ingredients and shake with cracked ice; strain into a cocktail glass.

STOUFFER'S FROZEN COCKTAIL

1/2 oz. Simple Syrup (page 223)
1/2 oz. lemon juice
2/3 oz. Cointreau
2/3 oz. light rum

Prepare drink as indicated on page 222 for frozen drinks. Serve in a saucer champagne glass, and garnish with a fresh strawberry and a mint leaf or two.

SUNRISE

3/8 oz. lemon juice
1/2 oz. triple sec
1/2 oz. benedictine
1 oz. light rum

Combine above ingredients and shake with cracked ice; strain into a cocktail glass.

TOM COLLINS

1 heaping barspoon powdered sugar
1/4 oz. lime juice
1/2 oz. lemon juice
1-1/2 oz. gin

Combine above ingredients and shake with cracked ice; strain into a 12-ounce highball glass with ice cubes. Fill with soda water and decorate with a stemmed cherry and a lime wedge.

TOM AND JERRY

3 tablespoons batter (below)
1/2 oz. brandy
1/2 oz. Jamaican rum
Hot milk

Place three tablespoons of batter in each hot Tom and Jerry Cup, then add brandy and rum. Fill remainder of cup with hot milk, just below boiling point. When pouring hot milk, keep stirring with glass rod to mix well. Grate fresh nutmeg sparingly on top of drink.

Batter: (makes 18 servings)
6 egg whites
3/4 cup granulated sugar
6 egg yolks
1 pinch cinnamon
1 pinch ground cloves
1 dash vanilla extract
2 pinches salt

Use an electric mixer at medium speed; beat egg whites; then add sugar. After sugar is beaten in, add yolks, spices, vanilla extract, then salt. Beat batter for 10 minutes until a heavy consistency has been obtained.

VELVET HAMMER

1 oz. heavy cream
1 oz. white crème de cacao
1 oz. triple sec

Combine above ingredients and shake with ice cubes; strain into a claret glass.

VERMOUTH CASSIS

1 oz. crème de cassis
2 oz. dry vermouth

Combine above ingredients and 4 or 5 ice cubes in a 12-ounce highball glass. Stir like a martini and top with soda water. There should be enough ice in drink so that 2-1/2 oz. of soda water are added.

VERMOUTH AND SODA

Pour 2 ounces of dry vermouth into an 8-ounch highball glass and add 2 large ice cubes. Fill with soda water.

VODKA COLLINS

Prepare the same as a Tom Collins (see page 263), substituting vodka for the gin.

VODKA MARTINI

Prepare the same as a regular Martini (see page 249), substituting vodka for the gin.

VODKA SOUR

Prepare the same as a Whiskey Sour (see page 266), substituting vodka for the whiskey.

VODKA AND TONIC

Prepare the same as a Gin and Tonic (see page 240), substituting vodka for the gin.

WARD EIGHT

1 level barspoon powdered sugar
1/3 oz. grenadine
1/4 oz. lime juice
1/2 oz. lemon juice
1-1/2 oz. bourbon whiskey

Combine above ingredients and shake with cracked ice; strain into a Ramos Fizz glass which is 2/3 full of cracked ice. Serve with straws.

WHISKEY MILK PUNCH

1 rounded barspoon powdered sugar
6 oz. milk
1-1/2 oz. 100-proof rye or bourbon whiskey

Combine above ingredients and shake with ice; strain into a 12-ounce highball glass. Top with nutmeg.

WHISKEY SOUR

1 heaping barspoon powdered sugar
1/4 oz. lime juice
1/2 oz. lemon juice
1-1/2 oz. bourbon whiskey

Combine above ingredients and shake with cracked ice; strain into a whiskey sour glass. Decorate with a stemmed cherry and top with a small amount of soda water.

WHITE CHRISTMAS

1 teaspoon granulated sugar
2-1/2 oz. coffee cream
1/2 oz. brandy
1-1/4 oz. light rum

Combine above ingredients and shake well with cracked ice; strain into a Ramos Fizz glass. Sprinkle with nutmeg.

WHITE LADY

1/4 barspoon powdered sugar
1/2 oz. Simple Syrup (page 223)
1/3 oz. lemon juice
1/4 oz. heavy cream
1/2 egg white
1 dash orange flower water
1-1/4 oz. gin

Combine above ingredients and shake with cracked ice; strain into a claret glass.

WHITE MINK

1 oz. white crème de menthe
1 oz. white crème de cacao
1/8 oz. brandy

Combine above ingredients and shake with cracked ice; strain into a cocktail glass.

WHITE RUSSIAN

1/4 oz. heavy cream
1 oz. white crème de cacao
1 oz. vodka

Combine above ingredients and shake with cracked ice; strain into an old-fashioned glass filled with ice cubes.

WHITE SPIDER

1 oz. white crème de menthe
1 oz. vodka

Combine above ingredients and shake with cracked ice; strain into a cocktail glass.

YELLOW GIRAFFE

3/4 oz. white crème de menthe
3/4 oz. Galliano
3/4 oz. vodka

Combine above ingredients and shake with cracked ice; strain into a cocktail glass.

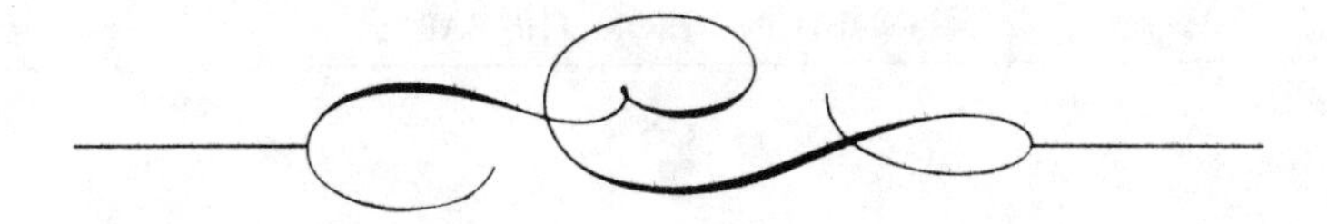

PICK-ME-UPS

Here are some drinks that are rejuvenators for that "morning after" feeling.

BLACK VELVET

2 oz. chilled stout
4 oz. chilled champagne

Tip glass and pour liquid down the side of a 12-ounce highball glass to prevent needless carbonation. Blend the two ingredients together by gently pushing ice cubes to bottom of glass two or three times. For a slightly heavier drink, use equal parts of stout and champagne.

BLOODY MARY

Dash each salt and pepper
1/2 teaspoon Worcestershire sauce
1 drop Tabasco
1/3 oz. lemon juice
1-1/2 oz. vodka
Tomato juice to fill glass

Combine above ingredients directly into an 8-ounce old-fashioned glass filled with ice cubes. Stir slightly to blend. Decorate with lime wedge on rim of glass.

NOTE: Tomato juice is added to the drink last.

BULLSHOT

1/3 oz. lemon juice
3 oz. beef consommé
1-1/4 oz. vodka
1/2 teaspoon Worcestershire sauce
Dash each salt and pepper

Combine above ingredients into a highball glass; add ice cubes and stir to blend.

GOLDEN FIZZ

See recipe on page 241.

PRAIRIE OYSTER

1 whole egg
Dash Worcestershire sauce
1-1/4 oz. brandy

Crack the egg into an 8-ounce old-fashioned glass; making every attempt to keep the yolk intact. Add dash of Worcestershire sauce and brandy. Stir easily so yolk does not break.

RED SNAPPER

1/3 oz. lemon juice
1-1/2 oz. gin
1/2 teaspoon Worcestershire sauce
Dash each salt and pepper
Tomato juice to fill glass

Put all the above ingredients directly into an 8-ounce old-fashioned glass filled with ice cubes. Stir to blend.

SALTY DOG

4 oz. grapefruit juice **1-1/2 oz. vodka**

Prepare an old-fashioned glass by rubbing the rim with a lemon wedge and then dipping the glass in salt. Combine above ingredients and pour over the ice cubes in the prepared glass.

SCREWDRIVER

4 oz. orange juice **1-1/2 oz. vodka**

Combine above ingredients in a highball glass filled with ice cubes. Stir to blend.

WHISKEY MILK PUNCH

See recipe on page 266. If you prefer, substitute brandy for the whiskey.

WHISKEY SOUR

See recipe on page 266.

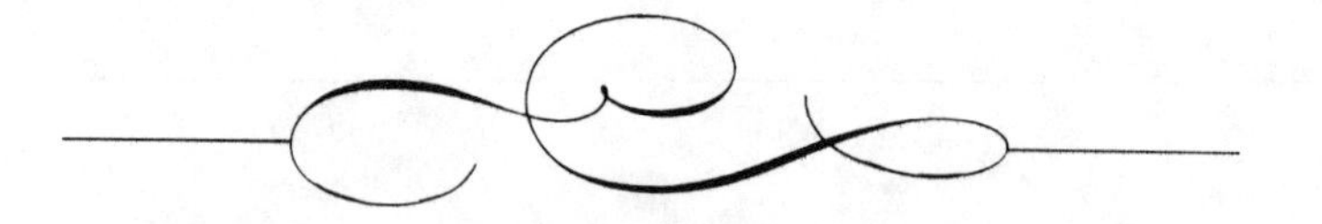

PARTY PUNCH SUGGESTIONS

All punches are based on 1/2-cup servings in a punch cup.

CHAMPAGNE PUNCH
(Serves 50)

2 cups orange juice (fresh or frozen, but strained)
3 cups lemon juice
2 cups pineapple juice (canned, unsweetened)
1/2 cup maraschino cherry juice
Simple Syrup (page 223)
Ice (several large chunks)
1 bottle brandy
4 large bottles chilled champagne

Combine orange, lemon, pineapple and cherry juices; chill thoroughly. Taste and add Simple Syrup, if desired. Pour into punch bowl containing fruit for garnish and chunks of ice. Add brandy and stir to blend. Add chilled champagne.

NOTE: Punch can be diluted with up to 2 quarts of soda water.

EGGNOG
(Serves 24)

9 fresh egg yolks
1/4 teaspoon salt
1/3 cup granulated sugar
1 cup bourbon whiskey
1/4 cup light rum
9 fresh egg whites, room temperature
3 cups milk
1 quart coffee cream

Beat egg yolks and salt together until thick and lemon colored. Add sugar gradually and beat thoroughly. Add bourbon gradually, beating it in well. Add rum gradually in the same manner. Beat egg whites until stiff and stir into yolk mixture. Add milk and cream gradually, blending them in well. Chill thoroughly, 2 or 3 hours. Garnish with freshly ground nutmeg.

FRUIT PUNCH

(Serves 32)

1 cup pineapple juice (canned, unsweetened)
4 cups orange juice (fresh or frozen, but strained)
1/2 cup lemon juice (strained)
1/4 cup maraschino cherry juice
1 cup Simple Syrup (page 223)
2 quarts ginger ale (chilled)
2 trays ice cubes (or 1 quart lemon sherbet)

Combine pineapple, orange, lemon and cherry juices with Simple Syrup and chill thoroughly. Just before serving, add ginger ale and ice cubes or sherbet. Garnish with pineapple slices (canned), fresh unpeeled orange, lemon or lime slices, or maraschino cherries. Omit fruit garnish if sherbet is used.

NOTE: Whiskey, rum, gin or other spirits can be added to this fruit punch base if desired. Be sure then to omit sherbet.

KENTUCKY CHAMPAGNE PUNCH

(Serves 32)

1 fifth bourbon whiskey
2 fifths chilled white grape juice
1 quart chilled ginger ale
2 trays ice cubes

Combine bourbon and grape juice; add ginger ale and ice cubes. Garnish with upeeled orange slices and fresh pineapple sticks.

WHISKEY PUNCH

(Serves 24)

2 cups pineapple juice (canned, unsweetened)
4 cups orange juice (fresh or frozen, but strained)
1/4 cup lemon juice (strained)
1 cup Simple Syrup (page 223)
1 fifth whiskey
2 trays ice cubes

Combine pineapple, orange, and lemon juices with Simple Syrup and chill thoroughly. Just before serving, add whiskey and ice cubes. Garnish with unpeeled lemon, lime or orange slices, pineapple slices or chunks, or maraschino cherries.

WINE PUNCH

(Serves 32)

2 cups orange juice (fresh or frozen, but strained)
1 cup pineapple juice (canned, unsweetened)
1/4 cup lemon juice
1 cup Simple Syrup (page 223)
1/2 cup brandy
2 fifths sauterne (chilled)
2 trays ice cubes

Combine orange, pineapple and lemon juices with Simple Syrup and chill thoroughly. Just before serving, add brandy, chilled sauterne and ice cubes. Garnish with fresh pineapple chunks or sticks, fresh strawberries, unpeeled lemon or orange slices.

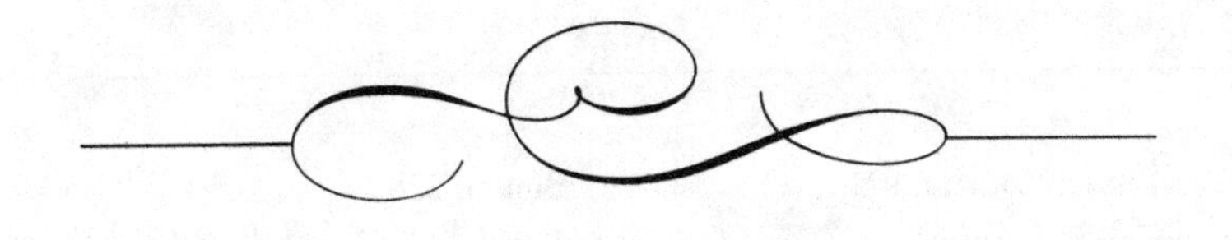

INDEX